ALL and Everything 2015

··· ∼ ···

The Proceedings

of the 20th

ALL and Everything 2015

International Humanities Conference

Anthony Blake

Lee van Laer

Ocke de Boer

Robin Bloor

Paul Beekman Taylor

Seminars – "Purgatory," *Beelzebub's Tales*

Seminar – "Professor Skridlov," *Meetings*

Seminar – "Prologue," *Life is Real Only Then, When "I Am"*

Darlene Franz

Farzin Deravi

First Edition Published 2015

Published by ALL & Everything Conferences (on behalf of the Planning Committee)
© Copyright 2015 by ALL & Everything Conferences

Any profit from the sale of these Proceedings will be devoted to the funds
for the organization of future conferences of a similar nature.

Published by ALL & Everything Conferences

Website: www.aandeconference.org
E-mail: info@aandeconference.org

First Edition Print
ISBN: 978-1515394419

Also Published as
First Edition eBook

Cover: One of the aims of the ALL and Everything Conference is to study all Three Series of G. I. Gurdjieff's writings. This year we added the Third Series to our on-going Seminars on *Beelzebub's Tales* and *Meetings with Remarkable Men*. The image is a detail from a poster that is pictured in the back matter of this volume along with a brief explanation.

Table of Contents

FOREWORD

The Planning Committee would like to take this opportunity of thanking all the Presenters for their help in producing these Proceedings. We hope that this publication will lead to further creative interactions between those in the Work in the future.

The 20th International Humanities Conference — All & Everything 2015 convened on Wednesday, April 29th to Sunday May 3rd, 2015 at the Van der Valk Hotel, Hoorn, NH, The Netherlands. The conference was attended by 47 delegates travelling from Germany, Greece, Israel, Italy, Norway, Russia, Sweden, the Netherlands, the United Kingdom and the United States.

From the Conference's inception, its members have worked toward making this "gathering of the Companions of the Book" to become more and more just that — a gathering of people from all over the world who come together for the purpose of "fathoming the gist" of Gurdjieff's writings, of sharing our insights and experiences, our questions, and our efforts to understand and grow into becoming remarkable men and women.

The final session of the conference on Sunday morning, traditionally entitled "Where do we go from here," provided an opportunity to discuss the achievements of the conference and the challenges facing its future editions.

··· ∾ ···

ALL and Everything
20th International Humanities Conference

Wednesday 29th April to Sunday 3rd May, 2015
Van der Valk Hotel, Hoorn, NH, The Netherlands

Conference Program

Unterschrift des Inhabers
Signature du porteur

Wednesday, 29 April 2015
 2:30 pm – Informal Session: getting to know one another
 3:45 pm – Coffee break
 4:15 pm – Tony Blake: "How to Read"
 7:00 pm – Dinner and open evening for renewing and building relationships
 7:30 am – Voluntary Sitting/Meditation each morning

Thursday, 30 April 2015
 9:15 am – Opening Remarks
 9:30 am – Lee van Laer: Intentional Suffering in *Beelzebub's Tales* and Meister Eckhart's
          Book of Divine Consolation: a perspective on meanings
10:45 am – Coffee Break
11:15 am – Paul Beekman Taylor: Centrigravital Love in Gurdjieff's Rhetoric of Time
12:30 pm – Lunch
 2:30 pm – Seminar: "The Holy Planet 'Purgatory'" *Beelzebub's Tales to His Grandson*
 3:45 pm – Coffee break
 4:15 pm – "The Holy Planet 'Purgatory'" continued
 7:00 pm – Dinner
 8:30 pm – Movie: "Chartres Cathedral – A Sacred Geometry"

Friday, 1 May 2015
 9:30 am – Seminar: "The Holy Planet 'Purgatory,'" *Beelzebub's Tales to His Grandson*
10:45 am – Coffee Break
11:00 am – Seminar: "Professor Skridlov" (from p. 230), *Meetings with Remarkable Men*
12:30 pm – Lunch
 2:30 pm – Paper – Ocke de Boer: Two Souls
 3:45 pm – Coffee Break
 4:15 pm – Seminar: Group reading of the Prologue to *Life is Real Only Then, When "I Am"*
 7:00 pm – Dinner
 8:30 pm – Piano Recital: Avrom Surath

Saturday, 2 May 2015
 9:30 am – Paper – Anthony Blake: Understanding Cosmic Laws
10:45 am – Coffee Break
11:15 am – Paper – Robin Bloor: The Diagram of Everything Living
12:30 pm – Lunch
 2:30 pm – Darlene Franz: Singing a Whole World: Chant Circle as Microcosmos
 4:00 pm – Coffee Break
 4:30 pm – Seminar: **Discussion of emerging themes during the conference**
 7:30 pm – Banquet Evening

Sunday, 3 May 2015
 9:30 am – 11:30 Seminar: Where do we go from here?
 Conference Closes

Lee van Laer: Intentional Suffering in *Beelzebub's Tales* and Meister Eckhart's *Book of Divine Consolation*

An investigation of the question of intentional suffering from Gurdjieff's point of view; Meister Eckhart's perspectives on suffering from the *Book of Divine Consolation*; a comparative discourse on the two sources, with a further examination of Buddhist and Islamic concepts, as well as Swedenborg's teachings.

The presentation contends that Gurdjieff's views on suffering address esoteric, or inner, questions, and not outer ones; that they are canonical in the sense of being traditional and well in keeping with established ideas within the great traditions; and that the idea of intentional suffering has practical aspects whose hidden depths are best revealed by comparisons to other teachings.

—Lee van Laer was born in Yonkers, NY. He spent his childhood in Hamburg, Germany, and now lives in Sparkill, NY. Mr. van Laer has a BFA from St. Lawrence University ('77) and is a global sourcing professional in the textile business. He is a senior editor at Parabola Magazine and the publisher of the *Zen, Yoga, Gurdjieff* blog, and the author of several books about the enneagram and the Gurdjieff work, as well as a book on esoteric meaning in the paintings of Hieronymus Bosch.

Paul Taylor: Centrigravital Love in Gurdjieff's Rhetoric of Time

The goal of this study is to fathom the gist of the scene in the "Prologue" to *Life Is Real Only Then, When "I Am,"* in which Gurdjieff inserts the word "centrigravital" (p. 39) to generate multiple senses within its narrative context and throughout the entire book. The scene has a threefold coded chronology in its recollection in 1935 of a moment in 1927 when Gurdjieff recalls an evening in early 1925 when he sits between his wife and mother on a bench, attended by two peacocks, a cat and a dog. His recollection of this scene in 1927 and 1935 is given a moral slant by the neologism "centrigravital" that he uses for the form of love he bears toward his mother and wife at a moment when he anticipates their deaths. The allegorical, teleological and anagogic meanings of the scene and its imagery are codes that my paper suggests ways to decipher.

—Prof. Taylor lived for some years with Jean Toomer in New York and Pennsylvania as a young boy and studied with Gurdjieff in Paris after World War 2, before turning to a teaching career in Medieval Germanic languages and literature, first in Iceland and for the past thirty years in Geneva, where he lives with his wife and two teenage children.

Tony Blake: Understanding Cosmic Laws

Treatments of Gurdjieff's cosmic laws often tend to render them as formulae revealing the mind of God. They are better approached as ways of understanding which require creativity and amplification. Taking them as point of departure, John Bennett developed 'systematics' as a discipline of understanding. This relates to Gurdjieff's distinction between knowledge and understanding. The paper will expand on the idea of 'Djartklom' as key to how experience is transformed into understanding. It will introduce material from mathematics showing why 3 and 7 are intrinsically linked and notions from Bohm on implicate and explicate order.

—Anthony Blake has a background in physics and philosophy. He studied with the systems thinker and mystic, John Bennett, as well as with the physicist, David Bohm, and other innovators and pioneers. He has followed the principle of integration without rejection, proposed by Bennett, and focuses on how to make this possible in real life. He is the author of several books - on the enneagram symbol of Gurdjieff, the meaning of time, intelligence, dialogue, globalization, systematics, etc.. As Director of Studies and co-founder of DuVersity, Anthony facilitates seminars and lectures on new methods.

Robin Bloor: "The Diagram of Everything Living"

Few people have made much effort to understand the scientific foundation Gurdjieff provided directly in his lectures to his Moscow Groups and indirectly through his descriptions in *The Tales*. The purpose of this presentation is to begin that task. This presentation and paper will thus consider: The Ray of Creation, The Hydrogens, The Side Octave from The Sun and The Diagram of Everything Living.

—Robin Bloor is the author of two books about *The Tales* entitled *To Fathom The Gist* Volumes 1 and 2. He has previously presented once at A&E. Bloor has been associated with the Work since the mid 1980s and became a pupil of Rina Hands in 1988. Rina was a one-time associate of J. G. Bennett, a student of Peter Ouspensky's, and later, a pupil of George Gurdjieff. She ran groups in London and in Bradford in the North of England.

Ocke de Boer: "Two Souls"

In the original chapter "The Holy Planet 'Purgatory'" (1931 edition) Gurdjieff speaks about two kinds of souls. In the 1950 edition he also does this, but he hides it. Ocke's presentation is about two kinds of souls. He will speak about the Kesdjan body and relate it to Mme de Salzmann's excellent book *Reality of Being*. There is emphasis on applying Work ideas on one's being without which one will not be able to make these ideas one's own.

—Ocke de Boer is the engine of a Work-group in Holland. This group has existed since 1990. He studied Esotericism in Amsterdam for 4 years at a Raja Yoga school for Universal Thinking, which is non-dualistic thinking. He gained a general education on philosophy, religion and esoteric systems at that school, without getting lost in any of them. His center of gravity is in the Fourth Way, our Work, which he refuses to call the Gurdjieff work. He is the author of *Higher Being Bodies*.

My Illustrious Presentation—A Collaborative Picturing

> ... then you will probably acquire the possibility of clearly picturing to yourself and well understand how,... (BT p. 618)

You are invited to participate in a collaborative picturing experiment during the A&E Conference, entitled "My Illustrious Presentation." This activity aims to explore a section of the text from *Beelzebub's Tales to His Grandson* (BT pp 613-619) in a novel and potentially groundbreaking way.

This collaborative painting/drawing will be created during the conference by any of the conference participants wishing to engage with it. The theme of the artwork is taken from a section of the chapter Russia in *Beelzebub's Tales.* This section of the text is rich in imagery and may contain significant material accessible through visualization and "mentation by form". The aim of this collaborative "picturing" is to bring out the imagery contained within the text from multiple perspectives of different participants, thus providing new insights that may not be otherwise accessible.

Similar to Tunisian Collaborative Paintings, any of the "artists" may add to the work at any time during the conference, but contributors all agree to follow the proposed theme and are discouraged from painting/drawing over anyone else's work. There is no need for an arbiter. No painting or drawing skills are required!

The medium for this work will be a Magic White Board and non-permanent markers. The board is installed and pens provided for participants who may "picture" simultaneously and at any time during the conference. Audio recordings of the relevant text are available for streaming or download at: https://soundcloud.com/user675274643/"

Darlene Franz

Darlene is a freelance oboist, music educator, singer, and chant composer residing in Seattle, Washington. Her love of the human voice as an expressive and spiritual instrument comes from her father's early lullabies, her Mennonite musical heritage, and many rich experiences singing with early music groups and Episcopal church choirs. She is grateful to count among her influences such musical luminaries as Paul Hillier, Margriet Tindemanns, Iegor Reznikoff, Bobby McFerrin, and Bronislawa Falinska.

—Darlene holds a doctorate of musical arts in oboe performance from the University of Washington. Her doctoral dissertation was on interrelationships among Brahms' early and late organ music and his vocal music.

Since 2006, Darlene has been writing chants and teaching music and attention throughout the US and Canada, and in New Zealand. Darlene's work with groups cultivates the expansion of attention and presence, deepening of embodied awareness, and freeing of personal and collective energies blocked by habit and conditioning. Singers and especially "non-singers" experience an integration of mind, body, and feelings through meditative practices using sacred chant drawn from the music of Taizé, the ancient tradition of psalm antiphons, and a growing body of newly-composed Christian inter-spiritual chant.

--- --- ---

— EVENING PRESENTER BIOGRAPHIES —

--- Avrom Surath ---

Avrom's musical studies began in his youth in Midland, Michigan thanks to the guidance of his mother and grandmother. His musical work experienced a renaissance in his adulthood because of the encouragement and support of Cesareo Pelaez and Michel De Salzmann. His studies in Cuban music over several decades were directed by Cesareo and his sister, Elisa Pedraza, who had been the director of the National Academy of Music in Santa Clara, Cuba before going into exile. He lives in Beverly, Massachusetts with his wife Ann and peek-a-poo Pooky.

— COMMITTEE VOLUNTEERS 2014 —

Planning Committee—John Amaral, Stephen Aronson, Paul Bakker, Marlena Buzzell, Farzin Deravi, Harry Gray, Michael Hall, Mariëtte IJsselmuiden, Bonnie Phillips, Toddy Smyth, Steffan Soule, Avrom Surath, Kristina Turner.

Reading Panel—Stephen Aronson, Toddy Smyth, Kristina Turner, Mariëtte IJsselmuiden.

Music and Sound—John Amaral

Advisory Board—Keith Buzzell, Sy Ginsburg, Dimitri Peretzi, Paul Taylor, Terje Tonne.

We would like to thank the hotel and the staff for their hospitality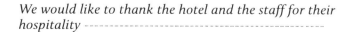

Van der Valk Hotel, Hoorn, NH, The Netherlands

Abaranian Abdest Abdil Abrustdonis
Absoizomosa Actavus Adashsikra
Adashtanas adiat Adossia Afalkalna
Again-Tarnotoltoor Agoorokhrostiny
Ahoon Aieioiuoa Aimnophnian Aisorian
Aiësakhaldan Aiëssirittoorassnian Akhaldan
Aklonoatistitchian Aksharpanziar Alan Kardec
Algamatant Aliamizoornakalu Alil Alillonofarab
Aliman Alisarine Alla Ek Linakh Alla-attapan
Almacornian Almznoshinoo Alnatoorornian
Alnepoosian Alnokhoorian Alstoozori Amambakhlootr
Amarhoodan Amarloos Amber Amenzano
Amersamarskanapa Amskomoutator Amu Darya
anasha aniline Anklad Anodnatious Anoklinism
Anoroparionikima Ansanbaluiazar Ansapalnian Antkooano
Anulios Appolis Arachiaplnish Aral Arax Arguenia
Arhoonilo Arkhatozine Armanatoora Arostodesokh
Arrack Ashagiprotoëhary Ashhana Ashhark
Ashiata Shiemash Asiman
Askalnooazar Asklay Askokin Asoochilon
Assadulla Ibrahim Ogly Assooparatsata
Astralnomonian Astroluolucizoïn
Astrosovors Atarnakh Ateshkain
Atlantis Atropine Autoegocrat
Autokolizikners Avazlin Bairam Balakhanira
Baleaooto Bambini Barmen
Beelzebub being-obligolnian-strivings
Belcultassi Berdichev Blagonoorarirnian
Blastegoklornian Bliss-stokirno Bluebeard
Bobbin-kandelnost Bokhara Boolmarshano

ALL and Everything

Presentations 2015

··· ∼ ···

An Invitation to Reading

... Anthony Blake ...

First, I am addressing the title of the session [the original title was How to Read]. It evokes an image of something like "the seven essential steps of leadership": I'm going to tell you do this and do this and do this, and these are the principles. And so that would give you a wrong impression. I hope during this discourse I rarely fall into the trap of telling you anything, because I have long been convinced you can't tell anybody anything, to effect.

I want to re-title the seminar *An Invitation to Reading*. It makes it more open-ended, and also conveys a sense, which is very important to me, that reading is actually another undiscovered country. It's something which everybody believes they can do, thank you very much. Here you are, all mature, educated people. But of course you can read. There is no problem. But, for me, it is a mystery. I have six children, and I thought, I'm going to find out how children learn how to read. Failed. I didn't spot what happened at all. How it happens, nobody knows how it happens. But there is more in reading than simply the child learning the mechanics of language. I will remind you of our dominant authority figure Mr. Gurdjieff saying to Ouspensky, "You do not know how to read. You can't even read your own books. If you could read your own books, I'd be at your feet. You'd be an enlightened person." So consider this. I took it very seriously, and did what I could to find out about reading.

I'll reiterate the title I'm giving now for this session. It's an invitation, it's not a telling. And I will add a request to be forgiven for my sins if I propose something too ridiculous, as I'm liable to; or too mystical, or too pretentious. I'm simply trying to share with you what I've come across in my puzzlement about reading. But to give you something which will give you pleasure to start with, and to enable you to feel better about me when I begin to talk later on, we're going to start with something really meaningful.

[Darlene Franz on oboe playing "Reading from a Holy Book" by Gurdjieff, accompanied by Anthony Blake on harmonium]

As many will know, the readings at the Prieuré, at least as far as I've read, were always prefaced by music. Why have music for the readings? I made my recordings of *Beelzebub's Tales* introduced by some of the music for some of the chapters. There are only two pieces which were known to be played at the Prieuré before readings of *Beelzebub*, the others I just guessed at. But why have the music? It might be a crude thing to say, but you cannot read this substantial material without your feeling. Most people when they sit down in their chair find it hard to summon their feelings. This has been known, or part of this has been known, for a long time. In the famous text of the Patanjali yoga sutras, you have the three steps. The first is dharana, which is preparation, to dispose yourself towards being receptive. So you have to become receptive. Music is one of the forms which enables this. To repeat, if you sit down in front of a text, simply with resolve, simply with the text, simply cold-bloodedly, it is unlikely to take root. You have to provide the soil for this to take root.

Now there is a peculiar, a main part, a very essential part, of the Qur'an when Gabriel comes to Mohammed and says, as translated into English (it has ambiguities and these are part of the story), "Read." And Mohammed says, "I can't read." And Gabriel says, "Read." "I can't read." And this word, it's 'read' and it's also 'proclaim', it's also 'recite'. It has all those intimations in it. So finally Gabriel imparts one of the main short suras, in which then Mohammed speaks.

In the early days you remember that the sense of reading was not so much like we have it now. So you sit down cold-bloodedly before a text or page, and usually you do some mysterious inner operation called reading in a little corner by yourself. And you remember St. Augustine talking about how strange it was for people to see a cleric with a text when his lips were not moving. He just sat in front of it and no longer needed to move his lips. When they first began to read they always recited aloud, then they just moved their lips, and then ceased to move their lips. Now nobody moves their lips as they are frightened for being taken for an idiot. If you sit there with a text going like this, people are going to look at you and say, "He's not very intelligent. He has to mouth the words to make sure that he knows what they are."

So we've lost touch with a lot of the immersion in reciting and saying aloud. With poetry we occasionally go to a meeting where someone is reading one of their poems, but it's rarer and rarer. We hardly ever meet someone on a street corner reciting their poems. So reading becomes this withdrawn activity. Yet we have the anecdotes of Mr. Gurdjieff saying that at a certain point in his life he would put his work into books. Even, he seems to imply, he had given up on people completely. People around him were useless. He could only trust the books. It seems a remarkable thing, because this was after his period when he had done this tremendous creation of the dances and music. And suddenly for him to say, "No, put it into books, they will be my soldiers." How is this possible?

If you remember the critique of Socrates in the Phaedrus where he is attacking the written word, he says, "How can the written word be intelligent?" You can't ask them any questions. You ask a book and say, What do you mean? And the book is silent. It just says the words which are printed on the page. Obviously books must be in principle unintelligent. Though if we want to read in a sense which possibly, because who knows what he wanted, which possibly Gurdjieff would have approved of, in which he was calling Ouspensky to task about, then clearly we have to invest in it. What comes to my mind by association is from the Odyssey: Odysseus called upon Tiresias and made blood sacrifices to enable Tiresias to acquire substance and give them his counsel which they desired. So they fight away the other spirits and let only Tiresias himself feed upon the blood. But for me this is an actual image of making the reading of a text because it's not only that side which Nietzsche pointed to, "Write with blood and you will find that blood is spirit," but for the reader to give of his blood or substance, too.

In a little while I go on speaking about how the reader and the writer must be very close together to make it work. The very first thing in front of reading, this is how it's been for me, is extremely difficult, and it has those similarities with what you've come across, many years ago most of you, in this various literature we all read where it was written and reported that you can't convince people, most people in the world, about developing consciousness because they're completely sure they have it already. And so you won't bother about reading as long as you're sure you can read already. And if it's for you not a problem, then what I say will be garbage. It's only once you've seen that you do not read, and this is the most, I confess it, for me the most difficult task of all. I was very grateful for the opportunity which came up for the recording of all of Gurdjieff's writings because it put me in touch with them in a different way. And I realised I couldn't have got closer to them just by staring at the pages.

The best impulse I ever had about Beelzebub came when I was about seventeen I think. I had a dream and, in this dream, I was looking through the pages of All and Everything and this conviction came that there really was objective science. But you know in a dream you can't actually read any text which you dream about, so all I was left with afterwards was that it really is there, somewhere. But how is it there? There are many ways to go, and many of you have diligently tried various ways–ways of working out the coding systems and the references, and diligent work can be done with this. But I will repeat, for me one thing above all is essential, which may seem a negativity, is the old adage,

"Must make vacuum." Unless you make a vacuum there is no space for anything. The ordinary way of the world is to add things on, but if you add things on they all sink to the ground under their own weight. To make a vacuum is to allow something to come in. So I will say, it's only when you actually begin to experience that you do not understand the text, cannot read what's there, that you begin to read.

Now many of you have got this chapter from Purgatory here [1931 version]. Now to start with a very simple experiment. [A participant] is going to read this first page, and he will have the task of reading from the feeling of it, and the rest of you I want you to hear what it actually says, the information in it.

"The next day, the ship set off for its final destination in the direction of the Planet Karatas, where Beelzebub is now dwelling. Shortly after the ship had started, Hassein sat down as usual at Beelzebub's feet, and said, "Grandfather, dear grandfather, please explain to me, why, as we have been told, on this holy planet Purgatory, on which we have just been, Our All-Comprehensive Endlessness so often appears?"

At this question, Beelzebub thought a little longer than usual and then said:

"It is a pity, my dear Hassein, that it is impossible at the moment to reply at length to this question of yours, because we shall soon be arriving on our planet. For a complete understanding, that is, such an understanding as I would like to give you of this holy planet, Purgatory, I should be obliged to talk a very long time. But do not fail to remind me of it, on a more convenient occasion when I may be able to explain it all to you. The understanding of the holy planet Purgatory is the most important thing for your education, and sooner or later, it will become decidedly necessary for every being, of whatever nature or form, to know of it.

"Nevertheless, my dear boy, as we shall not be arriving home at once, in order to shorten the time, I will try my best to reply in brief to your question, "Why Our Endlessness appears so often on that holy planet?" Then Beelzebub spoke as follows:

"Our Endless Creator appears so often on that planet, only because, there dwell the most unfortunate souls from among all the souls existing in the Universe. The souls who are on this planet Purgatory suffer as nothing and nobody suffers in the whole Universe. And for this reason Our All-Loving Boundlessly Compassionate Creator, His Endlessness, having no other possibility of helping them with anything, appears often on that planet, to soothe these souls in their terrible inevitable state and grief, by his presence.

"To understand these souls, it is first and absolutely necessary for you to know, in general, what a soul is. But even before you can understand this, you should understand why souls exist in the Universe at all, and why souls, as well as the whole of the Universe, were created by Our Almighty Creator.

"So listen attentively and try to assimilate these ideas into yourself.

"Our Creator was compelled to create the Universe for the following reason:

"When nothing else as yet was in the World, in the whole of the Universe, only the Sun-Absolute existed, and there on this Sun-Absolute, Our Almighty God existed with only His Cherubim and Seraphim.

TONY: This, as you know, is the 1931 version, and many of you have not heard this before perhaps, but just consider from what you've heard, was there anything significantly new for you?

COMMENT: I tried to imagine all the adjectives had more significance, more importance, like final destination. I came up with questions like, what is the final destination? And with many of the adjectives that I heard, that I had not thought of before.

TONY: Your question, what is the final destination?, you mean of mankind, of people and so on?

COMMENT: Yes. Some of the adjectives made questions pop up in my mind.

TONY: Okay, for you it was a question, that is fine.

COMMENT: What struck me right away was that in this first page the word 'souls' was used many times. Now I understood that a soul is a very scarce article, so to speak. It seems to me that souls are already being taken for granted here, and this is what I find new to me.

TONY: That's excellent. We don't want any discussion about what's true, what's false, or anything, but what strikes you.

COMMENT: It feels softer and less potent than what I've read before.

TONY: Somebody had a question, somebody had an observation, somebody had a feeling? What next? Active mentation, please! You've heard of that haven't you?

COMMENT: I have two things to say. First, as the text was being read, I wasn't sure if it was the same as what I had read or not. And then I wasn't sure if it wasn't a matter of I am not remembering the text or that I have new images of it. And towards the end I was sure that there was something new that I have heard which I forgot a few seconds later what it was. And I read it for another time just now in the text here, and by the time I started talking I have forgotten it again.

TONY: Well thank you for that, very much.

COMMENT: The sentence that struck me the most in this piece is, "Sooner or later it will become decidedly necessary for every being of whatever nature or form to know of it."

COMMENT: I smile because he uses the word soul, not higher being-body as he does usually, because Gurdjieff all the time shows the words that can convince people to be serious and he was afraid to be too spiritualist, to use soul and be connected to theosophy, so he used to create his own language, ... and Heropass, and coating of bodies, but here he uses the simple word soul. I think later he took it off because he claimed that there is no soul, so if there is no soul, most people don't have a soul, why should we be interested in Purgatory? Purgatory is to complete the building of the soul. So I like this version much more than the newer one because it's more simple.

Another thing is connected to what you said. You said you have to make a vacuum before you read. And this is exactly the first phrase: Hassein sits at the feet of Beelzebub and says, "Please tell me." This was taken from the *Bhagavad Gita*. The *Bhagavad Gita* starts with, "Please tell me what happened." And this posture, please tell me, is the right posture for the student in their study. This is the vacuum we spoke about.

TONY: What you say is significant. If you're really going to read, how are you going to begin the reading? Are you sitting at the feet of what you're reading? Or are you just arrogantly reading through what is in the text to find a few morsels which happen to please you? And, to exaggerate, there are very different attitudes. Do you actually want to learn anything by reading this text? How to get to that state of receptivity?

COMMENT: It struck me during the reading that it was possible to see some images. I cannot explain exactly how the images proceeded. I can tell something from the very end, and the cherubim and seraphim. Someone here has a website, and he has the angels on his website that are mentioned in *Beelzebub*, and I looked it up and I saw this picture. And in the end it was very interesting because the image came back. It started right from the beginning, from the ship. When you hear it, it is totally different from when you read.

TONY: The difference is when you hear you get the images powerfully, strong images, from hearing.

COMMENT: That's what I meant. That's new.

TONY: We have to use reading aloud here as all of you reading silently would be a rather awkward thing. I know a person facilitating often usurps the intelligence of his audience by making his summary, which is what he already believes anyway, and he ignores what he has heard from the people. I want you to know exactly what the people have said and the differences between them. I just ask this rhetorical question: Did any of you get the sense when you heard [participant]'s very excellent reading, I'm so embarrassed to put it this way, did any of you get the sense that you weren't hearing it at all? Nobody? You're all quite convinced you were hearing what he was saying?

COMMENT: I drifted away at a certain point to a completely different situation in Italy, and I came back and said uh oh. I went away and came back.

TONY: Imagine this picture, most of us probably have this in our minds: there is this book and you're supposed to know what these words are, and you look at the book and you suppose there's some kind of thing going on which is given fancy names like consciousness or that kind of stuff. So you're taking in this information. I myself am very suspicious as a teacher, I don't want to impose my image on you, this trying to suck out of you somehow something about this, because one observation that you had is of drifting away but there's something that attracts you and interests you in it, and you find for example that you stay with it. The text goes on but you stay with something that has struck you, that kind of thing.

COMMENT: What struck me was the words that,

> "Our Creator was compelled to create the Universe for the following reason:
> "When nothing else as yet was in the World, in the whole of the Universe, only the Sun-Absolute existed, and there on this Sun-Absolute, Our Almighty God existed with only His Cherubim and Seraphim.

Later on I know that the merciless Heropass was identified as being the reason for the diminishing of the Sun Absolute, but I find difficulty in understanding that.

TONY: Great. Wonderful. Again it just occurs to me that Gurdjieff always insisted when people started saying, "No I don't understand," he said, "You're beginning to understand." When people say they understand they understand nothing. I say I don't want to impose on you this version but possibly entertain the thought you're reading something and maybe you can catch yourself not actually reading it at all. The moment you catch yourself not actually reading it is, in my experience, the most valuable part of the reading. And it belongs to that narrative when put in front of you that the whole problem is that everybody, most of us with our mother tongue, say we've got skills, we've got mind and consciousness, memory, and we can read, we can move and dance, and let's add on some nice juicy bits on top of that. I'm just challenging this and saying the deeper learning, the deeper reading

(I'm pre-judging my case by saying the deeper) comes when you realise what you're missing. Only when you begin to realise what you're missing does some new spark appear to come. That's one idea. And you can take it or leave it.

Now [a participant] brought in a second idea, you got onto images. I'm going to ask you [a participant] to do the same passage please, if you don't mind. This time, remember what [participant] reported, all I want you to be aware of this time are the images that come to your mind. To put it crudely, you start seeing angels, or spaceships. Oh, give them the pleasure, do page two, to do it properly.

Reading from 1931 manuscript *Beelzebub's Tales*:

"Our Endlessness, Almighty God, once observed that the Sun-Absolute, itself, on which He existed was, owing to Time, diminishing gradually but perceptibly in volume, and He decided immediately to review all the Laws maintaining the existence of the Sun-Absolute.

"In the course of this search, He discovered that the cause of the diminution of the Sun is the Heropass, that is to say, Time, which gradually diminishes the substance of every force.

"As this question was very serious, He became thoughtful, and in these Divine reflections of His, He saw clearly, that, if this Heropass should continue to reduce the volume of the Sun-Absolute in this way, then sooner or later, it would eventually be to its complete destruction. Our Endlessness was then compelled to undertake several appropriate measures, so that this destruction of the Sun-Absolute from the Heropass should be averted.

"After great labours, He completely averted the whole of the threatened danger; and He accomplished this, in the following way:

"You must know that up till then the Sun-Absolute had in itself, for its existence, only the force of the 'Autoegokrat'; that is, an independent force depending on nothing external itself. This same force, in its turn, was formed only of two Laws, namely, the Law of 'Triamonia' and the Law of 'Eftologodiksis'. To these two Laws, Our Creator added the third force, called 'Fagolgiria', by means of which the 'Autoegokrat' became the 'Trogoautoegokrat', that is, a force depending on other forces exterior to itself. Or, as it might be said, after the addition of the Fagologiria, the Laws of Triamonia and Eftologodiksis could function only by feeding on the substances and forces coming from without.

"When I shall explain later, pay special attention, and try to understand very clearly these Laws of Triamonia and Eftologidiksis, since a complete understanding these two Laws will enable you to understand completely all other laws, both of the Creation, as well as of the maintenance of the Universe.

"I have already told you that the Sun-Absolute formerly existed only owing to these two independent Laws.

"The first of these two laws was just the Triamonia, or as it is also called, the law of 'Threefoldness'. This Law of Threefoldness, in its turn consists of three forces, called 'Surpotheos', 'Surpakiros', and 'Surpathanatos'. But, for convenience, mathematics calls these three forces of the Law of Threefoldness, the force 'Plus', the force 'Minus', and the force 'Neutralizing'; or 'Pushing', 'Resisting', and 'Equilibrium'. On certain planets, these three forces are also called 'God the Father,' 'God the Son' and 'God the Holy Ghost'.

"The second Law maintaining the Sun-Absolute is the law of Eftologodiksis; and this law is a force constantly evolving and involving in itself. The highest physico-chemical knowledge formulates this force as follows: 'The flowing of the line of a force which constantly deflects according to the law, with its ends meeting again.'

TONY: Thank you. Now I am asking you for just the images that came into your mind, whether they're special images or ordinary images. Anybody–images? Report on images. No images?

COMMENT: Yes, a lot.

COMMENT: When he talks about the sun diminishing, the image flashed of when the lights go down in a room and what that looks like.

TONY: When there was all that talk about laws what was in your minds? What were you picturing? Nothing?

COMMENT: There is a picture, I think it's William Blake, I saw it very clearly, but it was about the Heropass part, not about the laws; it was in the beginning.

TONY: He was depicting Newton in that painting?

COMMENT: Yes.

TONY: Anybody else? The actual images you have.

COMMENT: I have an image of God creating a world. And there are flashes and it's shining and exploding.

COMMENT: This whole thing really surprises me. I do not have the text that's published; I do not know the difference between the published and this 1931 manuscript but there seems to be a difference because this seems to be like the dog not altogether buried.

TONY: In this passage, what images came into your mind, not ideas?

COMMENT: I think that in this passage what Gurdjieff is trying to do is.....

TONY: No, no. What are the images in your mind? Doesn't something come up in your mind? You're hearing it and doesn't a picture appear?

COMMENT: What Gurdjieff is doing – that's what came to my mind in this passage.

TONY: You are picturing Gurdjieff?

COMMENT: Yes.

TONY: Okay, that's great. Make it concrete, you know. So you are picturing what Gurdjieff is trying to do; a man trying to convey something. That's great. Anybody else? Try and make it concrete, what is actually occurring in your minds.

COMMENT: I have an image of the diagram of Ray of Creation.

TONY: Yes, memory comes up. Does anyone get anything like a spontaneous image?

COMMENT: Eating and digesting impressions. Like in the dark of my stomach, swallowing things, not from within, but something happening inside of me that is eating and digesting.

COMMENT: I had an image of OUR ENDLESSNESS when he figured out that the planet would shrink and that he was desperate and it was completely new, seeing HIM realizing what was happening.

TONY: What did he look like?

COMMENT: He had long white hair with his robes billowing around, looking like, "What am I going to do??" And then I had a picture of you asking me for images and if you asked me again what was I going to do?

COMMENT: I had a problem with this in the sense that the form in my mind was almost like a balloon losing its volume, and then the question just immediately arises, and therefore creates a complete paradox, shrinking in relation to what? Are we to assume it is some kind of prank of the Absolute? It kind of just creates a paradox so that an image occurs and then gets destroyed.

TONY: Beautiful, beautiful. I hope you can see what I'm after.

COMMENT: Along with what he is saying, I had difficulty understanding why the necessity occurs.....

TONY: No I don't want difficulties, I want images.

COMMENT: I am trying to find an image of the need to create the Universe at that time. What happened prior to that? And why that time?

TONY: I'm a bit anxious about the time.

COMMENT: We have time to think about time? [comments and laughter]

TONY: I encourage you to actually watch what is coming up in you as you read it which is not argumentative, it's not to do with reasoning why or why not. What is actually occurring to you in your mind?

COMMENT: I have a question. You know sometimes psychologists do this experiment: what is the first thing that comes to your mind? That is one thing, but also what is your view about reading and re-reading? Is the image that comes first that is important or is it the image that comes after years of reading? What are we looking for here?

TONY: Ah. Well, it's unfair to you, but I am going to halt you on that word 'we.' This is a serious question you are asking. For example, when I was doing these readings [*The Tales, Meetings, Life*] I noticed very much that if, in a certain way, I followed an image coming up for me, then the reading went wrong. I had to be very careful to allow the imagery coming up to keep on flowing. As soon as it got stopped, it became a distraction, but it was necessary to have this because, in my words, in my expression, you have to tell yourself your own narrative of what is going on. It was providing a stream of images, it was providing a medium in which meaning can be communicated to me. So for me it is the liveliness and relaxation of the imagery which is important, and this does develop with practice certainly.

What I believe happens with a lot of people is that they may have images of this, that and the other, and they discount them as trivial. But I am saying, don't discount them as trivial because, in a sense, that is all you've got. And just appreciate that anyway all the time you've got images coming up in you, and when you begin to get into a text you must (I've got the 'must' word here so forgive me) at least have some sense of it happening all by itself in a way which may not be related to the text. And if you do it, I believe, then this stream of imagery begins to feed your understanding and support it.

COMMENT: Just contrasting the reading of the two for me was much more difficult to relate to the second page because I didn't have as much emotional connection with the concepts as I did with "Dear Grandfather" and Hassein and so on.

TONY: That's quite a point in itself. These elements which I am saying are important are realizing if you can (and it's like a psychological paradox) become aware that you are not aware. And becoming aware that you are not reading; or reading, and reading that you are not reading. Then there is the disposition that you can have this sense of feeling which usually needs to be invoked by some means. And music is one of the best ways for it.

Then this thing about the images: the images are always there in some way, I am suggesting. And if they are not acknowledged then they are liable to influence how you read unconsciously. So the more you appreciate them for what they are, directly as what they are, the freer you are from them.

I am going to another point, another perspective, in this. In a way this particular session arose from a remark I made, perhaps last year, when there was a study session on the chapter "Religion." Now in the chapter on Religion, those of you who know it, could you recall what it is about? Could you give me in a few words what you think that chapter is about for you?

COMMENT: I would say it's about people being misled in order to prevent a problem which was about drug addiction ... which bit where you talking about in the chapter "Religion?"

TONY: Just what you remember. Anybody else? What is the tzimus of that chapter for you?

COMMENT: Gurdjieff looks at religions from two opposing perspectives. He does acknowledge that the religion of the religion comes from higher beings. He is a very religious person, he believed in Jesus Christ etc.. But when he sees how religious people behave and what comes out of religion, he must object. So what he does is he explains, through each religion, how it started nice and how it went wrong. He has a very, very keen understanding of the problem of each religion. For example, seventy years ago he speaks, concerning the Muslims, about the "Shiite" and the "Sunnite" fight which we now see happening in the Middle East. He mentions it then. He tells about Judaism, about Christianity, about the building of the University in Jerusalem. What he said was amazing. He said, "When I heard they built the Jewish University in Jerusalem, it means to me that in 50 years they will make a parking place there. Exactly 50 years later, in 2013, they build a parking place.

So he could really see the problems of each religion and I feel very sorry for him because he is a very, very deeply religious person but somehow he has to attack the present form of religions because of, what he says, the "good and bad," the rigidity of religions. So what he tries to say is, yes, religion is genuine, religion is important, but religion is a living thing and once you try to lock it and politicize it and make it together with the state, it's no more spiritual. That's the chapter, what it is about.

COMMENT: What I remember very well is how he explains that religions always end in sects because they're always arguing. People cannot be together in this. It is very difficult for a group to stay related because it becomes a hierarchy, who is right and who tells it better. The sects are what end it all the time. That's what I remember.

TONY: Two things: first of all, why would any of this matter to you about the sects, about the deterioration of religion? Why does it matter to you?

COMMENT: To whom?

TONY: To you.

COMMENT: To me, I don't care. You asked what was said in the chapter "Religion."

TONY: Yeah, but you don't care?

COMMENT: It is not that I don't care. He is right, of course, but nowadays, we all now know that religious institutions are not the real spiritual centers. It's old news.

TONY: So it's old news, so you say this chapter actually tells you nothing new now and you can't find anything in it which is of any intrinsic interest to you personally, this archaic material.

COMMENT: I didn't find anything new because I read it forty years ago. [laughter]

COMMENT: I am wondering whether this is a lawful process–that when sacred ideas come in they may fall under more laws. There is a danger that we get distracted and maybe we can find out how to be alert or to be conscious of this process so we can reflect on what we can do so we do not take part in the distraction, and how we can try to come in contact with the sacred ideas, to the essence of the teaching.

TONY: Well that is what you feel for yourself you mean? Do you find the chapter gives you a means of doing that?

COMMENT: The chapter is telling me that this is a typical process, that the teaching gets destroyed after a short time because other interests like political or power interests get involved, and I would say very earthly aspects like vanity. This is a typical process, so I should have this in mind to be able to differentiate the teaching and what has happened to the teaching. I have to be able to see the difference.

TONY: You see I'm wishing, asking, looking towards, when you read material why would you do this in the first place? Is it because you've got nothing else to do? Is it because it is an entertaining story? Is it because you believe in it? Where are you in your reading?

COMMENT: I see this chapter almost as a warning about how we are, at any cost, avoiding what is needed in order to connect with religion. And as I see it, the basic structure of how we are misled, as somebody pointed out, is because of the consequences of the Kundabuffer. So in that sense, it points to what is needed in order not to be misled. So in that sense the chapter is a very detailed warning.

TONY: I'm still probing for this, why would it matter to you?

COMMENT: But none of this matters Tony. I mean what we take from it is what we can connect to when we read it, and that changes every time. So whatever it was that Gurdjieff intended, I don't know. What the chapter says, I don't know in totality. I only know what has touched me when I read it. I make my connection to my understanding at that point. In an objective sense, I don't know what the chapter is about.

TONY: I wasn't asking in an objective sense.

COMMENT: No, well good job too! Therefore it is interesting to hear what is means to other people because it might well not be the same that it means to me, but I can only receive what in it speaks to me at that time.

COMMENT: It matters because it happens in me. This degeneration is something that happens in me and that is why it matters to me. It is not just about exterior religion or sects; it is what happens when I receive something.

TONY: Yes, the thing to surface is the sense in which the material of the chapter which in this case describes events supposed to be happening thousands of years ago in other countries, and some possible events in recent times which Gurdjieff asserts are true, we don't know. So what is pertinent to us? My question is rather like saying: let's make it personal. You would go beyond your suggestion here, and suddenly it is you that speaks to you. I want to keep it as just an idea, a possibility, and please forgive me if I seem to be imposing it upon you.

I was very influenced myself by a lecture I heard by the Master of the Temple (that's in London) that it was the temple that featured in the book, in the movie, *The Da Vinci Code*. He gave this wonderful talk demolishing the novel and its ideas. But he said something at the end, and this is part of the narrative I want to share with you, he rhetorically asked the people listening to him about the Gospel of John. And he said, "What is the Gospel of John about?" And of course he had his answer prepared; he's written about the Gospels in a very profound way. And he said "it's about the reader." I felt this so strongly, I can feel it now, and I feel that I can't convey it; you can't impose it on anybody. To me, it is when I meet myself in the text, then I take it seriously. It's got my name on it. My name on it. Not "we," not "in general," not "humanity." Mine.

COMMENT: To me this warning can only have a meaning when it resonates with that within me–that wish for purity. And I agree with what you are saying that it has to be my name on it but, at the same time, I think that is the only objective that gives you the right to sign with your own name and in that way we share the same reason.

TONY: There are various stories, one of which, following on a little bit from what you say, which always stuck with me, from the Hui Neng I think it was, the Sixth Patriarch of Chan Buddhism. He was living in poverty with his mother, he was aged sixteen picking up sticks, and he heard the monk reciting the Diamond Sutra, which is one of the classics. On hearing it, he knew he was enlightened and then he revealed himself.

That is also in the literature. I'm referring to literature, because this is also about reading I think I'm allowed to. One of the great human narratives, which was primarily, I think, Gnostic, many of you will know it, is called "The Hymn of the Pearl." And I will summarise it for you briefly. There is this divine kingdom of the King, Queen and the Prince, the court. And the King and Queen say to the Prince, "Part of our substance, our treasure, is lost in the land of Egypt. You must go down and reclaim this pearl." So he sets off, enters the land of Egypt, and he has to disguise himself, put on the clothes of the people there, eat their food. And, of course, he forgets who he is. And so the King and the Queen, in their foreseeingness, know this, and in one version, which is my favourite one, they send a bird down to him, and he perches on the shoulder and whispers in his ear and tells him who he is. And he wakes up, recovers the pearl, takes it back to them rejoicing in them. To be told who one is–something like that.

With reference to when he talked about the higher beings in the origins of religion, I had a friend, who was also a Bennett student, Simon Weightman, and he was head of religious studies in the School of Oriental and African Studies in London University. I had periods when I had long conversations with him, and he said, "You know how basically it happens in all religions–you get some extraordinary event, which is a true event of the religion, and then the energy of this fades, and the second thing which happens is that they write the scriptures. So typically you write the scriptures in a discontinued dialect because the thing is to identify the scriptures with the event–but the only thing that then remains are the scriptures, not the event itself. And this is a conundrum in all religions and it is one of the core ideas in that chapter, which Gurdjieff appears to try to address.

It leads me to make the following, perhaps you will hear it as quite a ridiculous set of remarks, that is to say, it has appeared in literature, Calasso in Italy or George Steiner, and there has been this transformation, particularly in the last three thousand years which is the kind of written language which came from the alphabet, which was only invented once by the Phoenicians, in which we cease to talk about the Gods. Why? Because the Gods are in the literature. So it is no longer talking about anything, but they are there. And so today the Gods live in words, actually live in words. So there need be no barrier between the original revelation and the words at all.

I offer that to you as a possibility, not as a probability. The only rationale I can express to justify my even mentioning it is because I do not think that or feel that God would deny access to the truth as it is.

Still I go on my own quest, as I say starting with my children; I didn't know how they learnt how to read; I am sure I don't know how to read. As I get older I seem to be able to read less and less, but I know that this reading is no longer 'reading about' or descriptions of what has happened to other people or imaginations of another mind, but a way of gaining access to a truth. And, as many of you have hinted, it comes by appreciation of what one lacks, which makes the opening, and then trust in the reality being there, inasmuch as you are real. So it turns around. *Life is real only then, when I Am.* I can even be outrageous and say that "life is real only then, when I read."

Thank you.

Summary

Four levels:

Words	Outer
Images	Inner
'I'	Secret
God or the message	Deeply Secret

Hints can be found in the classic Lectio Divina (divine reading)

Reading
Meditation
Prayer
Contemplation

Anthony Blake — tony@toutley.demon.co.uk

··· ∾ ···

INTENTIONAL SUFFERING IN *BEELZEBUB'S TALES* AND MEISTER ECKHART'S *BOOK OF DIVINE CONSOLATION*:
A PERSPECTIVE ON MEANINGS

. . . LEE VAN LAER . . .

Introduction

The concept of intentional suffering occupies a place of priority both in Gurdjieff's cosmology and his instructions for inner work. As such, this concept bears close examination; exactly what did Gurdjieff mean by it, and what relationship does it bear to tradition and practice as encountered outside the scope of his own teachings?

The idea of suffering and its central position as an (if not the) essential dilemma of human existence pervades religious thinking across a wide spectrum of traditions and disciplines. The Buddha taught suffering and, above all, a search for the end of suffering; Ibn al 'Arabi, arguably the greatest authority of the Sufi tradition, contends that suffering is, *au contraire*, fundamentally essential to the human condition and furthermore inescapable. Christianity maintains that Christ suffered and died in order to pay for mankind's sins—giving it a central role, and evoking comparison to the Vedic concepts of karma and karmic debt, which tie sin and suffering together in a self-perpetuating bundle. The great Christian mystic Meister Eckhart's classic *Book of Divine Consolation* adds an indispensable human dimension to the question of suffering in Christianity. In a feat of sheer *legerdemain*, this text manages to substantially elevate and bring the question down to earth at the same time, recasting it in direct relationship to our personal lives; all this without excessive recourse to the classic parable of Christ's sacrifice, a matter of high theological discourse with limited practical value for the average reader.

Gurdjieff introduces his idea of intentional suffering in his chapter "The First Visit of Beelzebub to India," in which he attributes its origin to Saint Buddha. In this radical revision of dharma teaching, Buddha did not advise his followers to *go beyond* suffering, but, rather, to intentionally *engage* in it. This recasting of one of the central tenets of Buddhist thinking—the escape from suffering—is neatly framed by the simple explanation that its followers subsequently got it all wrong—an explanation, by the way, that Beelzebub cheerfully employs time after time as he recounts the foibles and follies of mankind.

The reason for this potentially perverse instruction—after all, who *wants* to suffer?—is to counter the noxious after-effects of the organ kundabuffer, a dubious appendage added to mankind in much the same way an angelic hacker might install an appealing, but ultimately malevolent, piece of hardware. The fact that no physical evidence whatsoever for this organ exists—driven home by the hard modern sciences of evolution and genetics—indicates an allegorical presence here, perhaps alluding quite directly to ego—which is, after all, an *inner* organ, if we are willing to acknowledge Gurdjieff's contention that everything , even the spiritual, is material.

In any event, the activity itself is introduced—and to some extent fundamentally defined—by a single passage in the book.

Before we begin our journey by examining that passage, it's worth noting that data searches turn up approximately fifty-seven instances where the word suffering is mentioned in *Beelzebub*, allowing for the several different flavors of translation. Of these, arguably, only about nineteen are of substantive value, in that they cast direct light on the meaning of the term; twenty four are of indirect value, that is, they mention the term but shed a less exact light on nature and meaning; and thirteen simply use the term suffering in a strictly vernacular sense, with no reference to the esoteric meaning of the term. (see footnote 1). There are a few additional instances where the word suffering turns up in the first translation and not in the second, but they are minor and have no real bearing on the discourse. (I might mention that this essay categorically does not address various arguments about the merits of different translations.)

We'll investigate the question of intentional suffering first from the point of view of what Gurdjieff said about it; second, review Meister Eckhart's perspectives on suffering from the *Book of Divine Consolations*; and then engage in a comparative discourse on the two sources, with further light shed on the question by Buddhist and Islamic concepts, as well as Swedenborg's teachings.

In the course of things, I will attempt to demonstrate that Gurdjieff's views on suffering address *esoteric*, or inner, questions, and not outer ones; that they are canonical in the sense of being rather strictly traditional and well in keeping with other established ideas within the great traditions; and that the idea of intentional suffering, a linchpin of the Gurdjieff teaching, has practical aspects whose hidden depths are best revealed by comparisons to other teachings.

Along the way, we may answer the question of who wants to suffer, and why, as well as come to some questions about the role of suffering in general, and the mystery of why suffering is needed at all. Gurdjieff and Eckhart shared, perhaps unsurprisingly, a number of opinions on this subject—and these points of view live, as we shall see, under the long shadows cast by the traditional and very (whether Greek or Roman) Catholic Christianity they were both raised in.

Intentional Suffering in *Beelzebub's Tales To His Grandson*

In recounting his visit to India, briefly put, Beelzebub imparts the following recap of mankind's contemporaneous condition to Hassein. Mankind's reason had by then already abnormally deteriorated to the point where it only functioned under corresponding shocks from without[1]—that is, man's Being was no longer influenced, as it ought to be, by inner development.

Saint Buddha—sent to rectify this matter—determined to enlighten man's Reason by imparting objective truths. Of those truths, the most important was the following:

> One of the best means of rendering ineffective the predisposition in your nature to crystallize the consequences of the properties of the organ kundabuffer is "intentional suffering"; and the greatest "intentional suffering" can be obtained in our presences by compelling ourselves to endure the displeasing manifestations of others toward ourselves. (*Beelzebub*, p. 241.)

I think readers can agree this is not a lot to hang one's hat on; and yet this is perhaps the most specific instruction we receive on the matter, despite the fact that the idea of intentional suffering (along

---

1 "Here it must be noted without fail that at that time there had already been crystallized in the presence of Saint Buddha, as my detailed investigations made evident, a very clear understanding that during the process of its abnormal formation, the Reason of the beings of the planet Earth becomes 'instincto-titillarian,' that is, it functions only under the action of corresponding shocks from without." (*Beelzebub*, p. 219)

with its partner-in-effort, conscious labor) is repeatedly offered up throughout the rest of the book as the only means whereby man's Being can be perfected.

In reviewing a wide range of descriptions of the properties of the consequences of the organ kundabuffer, one is likely to come to the conclusion that all of its maleficent effects are directly or indirectly attributable to actions of what we now call ego: vanity, greed, jealousy, a failure to fulfill personal obligations, and war are all specifically cited, with many others implied. As such, we can be left with little doubt that any instructions specifically aimed at removing the effects of the organ kundabuffer must, in a nutshell, be intended to counter the effects of ego.

Intentional suffering cannot, here, be in any way confused with outward suffering, which is a separate and distinct entity. The parable of the sect of Self-Tamers in Tibet, who turned the idea of intentional suffering into a distressingly extreme outward form of suffering,[2] serves as ample illustration of the principle; and does double duty by way of emphasizing (by negative example) the fact that intentional suffering must be engaged in and experienced *in relationship with others*.

The principle was forgotten; the Self-Tamers consequently manage to do the exact *opposite* of what Saint Buddha intended for them; and the solitude and austerities of monastic practices in general come under repeated fire during the course of the book. Only a specifically inward or esoteric suffering, engaged in relationship with other human beings, qualifies as meaningful.

In a perhaps prescient anticipation of new-age practice, Gurdjieff dismisses the modern and distinctly non-traditional offshoots of ancient esotericism. Theosophy, spiritualism, occultism and even psychoanalysis are cited as aberrant understandings.[3] If these supposed disciplines share any single common trait, it is perhaps in ascribing the power for change to the individual and the ego; and one might argue each one ultimately supposes a potential to escape suffering through personal effort. Agency, in other words, is in these practices ascribed to the individual and their own power to change situations. They do not, in a word, bring a person to an inner sense of their own nothingness.

One of the ultimate purposes of suffering, we learn, is to prepare one's self for service; and we soon learn that suffering itself specifically prepares one for the third and fourth obligolnian strivings.[4] Both

2 "This sect of the Self-Tamers arose owing to that distorted understanding of one of the principles of the Buddhist religion which, as I have already told you, they called 'suffering in solitude.' And it was in order to give themselves up to this famous 'suffering,' without hindrance from others like themselves, that these beings with whom we spent the night had settled so far away from their own people." (*Beelzebub*, chapter 22, page 256)

3 "Owing to the strangeness of their psyche, the intentional suffering and conscious labors specially actualized for them by that Sacred Individual, Saint Buddha, who had been coated with a planetary presence like their own, have since then hovered in vain over this planet, without having as yet produced any of the real results that could have been lawfully expected; but they have engendered only all kinds of pseudo teachings, like those existing there today bearing the names of 'occultism,' 'theosophy,' 'spiritualism,' 'psychoanalysis,' and so on, which, now as before, are simply means for 'obscuring' their psyche, already obscured enough without this." (ibid., p. 249)

4 "Even before my fifth sojourn there, that is, before the period when Babylon, as I have told you, was in full flower, those who were regarded by others as 'learned' were not such beings as become worthy to be considered learned everywhere else in the Universe, namely, those who from the earliest times, even on your planet, have acquired by their conscious labor and intentional suffering the ability to contemplate all the details of everything that exists from the point of view of world-arising and world-existence, which enables them to perfect their highest being-body to the degree corresponding to the sacred Measurer of Objective Reason, and later to sense the cosmic truths accessible to this highest body, according to its level of development." (ibid., p. 322)

strivings imply acts of selflessness in the service of others and of creation itself; in other words, they are the very antithesis of egoistic action. These actions confer objective merits that engender respect and trust in others.[5]

Finally, the reader is introduced to the idea that suffering itself is the essential root of existence and being:

> "In all the three-brained beings of the entire Universe including us men, owing to the data crystallized in our common presence for engendering the divine impulse of Conscience — in the whole of us and the whole of our essence—are and must be to the very root nothing but suffering." (*Beelzebub*, p. 372.)

This seemingly grim prognosis is cast in terms of a constant and, by implication, eternal struggle between the natural and spiritual sides of mankind's being. Without this struggle, reason cannot arise.

Even Gurdjieff's "Hasnamuss-individuals," objective villains with powerful egoistic impulses, must expiate their sin solely through this same action; so the question of inner development in the absence of intentional suffering seems moot. For Gurdjieff, there is no other available path.

Throughout his teaching, Gurdjieff steadfastly refuses to lay out any optimistic foundations for the attainment of yogic bliss, ecstatic Christian or Sufi rapture, or Buddhist enlightenment. This is worth examining in light of Ibn al 'Arabi's views on the matter:

> "In our situation we only need an explanation of the realm of this world, which is the place of responsibility, trial, and works."
>
> "Know that since God created human beings and brought them out of nothingness into existence, they have not stopped being travelers. They have no resting place from their journey... Every rational person must know that the journey is based upon toil and the hardships of life, on afflictions and tests and the acceptance of dangers and very great terrors. It is not possible for the traveler to find in this journey unimpaired comfort, security, or bliss. For waters are variously flavored and weather changes, and the character of the people at every place where one stops differs from the character at the next. The traveler needs to learn what is useful from each situation...
>
> "We have not mentioned this to answer the people fond of comfort in this world, who strive for it and are devoted to the collection of worldly rubble... we mention it as counsel to whoever wishes to hasten the bliss of contemplation in other than its given realm, and to hasten the state of annihilation elsewhere than in its native place, and who desire absorption in the real by means of 'fana', obliteration from the worlds... The masters among us are scornful of this ambition because it is a waste of time and a loss of true rank, and associates the realm with that which is unsuitable to it."—Ibn al 'Arabi, *Journey to the Lord of Power,* trans. Rabia Terry Harris

Earth is, Ibn al 'Arabi advises us, a level where inner work must be done; and here perhaps lie the roots of Gurdjieff's conscious labor, the prerequisite for and partner in intentional suffering.

Although this covers the overall gist of intentional suffering, a few other notable points can be gleaned from the text. A special, higher kind of being property called "ikhriltatzkakra" results from

---

5 "According to the first meaning it is used, as in the past, to designate those beings who become 'initiates' thanks to their personal conscious labors and intentional sufferings, and who thus acquire in themselves, as I have already told you, objective merits that are perceptible to other beings of any brain-systems and that evoke trust and respect." (*Beelzebub,,* p. 350)

conscious labor and intentional suffering; and the salient property of this new 'egoaitoorassian' form of will as cited in *Beelzebub's Tales* is that it allows the adept to play a role at the club of the Adherents of Legominism.[6]

This allegorical representation of role-playing in life is a known feature of the Greek schools of Stoicism, and the practice still features prominently in the active legacy of Gurdjieff's personal teachings. Here we might note the extensive connections between Gurdjieff's practice of external considering, the idea of action detached from the ordinary action of ego, and the actor's craft of representing not his own, but an entirely different other person's actions and feelings.

Furthermore, the full and complete digestion of the impressions of the second and third being foods (air and impressions) which are indispensable for the formation of the astral body — another noteworthy feature in the cosmological landscape of the Gurdjieff work — can only be accomplished through the same action.[7]

Mankind's ordinary moral suffering is, according to Beelzebub, "futile,"[8] and the actions of conscious labor and intentional suffering produce actual physiological and chemical results.[9] This remark underscores Gurdjieff's contention that conventional outward morality is in effect useless; here, he ties it firmly to the need for an action of inner suffering, the only means whereby a real or objective morality can develop.

In what may be the final substantive comment on the nature of intentional suffering, we are informed that this particular inner work is necessary for planetary, as well as personal, reasons.[10]

Suffering According to Eckhart in *The Book of Divine Consolation*

Like Gurdjieff, Eckhart places suffering high on the list of inner actions that lead a human being towards self-development. In Eckhart's spiritual landscape, all actions we refer to as egoistic in today's terms are considered as willful. All suffering, in Eckhart's teachings, ultimately arise from a misalignment of a person's will with God's; and the aim of all suffering is to turn a human being back towards God's will, such that he is shorn of all ego.

6 "Three-centered beings can acquire this being-property called 'ikhriltatzkakra' only after having personally acquired in their presence what is called 'egoaieritoorassian-will,' which in turn can be obtained only thanks to being-partkdolg-duty, that is, to conscious labor and intentional suffering". *Beelzebub*, p. 485

7 "To tell the truth, my boy, I did not understand at once all that he told me; it all became clear to me only later when, during my studies of the fundamental cosmic laws, I learned that these sacred substances, 'abrustdonis' and 'helkdonis,' are precisely those substances which enter into the formation and perfecting of the higher being-bodies of the three-brained beings--that is, the 'kesdjan body' and the 'body of the soul'..." Ibid, p. 1106

8 "Because of this constant indignation, the ordinary being-existence of these unfortunates almost always flows accompanied by unproductive 'moral sufferings'; and these futile 'moral sufferings' of theirs usually continue by momentum to act for a long time on their psyche 'semtzektzionally' or, as they would say on your planet, 'oppressively'; in other words, they ultimately become 'instruarnian,' or 'nervous,' of course without the participation of their consciousness." (ibid., p. 1077)

9 ... and that the separation of the sacred 'askokeen' from the two other substances proceeds when beings, on whatever planet they may be, transmute these sacred substances in themselves for the forming and perfecting of their higher bodies, by means of conscious labor and intentional suffering." (the continuation of footnote 7, ibid, p. 1106)

10 "And so, my dear Hassein, when it became clear that there had entirely disappeared from the psyche of your favorites the instinctive need for conscious labor and intentional suffering in order to take in and transmute in themselves the sacred substances of abrustdonis and helkdonis--thus releasing the sacred askokeen for the maintenance of the Moon and Anoolios--Great Nature was constrained to adapt herself and to extract this sacred substance by other means, one of them being precisely that periodic terrifying process of reciprocal destruction." (ibid., p. 1107)

God never tires of loving and working, and whatever He loves is one love. Therefore it is true that God is love. And that is why I said above that the good man always wants and desires to suffer for God's sake, not to have suffered: in suffering he has that which he loves. He loves to suffer for God's sake, and he suffers for God's sake. Therefore and therein a man is God's son, formed after God and in God, who loves for his own sake, that is, he loves for the sake of loving, works for the sake of working; and for that reason God loves and works without ceasing. And God's work is His nature, His being, His life, and His felicity. Thus in very truth, for the son of God, for a good man insofar as he is God's son, suffering for God's sake, working for God is his being, his life, his work, his felicity, for our Lord declares, "Blessed are they that suffer for righteousness' sake" (Matt. 5:10). (Meister Eckhart, *The Complete Mystical Works*, p. 543.)

This passage, with its strong and repeated emphasis on working and love of work, reminds us not only of Gurdjieff's aphorism "I love him who loves work," but also of the fundamental principle of conscious labor; and it is introduced in direct conjunction with a will to suffer, that is, an intention to suffer. This suffering is selfless suffering, that is, it is engaged in *on behalf of God*; and the two ideas—which precisely mirror the twin activities of conscious labor and intentional suffering—are engaged in out of a loving action, and on behalf of an effort at unity with God.

This is no coincidence; the ultimate striving of every Being in Beelzebub's universe is an identical reunion with His Uni-Being Endlessness.

The actions are, furthermore, aimed at performing a service on behalf of God (he *suffers for God's sake*); the phrase not only reminds us of Gurdjieff's fourth obligolnian striving, it also echoes the Gurdjieffian adage that one work for the sake of work itself, and not for results.

Eckhart definitely believes that suffering of itself exists for a higher purpose.

> Seneca, a pagan master, asks, 'What is the best comfort in suffering and distress?' and says it is that a man should take all things as if he had wished and prayed for them... (ME, p. 530)

Here he introduces, via the stoics, the idea that we ought to form a very different inward intention towards our suffering than the ones our ego would adopt. Epictetus mentions the same adage; and the inference is that one's inner attitude must be brought *intentionally into alignment with the object truth of outer events*. Saint Buddha's instruction to achieve this principally by bearing the unpleasing manifestations of others is exquisitely tuned to put us, on a daily basis, face to face with exactly that which is *not* as we would wish it. The practice of outer considering dovetails neatly into this in a tight-fitting piece of joinery any good spiritual carpenter can well appreciate.

This action must, by default, involve a conscious labor of inner effort, and a going-against the now instinctive egoism that infects humanity: ergo, the process of intentionally suffering.

This call to ruthless objectivity in regard to outer events (a familiar piece of furniture in Gurdjieff's living room) furthermore mirrors the alignment between conscious labor, intentional suffering, and the development of Objective Reason, one of the chief features appearing in beings who labor consciously and suffer intentionally. It is, in short, a form of mindfulness; and perhaps modern Buddhism's emphasis on this aspect of practice represents a belated return to some of the radical values the Buddha originally introduced.

> A good man should trust in God, believe and be assured that God is so good that it is impossible for God, His goodness, and love to endure that any pain or suffering befall a man unless either to save that man from further suffering... (ME, p. 530)

Eckhart's contention is that suffering is not only fundamentally purposeful but necessary, is reminiscent of Gurdjieff's remarks in Ashiata Shiemash.[11]

But to say that suffering is necessary and sufficient is not going far enough. Suffering is not only necessary, it is *virtuous*; and although Gurdjieff fails to state this outright, the inference in *Beelzebub* is so obvious and consistent it is nearly impossible to overlook.

Eckhart sees it thus:

> In the same way I say of virtue that she has an inner work: a will and tendency toward all good, and a flight from and a repugnance to all that is bad, evil, and incompatible with God and goodness. And the worse an act is, and the less godly, the stronger the repugnance; and the greater the work and the more godlike, the easier, more welcome, and pleasanter it is to her. And her sole complaint and sorrow - if she could feel sorrow - is that this suffering for God is too little, and all outward, temporal works are too little for her to be able to find full expression, realization, and shape in them. (ME, p. 540)

In Eckhart's world, we cannot divorce inner work from work towards the good; and it is an inner work alone that can fully express this properly. Hence Beelzebub's revolving critique of mankind's many outwardly directed works which attempt to create mechanical forms whereby suffering can be outwardly—physically—engaged in, represented, or otherwise put on display. Eckhart shared an equal skepticism of such outward displays, which same crops up in numerous sermons."

> But some people want to see God with their own eyes as they see a cow, and they want to love God as they love a cow. You love a cow for her milk and her cheese and your own profit. That is what all those men do who love God for outward wealth or inward consolation — and they do not truly love God, they love their own profit. (ME, p. 117)

Suffering in Gurdjieff's universe is the only source from which real happiness can arise:

> 'Every real happiness for man can arise exclusively from some unhappiness—also real—which he has already experienced. (*Beelzebub*, p 346)

This passage presents less overt challenges if we consider it in light of Eckhart's remarks on the same subject:

> She (virtue) does not wish to have suffered and to have got over pain and suffering: she is willing and eager to suffer always without ceasing for God and well-doing. All her happiness lies in suffering, and not in having suffered, for God's sake.

---

11 "And we must be suffering, because this being-impulse can come to its full manifestation in us only through the constant struggle between two quite opposite complexes of functioning issuing from two sources of quite opposite origin, that is to say, through the constant struggle between the processes of the functioning of our planetary body and the parallel processes of the functionings arising progressively in accordance with the coating and perfecting of our higher being-bodies within this planetary body of ours, which processes in their totality actualize every kind of reason in three-centered beings." (*Beelzebub*, p. 372.)

And therefore our Lord says quite deliberately: "Blessed are those who suffer for righteousness' sake" (Matt. 5:10) (ME, p. 540).

We ought to perhaps be reminded here a directly related idea: that Gurdjieff proposes a universe locked in an eternal struggle between joy and sorrow:

> ... this sorrow is formed in our All-Maintaining Common Father from the struggle constantly proceeding in the Universe between joy and sorrow. (*Beelzebub*, p. 341)

These two forces are mutually dependent. One cannot be recognized without the presence of the other. So with happiness and suffering; yet mankind seeks happiness even at the expense of suffering, presuming it is his right and destiny. Yet like Gurdjieff, Eckhart asserts the opposite, and goes one step further:

> One should also know that in nature the impress and inflow[12] of the highest and supreme nature is more delightful and pleasing to anything than its own nature and essence...
>
> From this a man may know whether it would be right for him, if it would be pleasant and delightful for him to abandon his natural will, to give it up and to deny himself totally in everything that God wants him to suffer. And that is the true meaning of our Lord's words, "Whoever will come to me, let him go out of himself and deny himself and take up his cross" (Matt. 16 : 24)... For assuredly, whoever had abandoned self and completely gone forth from self, for him nothing could be a cross or pain or suffering: it would all be a joy, a pleasure, and heart's delight, and that man would come and truly follow God. (ME, p. 547)

To intentionally suffer on behalf of God, in other words, is an act of joy. These two masters bring us, each in their own way, to a comprehensive theology of suffering, both inner and outer, which reconfigures it as a joyful and intentional act of submission to God's will: not through fear, obligation, or threat of eternal damnation, but willingly, and, furthermore, *through an alignment of one's own will with the will of the absolute.*

Some few Tibetan Buddhist traditions have preserved the understanding of inner work as an effort that lies well outside the range of any search for happiness, as we conventionally understand it; one is prompted to think, for example, of Dzongsar Jamyang Khyentse's *Not For Happiness*.[13]

Gurdjieff's conscious labor and intentional suffering are, in other words, deeply tied to the idea of complete surrender to God's will; and as we first meet him, Beelzebub's own life-task is to re-align

---

12 See Swedenborg's mention of the selfsame inflow, footnote 15. Both men are referring to the intimate, organic, and physical receiving of the divine inward presence of God.

13 "Buddhist practices are techniques we use to tackle our habitual self-cherishing. Each one is designed to attack individual habits until the compulsion to cling to "self " is entirely eradicated. So although a practice may look Buddhist, if it reinforces self-clinging, it is actually far more dangerous than any overtly non-Buddhist practice.
The aim of far too many teachings these days is to make people "feel good," and even some Buddhist masters are beginning to sound like New Age apostles. Their talks are entirely devoted to validating the manifestation of ego and endorsing the "rightness" of our feelings, neither of which have anything to do with the teachings we find in the pith instructions. So if you are only concerned about feeling good, you are far better off having a full body massage or listening to some uplifting or life affirming music than receiving dharma teachings, which were definitely not designed to cheer you up. On the contrary, the dharma was devised specifically to expose your failings and make you feel awful." Adapted from Not for Happiness: A Guide to the So-Called Preliminary Practices, by Dzongsar Jamyang Khyentse. © 2012 by Dzongsar Jamyang Khyentse.

his own rebellious will[14] with the Will of the divine. The entire premise of the book, in other words, is framed by this effort: Islam, the act of submission to God.

The Aim of Suffering

> A good man should trust in God, believe and be assured that God is so good that it is impossible for God, His goodness, and love to endure that any pain or suffering befall a man unless either to save that man from further suffering, or else to give him greater consolation on earth, or to make thereby and therefrom something better which should redound more largely and fully to God's glory. Yet be that as it may: by the mere fact of its being God's will that it should occur, the good man's will should be so much at one and united with God's will, that that man would will the same as God, even though it were to his own harm or indeed his damnation. (Meister Eckhart, *The Book of Divine Consolation*, p. 530)

In order to come to grips with Gurdjieff's intentional suffering, one must first draw a line between external sufferings such as mortification of the flesh, physical and moral abstinences of whatever variety, and the inner sufferings of the soul itself. Gurdjieff was never one for abstinence; and purification through mechanical or exterior means, no matter how severe, stand apart from the inner suffering he proposes in remorse of conscience. It is the suffering of the soul, of one's spiritual nature, that one must aim for; and any subjugation of the body is a merely preliminary measure. This struggle between man's natural and spiritual nature, a prominent feature in Swedenborg's writings, is outlined in *Beelzebub*:

> "'And we must be suffering, because this being-impulse can come to its full manifestation in us only through the constant struggle between two quite opposite complexes of functioning issuing from two sources of quite opposite origin, that is to say, through the constant struggle between the processes of the functioning of our planetary body and the parallel processes of the functionings arising progressively in accordance with the coating and perfecting of our higher being-bodies within this planetary body of ours, which processes in their totality actualize every kind of reason in three-centered beings.'" (*Beelzebub*, p. 372)

Swedenborg's conception of the matter is in its essence very nearly identical; and Swedenborg ascribes mankind's spiritual failings to a continual inability to discern and understand the difference between the natural, physical and biological world, and the spiritual world that engenders it.[15]

---

14 "...owing to his youthful and still unformed Reason, as well as to his callow and impetuous mentation with its unequally flowing associations, that is, a mentation based on a limited understanding—which is natural for beings who have not yet become fully responsible—Beelzebub once saw something in the government of the world that seemed to him "illogical" and, having found support among his comrades, unformed beings like himself, interfered in what was none of his business."

"Thanks to the force and impetuosity of Beelzebub's nature, his intervention, supported by his comrades, soon captured all minds and brought the central kingdom of the Megalocosmos to the brink of revolution."

"Having learned of this, His Endlessness, notwithstanding His all-lovingness and all-forgivingness, was constrained to banish Beelzebub and his comrades to one of the remote corners of the Universe, to the solar system "Ors"... *Beelzebub*, p. 50

15 "People who do not acquire a grasp of these levels have no way of knowing how the heavens are arranged or the arrangement of our own deeper and more outward abilities, or the difference between the spiritual world and the natural world, or the difference between our spirit and our body. This also means they cannot understand what correspondences and images are or what inflow is like. People who are attentive only to their physical senses do not grasp these differences, but regard them as instances of increase and decrease on the model of continuous levels. As a result, they cannot think of the spiritual except as a kind of purer natural; so they stand outside, far removed from intelligence." (Emmanuel Swedenborg, *Heaven and Hell*, p. 58)

Suffering, in the Christian universe, is an act of expiation, of purification, in atonement for what is called original sin. Gurdjieff— remaining, as ever, the quintessential iconoclast — recasts the entire sum of mankind's sin as something a good bit less than original; it represents not, at its root, a failing on man's part, but the result of a cosmic accident involving a collision with the comet Kondoor, and the subsequent failings of cosmic individuals whose tragic lack of foresight regarding the organ kundabuffer brings results which reverberate down through human history with a steadily degenerative effect.

In the cosmic machinery Gurdjieff has created, mankind ultimately owns nothing in this picture; not even his own sin. This might appear to be a unique proposition were it not, in its essence, so distinctly and identically expressed by Eckhart's writings. Even sin, in this sense, is not the property of the ego, which can lay no legitimate claim to it. We come once again to Eckhart, in a highly unorthodox passage that was ultimately condemned as heresy by the inquisition:

> And so, since God in a way wills that I should have sinned, I would not wish that I had not done so, for thus God's will is done "in earth " {that is, in ill-doing) as well as " in heaven" (that is, in well-doing). In this way one wills to do without God for God's sake, to be sundered from God for God's sake, and that alone is true repentance for my sins: then I grieve for sin without grief, as God grieves for all evil without grief. I have grief, the greatest grief, for my sins, for I would not sin for everything that is created or creaturely, even though there were a thousand worlds existing to all eternity - and yet without grief, and I accept and take the suffering in God's will and from God's will. Such suffering alone is perfect suffering, for it arises and springs from pure love of God's sheer goodness and joy. Thus it is made true, and one comes to know it, as I have said in this little book, that the good man, insofar as he is good, enters into full possession of that goodness which God is in Himself. (ME, *The Complete Mystical Works*, p. 531)

In sin, however, there is no escape from responsibility; regardless of cause, it becomes the responsibility of every thinking, three-brained being to rise above the machines of degeneration by exercising conscious *choice* to go against these insults and adversities; and God Himself, endlessly true to His own infinitely merciful form, repeatedly sends help.

The critical mechanism here is choice; humanity must choose, that is, *intend* to go against the active forces of inner degeneration, which are represented by the organ kundabuffer, or, as we call it, ego. All of the adversity and suffering a human being encounters during a lifetime are no more than agencies that create the opportunity for choice. One is asked to *go against one's self*; and this is the very root and essence of unselfishness. The perennial philosophical questions of agency and personal will loom large here; in mankind, esoteric tradition argues, these faculties are either severely atrophied or even absent. In the stoic tradition, volition is what constitutes the real self;[16] and Gurdjieff's teachings owe more than a bit to the stoics.

Gurdjieff's cure for this malady is inner effort. In conscious labor, we use our potential for agency to make an effort to choose for the good; and in choosing, we must intentionally suffer, because that choice inevitably involves giving up what we are in our own inner sense in order to serve a greater

16 "It is the volition that is the real person, the true self of the individual. Our convictions, attitudes, intentions and actions are truly ours in a way that nothing else is; they are determined solely by our use of impressions and thus internal to the sphere of volition." (*Stanford Encyclopedia of Philosophy*, entry on Epictetus)

good. The outer circumstances, which humanity places so much focus on, are merely a mechanism, a distraction from the real issue; and it is, without exception, the *inner* forces of suffering alone which provide mankind with a path towards liberation.

The efforts to find a path that alleviate outer suffering seem laudable, but they are a red herring. In Gurdjieffian terms, outer suffering is entirely mechanical, not conscious: in and of itself it has no agency. Only inner suffering has real value in this regard. This echoes Epictetus' stoic views on the matter.[17]

Our powerful attraction to outward forces and outward actions obscure the real issue, which is that all outer relationships are a reflection of inner attitudes and actions which must be suffered in order to purify us, or, as Gurdjieff puts it, free us from the noxious consequences of the organ kundabuffer.

This criticality of choice is the exact same mechanism Swedenborg puts at the heart of mankind's inner effort of regeneration. In his cosmology, as in Eckhart's, God has an urgent and never-ending wish for man to choose God, which is to choose love; and that choice must be a free choice, engaged in without coercion, up to and including the coercion of miracles, a form of holy action both Gurdjieff and Swedenborg eschewed; and, we might note, a form of action also consistently absent from Eckhart's landscape, where a person's choice to serve God looms equally large.

But why should intentional suffering be, as the Buddha originally taught, engaged in only in relationship with others? Here we need to refer to a page in Swedenborg's encyclopedia; and in fact it is the central page, so to speak, the axis around which all of Swedenborg's teachings align and center themselves.[18]

The crux of the matter is this difference between selfishness and selflessness; the fundamental effects of the organ kundabuffer are that it *imparts features of selfishness in mankind*. All of the impulses that counter it are selfless, that is, they go against our inner self-serving impulses; and of course we can only see our self-serving impulses in the light of relationship with others.

This emphasis on service, and on unselfishness, pervades Gurdjieff's teachings throughout, from his practice of inner and outer considering to his elevation of the *obyvatel* over the conceit of the earnest spiritual seeker; and it could easily be argued that one of the overarching themes of *Beelzebub* is that of service to and positive action on behalf of others; all, of course, ultimately aimed at service to God. All of this service is impossible without full submission to the will of God; and Beelzebub, as the protagonist who finds himself, so to speak, banished to the edge of the universe, enters the stage as a rebel who refused to submit to God's will. It takes one to know one, of course; and he thus becomes a critic well suited to the task of recounting mankind's failings.

---

17 "The appearance and comfort of one's body, one's possessions, one's relationships with other people, the success or failure of one's projects, and one's power and reputation in the world are all merely contingent facts about a person, features of our experience rather than characteristics of the self. These things are all "externals"; that is, things external to the sphere of volition." (*Stanford Encyclopedia of Philosophy*, Epictetus)

18 "Selfishness is what closes off our deeper natures from the Lord and heaven and opens our outer natures and turns them toward ourselves. So all people in whom that selfish love predominates are in the depths of darkness as far as heavenly realities are concerned, no matter how much light they may enjoy in regard to worldly matters. In contrast, since angels are free of that love, they enjoy the light of wisdom. The heavenly loves in which they are centered—love for the Lord and love for their neighbor—open the deeper levels because these loves come from the Lord and the Lord himself is within them." (ES, *Heaven and Hell*, p. 272)

In summary

Beelzebub's Tales uses an allegorical form to recapitulate, in considerable and sophisticated detail, a wide range of fundamental esoteric principles in common with both Eckhart, al Arabi, and Swedenborg. The comparisons firmly place *Beelzebub's Tales* in an identifiable traditional context; yet, in what might be called a near-perfect symmetry, that traditional context stems from other figures who were, in their own right, as unique, unusual, and iconoclastic as Gurdjieff himself. All are unabashedly mystical, coming from what Gurdjieff would have called influences C; and one is given to believe that Gurdjieff's insights must stem from the very same branch of the great river of Divine influences.

Beelzebub reminds us that such influences and their aftereffects are, after all, heritable:

> And I must tell you about the history of its arising and existence so that you may realize that if something is attained by the three-brained beings on your planet thanks to their 'being-partkdolg-duty'–that is to say, their conscious labor and intentional suffering–not only are these attainments utilized by them for the welfare of their own being but also, as with us, a certain part of these attainments is transmitted by heredity and becomes the property of their direct descendants. (*Beelzebub*, p. 292)

In tracing the trajectory of Gurdjieff's ideas on intentional suffering, we discover a surprising consonance with Buddhism; surprising, because Gurdjieff mentioned it so rarely outside the early, and strikingly central, role Buddha plays in *Beelzebub's Tales*. The book unmistakably assigns Saint Buddha the correct historical priorities of both time and circumstance in the genesis of the great traditions. The point ought to be more directly underscored as a cornerstone of the Gurdjieff teachings.

Once examined, the grounds for agreement on the question of suffering run deep enough to argue for the veracity of Gurdjieff's radical reconfiguration of Buddhist teaching; deconstructed, they reveal a consistency which is not at all apparent on the surface of the story. The demonstrable, and equally compelling, links to esoteric Christianity tie these practices together in an integrated manner that softens or even erases some of the long-standing barriers between eastern and western inner traditions; barriers that are now ever more rightly challenged. And the obvious relationship between intentional suffering and Islam, the practice of submission to the will of God—underscore the fact that esoteric Islam cannot reasonably hold itself apart as unique or separated from its brother and sister traditions in east and west, no matter how ardently its fundamentalist sects may insist on such separation. Ibn al 'Arabi, as it happens, certainly drew no such distinctions; for him, each religion was good enough unto the man who practiced it, insofar as he was sincere.

We have thus outlined the spiritual DNA of Gurdjieff's magnum opus; but whether he arrived at it independently of Ibn al 'Arabi, Eckhart, and Swedenborg (which seems, on examination, most unlikely) or through his own inner revelations, the consonance between these various masters validates, reverberates, and reinforces his message, underscoring the importance of *Beelzebub's Tales* as a spiritual revelation worthy of its place not just alongside, but within, the greatest traditions of mysticism and inner work from earlier centuries.

··· ∽ ···

Conference Presentation

I'm going to open here with a very brief passage from the book of the Wartime meetings in which someone asked Mr. Gurdjieff,

> I wanted to ask you if there was, for developing attention, only the method of "I am," or if there are other special methods.

Mr. Gurdjieff replied:

> One thing I can tell you. Methods do not exist. I do not know any. But I can explain now everything simply. For example, in *Beelzebub*, I know, there is everything one must know. It is a very interesting book. Everything is there. All that exists, all that has existed, all that can exist. The beginning, the end, all the secrets of the creation of the world; all is there. But one must understand, and to understand depends on one's individuality.[19]

And now, a quote from Meister Eckhart, who lived from about 1260 to 1328; his actual name was Eckhart von Hochheim, and he was a highly orthodox Catholic of the Dominican order, and he said:

> When I preach it is my wont to speak about detachment, and how man should rid himself of self and of all things. Secondly, that man should be informed back into the simple good which is God; thirdly, that we should remember the great nobility God has put into the soul, so that man may come miraculously to God; fourthly, of the purity of the Divine Nature, for the splendor of God's nature is unspeakable. God is a word, an unspoken word.[20]

These two men lived in entirely different millennia, so to speak; and although Gurdjieff openly acknowledged his Christian heritage, I don't know that too many people see the Gurdjieff work as an orthodox Christian practice. So one might think, well, there isn't a lot of commonality between these two men; and we're going to take a look at that through a very specific lens this morning, that is, the question of suffering; but before we get into that I thought I might tell people a little bit about how I first encountered this book.

I grew up in Germany, as was said earlier, and when I ran out of children's books—which was probably at about the age of seven or eight—I started reading my mother's murder mysteries, so by the time I was eight or nine years old I had read everything Agatha Christie ever wrote; and so I was a rather precocious reader by accident, but that's how it worked out.

When I came back to the United States for a brief tour in sixth grade, I read Dostoevsky's *Crime and Punishment* which is also, of course, about suffering, and the English teacher was astonished that I actually read the book and appeared to understand it. He suggested (rather archly, as I recall) that I read a book called *Beelzebub's Tales to His Grandson*. I said, "well that sounds kind of weird, isn't it about the devil?" and he said, "No, it's kind of science fiction, it's about a guy on a spaceship, the devil is on a spaceship," blah blah blah.

19 *Gurdjieff's Wartime Transcripts 1941-45*, (London: Book Studio 2009) P 59.
20 Eckhart, Meister. *The Complete Mystical Works of Meister Eckhart*, translated by Maurice O'C Walshe (New York: Crossroads Publishing 2007) P 543.

Well, I went to the local library, and to no one's surprise they didn't have a copy of the book, and so I read Ambrose Bierce's *The Devil's Dictionary*, which is really not a good substitute, but there you are.

In any event, the point is that even though I wasn't looking for the book, even at a very early age, the book was looking for me.

So anyway, about the paper, it's a fairly academic work, it's rife with quotations and a bit dense, and I was given the challenge of boiling it down into something simpler, and I did that and then I had to boil it down to something even simpler still, to the point that I think that what I've got is something produced by a simpleton—that but that's what we have here, so let's talk a bit about the overarching premises.

Every man or woman views suffering through the lens of their own agency; and perhaps this is where we go wrong, already, up front. We simply don't believe we are nothing; and to the ego, the idea that others ought to be considered before we gratify our own lusts and urges is—to put it bluntly—absurd. We can trust the devil in us—and what we can trust most is that he always wants our own satisfaction to come first.

This question of intentional suffering explores the intersection between outer, material suffering—which is what mankind generally understands by the word—and *inner* suffering, which is of a different quality and requires a different response. We can't come to the understanding of intentional suffering until we clearly distinguish between our inner and our outer lives, and develop an organic and tactile experience of the inner life.

Our difficulty lies in the fact that so much of our attention is directed outwardly, lacking the connection to sensation and feeling which is so necessary in life if we are to know our inner experience in the first place. We *think* a lot; we don't *sense*, and we don't *feel*. When we *do* sense and feel, they are almost entirely reactive; the minds that govern these parts of ourselves are untrained and unconscious.

Intentional suffering involves going *towards* that which we don't like. We don't like people to be cruel or unkind to us; yet in our sleepy confusion, we respond in kind. This is what ego and self-defense are all about. The proposal that we become aware enough of ourselves to say *no* to this habit is a thread that runs through all the great religions, in one way or another; yet it forms the warp and weft of them largely as a creature of the thinking mind. We're adepts at rationalization; yet the world around us proves over and over again, on both a microcosmic and macroscopic scale, that the thinking mind is fundamentally deficient. One might argue, in light of recent human events (by recent, I mean the last 5 to 10,000 years or so) that it's *not* a mind, and it *doesn't* think. We routinely engage, as a species, in entirely irrational acts that are demonstrably selfish and destructive. That is a nutshell into which you can stuff most of Beelzebub's advice, if you're in the mood for stuffing things.

Beelzebub is, among many other things, a chronicle of disasters. The products of disasters are varied and unpredictable; all are extraordinary, but not all are bad. For example, the Austrian psychologist Victor Frankl survived Auschwitz and wrote an astonishing book called *Man's Search for Meaning*. One essential point of the book (among many) is that *meaning emerges through suffering*. It is much like emergence in the biological world: a series of actions, in this case destructive ones, produce a whole much greater than the sum of their parts. It brings to mind the essential difference between those in Hell and in Purgatory in *Dante's Divine Comedy*. The punishments are the same in both places; yet in Purgatory, those who suffer agree that their punishment is just. Unlike those in hell, they understand that suffering has a purpose. The bad, in other words, is the servant of the good, for without it we would not know what good is.

In suffering, we endure; and we ought, furthermore, to intend to endure in an inner sense. Put differently, we develop the inner will to endure; so in intentional suffering, what is proposed is a path of intentional will.

This is the point of our lives: endurance is what we are built for, and we endure in order to become decent. It's said that Lord Pentland told folks the Gurdjieff work was meant to produce a decent human being; but no decent being emerges from our larval stage without suffering and overcoming it.

So the concept of intentional suffering occupies a place of priority in Gurdjieff's cosmology and his instructions for inner work, and the paper is an attempt to take a look at exactly what he means by the term, and how it compares to esoteric and other Christian practices.

I think that the following statement is, after an exhaustive review of his comments about intentional suffering in the book, the most succinct statement that he makes in defining the nature of intentional suffering:

> One of the best means of rendering ineffective the predisposition in your nature to crystallize the consequences of the properties of the organ Kundabuffer is intentional suffering, and the greatest intentional suffering can be obtained in our presences by compelling ourselves to endure the displeasing manifestations of others towards ourselves.[21]

So let's take a look at the organ Kundabuffer and what exactly the consequences of the organ Kundabuffer consist of.

In essence, Kundabuffer is ego manifestation is characterized by selfish behavior. It imparts agency to man and his own will. We think we can *do*; that's a typical characteristic of egoism, and it acts destructively in regard to other beings and circumstances; so if you review all of the features that Kundabuffer imparts, you'll see that almost without exception they are egoistic features.

A brief summary of some of the features of intentional suffering are as follows:

~ It takes place in relationship to other beings. It's not a solitary discipline, and he takes the example of the Self-Tamers to contrast how drastically wrong it is to attempt to suffer in the absence of others.
~ It requires submission of one's own will in the midst of circumstances.
~ It is a surrender of agency, it is non-judgmental; it takes on an attribute of service to others, and it is in essence an unselfish inner action that is aimed at a higher principle than the material reaction we usually engage in outer life.

Practices, organizations and systems to describe the power for change to the individual and the ego ultimately suppose a potential to escape material suffering through personal effort. Agency in these practices is ascribed to the individual; one can *do* something. This is very typical of what we think about efforts to ameliorate suffering. Gurdjieff categorically dismissed such efforts because they don't do enough to bring a person to an inner sense of their own nothingness.

One purpose of intentional suffering is to prepare oneself for service, a principle expounded in the third and fourth obligolnian strivings. Both strivings imply active selflessness in the service of others, and they are the antithesis of egoistic action.

Finally, we're introduced to the idea that suffering itself is the essential root of existing, existence, and being.

21 Gurdjieff, *Beelzebub's Tales*, (Triangle Editions: 1992) P 223

"'In all three-centered beings of our entire Universe without exception, including us men, owing to the data crystallized in our common presences for engendering in us the divine impulse of Conscience, "all-of-us" and the whole of our essence, are and must be already in our foundation, only suffering.[22]

This sounds like a grim prognosis cast in terms of an eternal struggle between the natural and spiritual side of mankind's being, but it isn't, because without this struggle the redemptive force of conscience cannot arise.

In mankind, ordinary moral suffering is, according to Beelzebub, futile. Conventional outward morality is in effect useless; the action of inner suffering is the only means whereby an objective morality can develop.

So that's a brief recap of some of the features of Gurdjieff's use of suffering; and we're now going to turn to Meister Eckhart. He, like Gurdjieff, assigned suffering priority in the development of the soul, and in Eckhart's spiritual landscape, egoistic action is willful action.

Suffering in Eckhart's teachings ultimately arises from a misalignment of our own will with God's. The aim of suffering is to turn human beings back towards God's will shorn of ego.

> The good man always wants and desires to suffer for God sake; he loves to suffer for God's sake. He loves for the sake of loving, works for the sake of working, and for that reason God loves and works without ceasing.[23]

This emphasis on work and long echoes Gurdjieff's famous aphorism, "I love him who loves work," and it mirrors the principle of conscious labor.

The suffering is a selfish selfless suffering that is engaged on in on behalf of God and in service of an ultimate reunion with God: the ultimate striving of every being in Beelzebub's universe is an identical reunion with his Endlessness.

Eckhart says that humanity is called on to perform a service on behalf of God: he *suffers for God's sake*. The phrase not only reminds us of Gurdjieff's fourth obligolnian striving; it also echoes the adage that one works for the sake of work itself and not for results.

So let's take a little bit of a look at what Eckhart says about suffering in summary: how did he view the question?

It takes place in a relationship; it's not a solitary discipline. It is of the world and in the world, but it is not aimed at the world. It requires submission of one's own will; it involves an inner effort, and Eckhart emphasizes that inner effort again and again; it is unselfish, non-judgmental, meritorious, and it is also aimed at a higher principle; and I would argue that intentional suffering as Gurdjieff proposed it encapsulates essential Christian and Buddhist virtues of patience, tolerance, and kindness.

These ideas go back to Plato and even earlier, really; the Stoics had a conception of the idea of acceptance that is encapsulated, perhaps, in this quote:

> What is the best comfort and suffering in distress is that a man should take all things as if he had wished and prayed for them.[24]

So the stoic concepts that Eckhart introduces here is that we ought to form a different *intention* towards our suffering, a different inward intention than what our ego adopts. Epictitus mentions

22 Gurdjieff, *Beelzebub's Tales*, (Triangle Editions: 1992) P 340
23 Eckhart, *The Complete Mystical Works of Meister Eckhart*, P 543.
24 Ibid., P 530.

the same adage, and the inference is that our inner attitude must be brought *intentionally into alignment* with the objective truth of outer events. St. Buddha's instructions to achieve this principally by bearing the unpleasing manifestations of others is exquisitely tuned to put us, on a daily basis, face to face with exactly that which is not as we would wish it.

So let's talk a little bit about what voluntary and *intentional* action are because there is a difference. To volunteer is to offer oneself outwardly, to go *towards* created things, which is certainly not the direction Eckhart pointed us in; and to *intend* is *tend inwardly*, that is, to direct one's attention inwardly. This is to go away from created things and towards the divine spark of the soul which exists before creation in Eckhart's conception of the universe.

It is an effort to *attend to being.* I think that the points of contact between Eckhart's teachings and de Salzmann's comments on this in *The Reality of Being* form a powerful link between the esoteric Christian tradition and the Gurdjieffian tradition

As to outwardness, Eckhart had some rather amusing things to say. This is one of my favorite Eckhart quotes:

> Some people want to see God with their own eyes as they see a cow, and they want to love God as they love a cow. You love a cow for her milk and her cheese and your own profit; that is what all those men do who love God for outward wealth or inward consolation. They do not truly love God, they love their own profit[25]

So in our outwardness we think that loving the cow brings us happiness; that's our conception of the world, and I think we all share. But Gurdjieff really had a much higher vision of this; he said that "Every real happiness for man can arise exclusively from some unhappiness which he has already experienced.

… and to take the whole paradigm one step further, Eckhart believes that suffering and joy actually have a consonance to one another, that they are linked experiences and that suffering and joy, or joy and sorrow, can't be separated from one another and that in suffering and sorrow, actually, is where joy is found. This is a very peculiar formulation; the church was not always comfortable with things Eckhart said; it's very possible this was one of them, but he really felt that suffering was a key to understanding our inner life; and of course Gurdjieff proposed a cosmos where that tension was one of the engines that drove the *feeling nature of God himself* which is an enormous idea—an enormous idea.

The forces are mutually dependent; one cannot be recognized without the presence of the other, yet we tend to seek happiness at the *expense* of suffering, presuming that it is our right and destiny.

Gurdjieff asserts the opposite, and Eckhart goes one step further:

> … one should also know that in nature the impress and inflow of the highest and supreme nature is more delightful and pleasing to anything than its own nature and essence. From this a man may know whether it would be right for him if it would be pleasant and delightful for him to abandon his natural will and to give it up and deny himself totally in everything that God wants him to suffer.[26]

So the two masters here, Gurdjieff and Eckhart, are bringing us closer and closer to an idea of suffering that I think is radical and common to all the great religions if we peel back the layers.

---

25 Eckhart, *The Complete Mystical Works of Meister Eckhart*, p 117.
26 Ibid., p 544.

The surrender of agency is also a big feature in Eckhart's teachings: we should trust in God; we should not believe that *we* can *do*, we should believe that *God* can do, and that we cannot—and it is that trust in faith in Eckhart's teachings that comes closest to touching Gurdjieff's adage that *man cannot do.*

So we're brought here to a theology of positive suffering, to intentionally suffering on behalf of God, in other words, is an act of joy—it's a comprehensive theology of suffering, inner and outer, through an alignment of one's own will with the will of the absolute—and let's remember that when Gurdjieff wrote *Beelzebub's Tales to His Grandson,* he chose as the protagonist a character who had chosen his own will over the will of His Endlessness, and because of that choice was banished to the solar system Ors; so Beelzebub himself is an illustration of the idea that ultimately one has to come back into realignment with the will of the absolute—that is his life task when we meet him, the task which by the end of the book he accomplishes.

In any event, my argument here is that Gurdjieff's conscious labor and intentional suffering are in other words deeply tied to the Orthodox Christian idea of complete surrender to God's will, and the entire premise of the book is framed by this effort of the act of submission to God.

It's worth taking a look at what the book and Meister Eckhart say about our fallen nature. In Gurdjieff's universe, our degenerate condition is the collective result of mistakes by cosmic agencies; we are not the owners of sins that have driven us to where we are; and in a passage that we *know* the Inquisition wasn't happy about, Eckhart said:

> ... and so, since God in a way wills that I should have sinned, I would not wish that I had not done so, for thus God's will is done in earth—that is, in ill doing—as well as in heaven, that is, in well doing. I accept and take the suffering in God's will and from God's will. Such suffering alone is perfect.[27]

So Eckhart did not see our sin as our own, in the same way than in *Beelzebub's Tales,* catastrophes that befall mankind are not of his own agency; that is to say, they came from an outside source.

In any event the critical mechanisms here that both masters share is that one has engage in conscious labor; there's a *theology of positive choice.* Mankind has to choose to go against his ego—I think that that's at the heart of the idea of intentional suffering—and that choice cannot be coerced either through form—that is to say, the religions—or through miracles. The individual has to undertake an inner choice, an intentional choice, to go against this, and Gurdjieff's essential message, which I think is an expansion of Eckhart's ideas in some ways, is that the work takes place in *ordinary life*—it can't take place in a monastery, it has to take place *now*—as we are today, and that is, *today.*

I think that it echoes something that Swedenborg said over and over again, which is that a person's intention is paramount in the action of spiritual development. Swedenborg was adamant that intention was everything; it determines whether a man goes to heaven or hell. It's also a theology of relationship; The Gurdjieff work is a work of relationship, and the whole book, really, *Beelzebub's Tales,* is about relationships—it's as much a work about human beings and their relationships with one another as it is a work of cosmology or theology of philosophy. We can only suffer in relationship with one another, we can't do it through a set of laws, we can't do it in a cave—and we do this in order to go against our selfishness; and if there's one thing I'm certain of it's that Mr. Gurdjieff was a man who unselfishly devoted himself to development both of himself and others. I think that is a

27 Eckhart, *The Complete Mystical Works of Meister Eckhart,* P 531.

core concept in this book and in our practice; and we can't really see our self-serving impulses unless we come up against other people and we are honest with ourselves and with them, which is of course the court the greatest difficulty we face in this work.

So it's a lot to swallow; but those who actually read the paper will see that the one of the points, and it does bring in a number of other teachings, is that Gurdjieff's intentional suffering bears notable relationships to a wide range of other teachings. He was a highly unorthodox teacher who brought a highly Orthodox teaching; and that's his value—his teaching is very much of the traditions, he's not a marginal figure in religious tradition, he is a major figure—and he's part of the spiritual DNA of mankind. This book we study together is part of our spiritual DNA: Gurdjieff certainly conceived of it as a heritage, and I think that this passage summarizes that:

> I must tell you about the history of its arising and existence so that you may real-ize that if something is obtained by the three-brain beings on your planet thanks to their being Partkdolg-duty—that is to say, their conscious labor and intentional suffering—not only are these attainments utilized by them for the welfare of their own being, but also, as with us, a certain part of these attainments is transmitted by heredity and becomes the property of their direct descendants—which is in this mo-ment a place in which we all stand together; and these are the credits for those who are interested in where the imagery came from.

And now it's time for questions...

Lee van Laer — doremishock@gmail.com

QUESTIONS AND ANSWERS

COMMENT: Thank you very much. It's very comprehensive. I just have a question that is kind of minor, in passing, you said something about the strivings; you mentioned the third and fourth striving together, and I wanted to know more about your feeling about the third striving as somehow linked with suffering. I think that's what you said.

VAN LAER: Well, that's a good question ... the effort to know more and more about the laws of world creation and world maintenance is deeply tied to the idea of suffering, because we are responsible for a world—an inner world—a cosmos within ourselves, and we suffer in order to understand the laws of maintenance in that inner Cosmos; so it's actually very closely tied to that, as an inner ques-tion. When impressions fall into us, we're a gravitational field, we're the surface of a planet— and everything that enters us stays inside our gravity field, we can't get rid of any of it over the course of a lifetime. That material, as it's accumulated, forms a solar system within us, as it were. Over the course of a lifetime when we take in these impressions, we're required to live with all of them. In my own case— I speak only for myself—I was an alcoholic when I was young; I abused drugs, I did some things that I've had to live with the consequences of. I can't expunge them; I have to *incorporate* every experience and understand the laws that govern this world that has fallen into me over the course of a lifetime, and I think that that's why I equate the study of that particular law with suffering who I am, and what has happened to me over the course of a life.

That's my impression of it, and of course he says in the fourth striving you have to pay as quickly as possible for one's arising and individuality in order afterward to be free to lighten as much as possible the sorrow of our common father; so this inward tuition, this intuition or *payment*—and it is an intuition—is necessary because it leads me towards an appreciation of suffering that is no longer personal. My conception of suffering is generally very personal and egoistic; and I think that this calls us to an experience of suffering that is greater than my own individuality.

COMMENT: Thank you very much for a wonderful presentation on a very important part of the work.

What I would address is something that would challenge our formatory thinking about suffering. I understood you to point out in your presentation that we tend to look at suffering with some sort of grimness. That would challenge my formatory thinking about suffering. What is the joy of suffering? What is my experience of the joy of suffering? That would bring both of them together, and anyone, for example, who has seriously worked with diminishing unnecessary talking, I believe have had that experience of flexibility which is emotionally unexplainable; but it's there. In addition to this flexibility, could you point at something that can manifest as joy and suffering?

VAN LAER: Well, the feeling experience of suffering takes place within the circulation of an octave as all of the lawful events, so there's a hierarchy, as it were, and so the question is a complex one—there are orders within, it is ordinary because there is an order to it—we don't always see that very clearly—but suffering goes from the basest notes in the octave like *Re*, where it's, you know, my girlfriend breaking up with me—just very material and ordinary things—to suffering the fact that I *am not,* which would really be a suffering related to being and of a truly higher-order because it represents a movement through the evolution of the octave that has come to a realization that isn't there when I'm just worried about the fact that I don't have a girlfriend any more.

But the question is an extraordinarily subtle one… that I think every individual has to bring their own experience to; the comments I would make directly to your question are that the experience of suffering, when it *approaches* the understanding of this word we use, joy—which is a very inadequate word—is that it is very closely related to sensation, that it is a material vibration of a much finer quality, and that it is an *inward payment*, and when one pays inwardly—when one's intuition becomes active—one knows organically, in the marrow of one's bones, that it is right, and although the emotional experience is one of what I think we would, with our ordinary parts, call anguish—it is a *true* experience, and because it is true, has an inestimable value that is so much greater than my ordinary parts because I rarely touch truth, you know; and when truth touches me in this way, and it cannot be denied, the fact that it is a form of sorrow or anguish; it is joy—it *is* joy.

I don't think they are different, in my experience; but it's a material thing, you know; the universe is penetrated to the finest level—even the subatomic level— with this vibration of the sorrow of His Endlessness, and we are receivers that are capable of developing the organic capacity to receive that material. He teaches that in this book; it's possibly for me one of the most extraordinary and true things in the book; after you throw everything else in the book out, the fact that he says that sets this work apart from every other religious and philosophical discipline that I've ever encountered.

In my experience I know that he told us truth about this; it's a form of nectar that's being given to us, suffering, and we have the opportunity to come to that. When we do, we can know at the lowest level, because we can't touch anything but the bottom of heaven, we can know what God is. So that's what I work for, to suffer, and that's the right word for it, and hoping others may have had a taste of this.

COMMENT: My question actually emerged at the point that you talked about your "youth sins" and the fact that you live under the knowledge that there is nothing you can do to annul them; they're there, so to speak, and I believe really that this is what real suffering is, that you live in front of things, that you know the way they are and there's nothing you can do about them; and in a way this is what's going on in purgatory; the endless suffering there is, being faced with this kind of inevitability. My question is, do people in Purgatory go someplace that they're free from their suffering, and what kind of place does bliss have in this whole process?

VAN LAER: Well, you know, Gurdjieff didn't ... and there are others who probably I'm sure know the chapter even more intimately than I do on that, I'm probably not the world's foremost authority of purgatory ... he seems to infer that there is no resolution in purgatory as it were ... I don't recall. Does anybody else, can anybody else respond to that particular point, does he give us in a doorway out from purgatory? R., what do you think?

COMMENT: Well, yes, because purgatory is to purge ... due to the fact that having descended, we became somewhere infected with an imperfection that we could not take back to the level of the absolute, so we are in purgatory until that imperfection is removed ... which is as long as it takes.

VAN LAER: It's open ended in a sense ...

COMMENT: It's open ended, completely ... in the way that I read it, for sure.

VAN LAER: I tend to agree with that; I don't think that he has a remedy where he says, "well, if you do this, then you're covered. It's ... that's not in there. I personally, in my experience, have an understanding of an absolute redemptive power which would imply that there is the possibility of purging, of purification ... and then you had a second part your question, which was ...

COMMENT: ...What's the place of bliss?

VAN LAER: Well ... bliss is something that is oversold in today's New Age teachings; everybody wants it, and there are magazines that can tell you how to get it; I subscribe to a few of them, and they're really very good magazines. I can't say anything: I can't say anything bad about them. For example, Shambala Sun is a Buddhist publication; it's a wonderful magazine with very upbeat articles about bliss and how to obtain it.

I'm getting to an age where I should probably just frankly speak about some things ... you know most of us are familiar with the literature on religious ecstasy, at least I think many of us have probably encountered religious ecstatics and heard what they had to say about religious ecstasy; and I can assure you that, for example, what St. Teresa had to say about it was quite accurate. Religious ecstasy is not ecstatic in the way that we would expect it to be, and bliss is not bliss in the way we expect it to be, because the great religious ecstatics—and you can know them by their words—they did not see beautiful pictures; that's not what religious ecstasy consists of—had experiences where they had an extraordinary bliss, physical bliss, that was a pleasurable ecstasy that was so powerful that it was cosmological in nature. At the exact same time it produces a feeling of emotional anguish that destroys everything that one is, that could not be sustained without the bliss. So that you couldn't bear the anguish if the ecstasy wasn't sent along with it at the same time; and it's done that way because the purification can't take place unless forces are balanced, you'll die if they aren't.

There a number of yogic practices related to the two secret chakras that lie around the heart that talk about this but I'm not the expert on that—I know someone who is if there are people who want to talk about, but it's not really talked about much in yoga, because it's technically forbidden. And it's certainly forbidden to open those places yourself, completely forbidden, it's only allowed if they are opened for you.

But in any event that the point is that bliss *isn't bliss*; it's actually a form of anguish, and that anguish is a gift, so I think the question of bliss itself is misunderstood. It's like the cow; it's happiness, but it's not a cow.

What we're searching for is the immolation of everything we are in a fire that purifies us; we have to be willing to confront that at some point and be destroyed, as it were, because that's the only way that we can exit purgatory, is a complete burning in the fire of what we are, and a movement into a new piece of territory.

COMMENT: I would have wanted to hear more about the images, your choice of images, particularly Hieronymus Bosch; could you tell me a little bit about how you've worked in bringing Bosch and intentional suffering together? How could I approach reading the language of Bosch better?

VAN LAER: Well, most of Bosch's paintings are wisdom paintings that contain deeply encoded teachings about the nature of our being, and they're certainly viewed through a Christian lens, but that doesn't invalidate them in any sense. I picked a few of these because they had a sense of humor—for example the man and the pig dressed as a nun-clearly to me seems to suggest the man is having to bear the displeasing manifestations of another—and I chose the images from the left-hand panel of the "Garden of Earthly Delights" because of the image of Christ. Indeed, all of the images in the Garden of Eden seem to bring us to a higher conception of man. That particular panel isn't the most sensational thing Bosch ever painted, but it is probably one of the most extraordinary paintings in the entire Western ouevre, because the fountain that comes down from above in that painting represents the divine inflow, not just into the earth, but into our being. It is the higher energy that Mme. talks about in her books, and he *painted* it —it's an outrageous proposition; but he *did* that.

Actually, that fountain ... I was talking to someone from the New York Gurdjieff Foundation on Christmas Eve four years ago and we were chatting about Bosch and this and that, and suddenly I saw the painting, and it came to me in a flash; that's why I wrote the book about the painting.

Bosch was deeply involved in trying to obtain an inner understanding of who we are and many of his paintings dealt with the subject of suffering and he's a logical source for visual material. Van der Weyden's crucifixion was put there largely because it's another extraordinary painting, and of course we just saw a fragment of it, but it's unlike most of the altarpieces of its time, it's very minimalist. The image of Christ's suffering is the signature icon of the Christian understanding of suffering, and of course there is everything from a very superficial to a very deep level of understanding we can come to in that.

Christ's sacrifice is in a certain sense a Hindu sacrifice, because he took on the karmic role of taking on the sins of all mankind, which is what a guru does for his followers. He takes on their karmic burden.

The adoration of the Magi—another Bosch painting—was chosen largely because of the prayerful attitude that the characters around the virgin adopt and that is actually an enneagram painting; the circle represents a progression of spiritual understanding as you circle it; it's very fascinating because it looks very simple but it's actually very complicated. The ecstasy of St. Teresa... well, we talked a little about religious ecstasy-I didn't really plan to talk about that in this presentation, but it's an important subject, because suffering is deeply tied to religious ecstasy, and actually there isn't any ecstasy—ecstasy is suffering—so I think it once again people get it wrong; what they're after is happiness and all this wonderful stuff, and actually what we're after is to be destroyed—and we do that through suffering.

The temptation of St. Anthony's is a painting I'm writing a book on now; it'll probably have some other paintings in it, but that is an extremely complicated painting, and unlike almost every other painting about St. Anthony's temptations, it's very clear to even the average critic who writes about the painting that the temptations that St. Anthony experienced were inner temptations. And the painting is presented in that way; the typical image we have is all these demons tearing him apart, that's the crowd favorite. But the painting that Bosch did is a different kind of work, as it were.

The vision of the hereafter which came after the earth and the comet is from a painting in Venice which has a picture of what is undoubtedly a near-death experience. NDEs were most famously described by Swedenborg; he was one of the first persons that wrote about them in any detail in Western literature. Here's a painting that was done several centuries earlier that shows you exactly the same conception of the vision of entering heaven.

The Wayfarer is a painting of a journeyman, a spiritual searcher, so that's why we ended up there towards the end of the presentation. But the visual language of the Northern Renaissance has the capacity to open up the feelings in the same way that music does; certainly it's not quite the same, but the purpose of art and music is supposed to be to offer us an avenue, a nonverbal avenue, into being; this is why I opened up with that quote by Eckhart, where he said God is an unspoken word.

COMMENT: Gurdjieff says that the one thing we are most unwilling to give up is our suffering; and I must say to me that has always tied in more to what Eckhart says about suffering belonging to God, in the sense that if we can give up our suffering, I mean literally offer it up, then it becomes transformed, and that's always seemed to me what Eckhart says... I mean, it's very interesting that's not a comparison you've drawn in your talk.

VAN LAER: It's in there ... I think it's a very good point; perhaps to me it's obvious enough that I didn't expound on it, but you're quite right. I think that the fulcrum that I was turning on here was more the idea that our own suffering is always interpreted from an egoistic point of view. Victor Frankel said that every human being thinks their own suffering is the largest suffering that there ever was, you know; and it's quite true—I think that I've got it worse than everyone else, and I think that there's an egoistic aspect of suffering that we have to surrender if we want to go deeper. Again, when you say you want to give up your suffering I think that the language that I was using in this presentation was that one has to align one's will with that of God, which is essentially the same action. If one is thankful for the sufferings one endures then one is, in essence, offering to a higher power much like those in AA do; that's where you begin when you get sober, you are turning your suffering over to a higher agency because you recognize that you are weak.

It was a shock to me many, many years ago when my group leader Henry Brown came in one day—you never knew what Henry was going to say—and said, "we're weak. Without this work we're weak— we wouldn't need this work if we were strong."

And so I see that I'm weak, and my offering can begin there if I see that.

COMMENT: Relative to this question of aligning one's will and the image of Beelzebub when he had his revolt and was banished and Looisos came down with this job for him, his impulse was immediately—I never get the feeling that he was out of sync with the will of Endlessness—even though he saw something that just didn't make sense ... so that's one question ... the other question is, what about the relationship of suffering and degrees of reason? Because in the image of Beelzebub there's never a hint of what you say, the personal suffering and yet there is this constant active, inquiry into where he ended up, in this system Ors, and his researches—all these active inquires he went through— there's something about that aspect of suffering that seems a little different; and it also seems that without that banishment he would not have acquired the high degree of reason that he has acquired. So how do you relate these two?

VAN LAER: Well, *Beelzebub's Tales* recount the doings of many active agencies, messengers that were sent from above to correct things. Beelzebub's an observer; his role throughout the book is as an observer, and I think that there may be a clue to redemption there, because he doesn't interfere or try fix anything in the same way that many of the other even higher, supposedly higher, cosmic beings do, and you'll notice that in the book flaws exist from the top to the bottom; even the highest cosmic agencies make horrific mistakes and can't foresee the consequences of their actions; but Beelzebub, if we want to speak about objective reason, his objectivity comes from his willingness to observe; and it's a critique, it's a very measured one; it's done with humor and compassion, and he also *tolerates*.

I've been interested in this idea of objective reason for some time and I'm not sure any of us know exactly what it means I actually embarked on a few stabs at what Eckhart says about reason and what Gurdjieff says about it, but that's a very incomplete work—but this role of Beelzebub as observer, I think, is important to your question—he *sees* what takes place—and I doubt that helps. You know we're asked to *see* over and over again and if there's one thing I don't want to do it's look at myself—and I'm speaking for myself here, so others can judge this from their own perspective—but you know I'm afraid of myself; I don't want to engage in the intimacy that I need to engage in the *inner* intimacy that's required for real inner, inward, experience... I'm always afraid of something. I can't tell you what it is because it's not like it's one thing, but there's a constant willingness to turn away; a will to be fearful of myself and what I am, and Beelzebub seems kind fearless to me—he's a hero because he's not afraid to see everything—kind of wonderful—he doesn't turn away.

COMMENT: Could you explain to me again what's the word intentional, just the word intentional, in very, very simple means.

VAN LAER: Well, an *intention* is what takes place inwardly, and it represents both a direction, a tendency toward, what tends to go in a direction—to go inward—and to *tend* is to also to tend *to*, care for.

So when I use the word intimacy there is an *intention* in its esoteric content; to go inward, intimately, to myself and to *attend* to my being.

It's an action where I get very close to myself, it's tied to the action of sensation—organic sensation. For those of you who have read it,—and I think it's well worth reading for those of you that haven't—Gurdjieff, in I think the seventh or eighth wartime meeting, says that *your organic sensation of being is what creates your individuality*; and this organic sensation of being is very closely tied to intentionality—to an inward attention—it's got nothing to do with whether I am unable to listen to you or not, because I'm not. We all know how poor our attention is; it's an inward attention, not something that we're often very close to.

COMMENT: I just wanted to address the question that was brought from T. I certainly agree that Beelzebub is a seer, an observer, but I think that's the half-truth; he is also so much an advisor, and this ability to give us advice and warnings grows out of this thing; and I think that when we can learn to see a little more, we can also get in touch with something in ourselves that can give ourselves some advice; and I think then we are talking about the contact with conscience.

VAN LAER: I think that's true. Well said.

COMMENT: I have the mike, and I wasn't intending to say something; but I'm going to. In *Beelzebub's Tales*, all the messengers from above are sent down to earth—except Beelzebub; he isn't *sent*, he is *banished*—and he doesn't have to deal with us, actually he's going to deal with us, because he's surprised that we kill each other all the time, when he's looking at us with his Teskooano; and for me that was a very interesting image: that he wasn't sent.

COMMENT: Intentional suffering and conscious labor are being Partkdolg-duty, and as a result of practicing that, Abrustdonis and Helkdonis are created to coat our higher being-bodies. Would you comment on what coating is and what is Abrustdonis and Helkdonis?

VAN LAER: Hmm. We're being offered to take an excursion into a vast piece of territory that I think opens like a chasm towards the very end of the presentation. Well, material is deposited, in this, that's clear enough—our impressions as we take them in fall either more or less deeply into our being, and we digest them. That's true of all the foods we take in; and as to exactly what the nature of those substances is, I think that one comes to an understanding of these things through one's own unspoken inner encounters with the truths that we digest over the course of a lifetime; so I think that it's one of those pieces of territory that's best left to the mysteries rather than... It reminds me of something that Ravi Ravindra said many years ago at a work period... "some things do not fare well under the cold light of analysis." That may sound like a cop out, but I have to leave you with that one, and I think that probably it's 10:35, we should probably wrap up here with whatever comes next.

··· ～ ···

Boordooks Bunsen Cagniard-de-la-Tour Caironana
Canaan Canineson Caravanseray Caspian
Cathodnatious centrotino Cevorksikra
Chai-Yoo Chaihana Chainonizironness Chakla
Chaldean Chaltandr chambardakh
Chami-anian Champarnakh Chatterlitz Cherub
Chiklaral Chiltoonakh chinkrooaries Chirman
Chirniano Chirnooanovo
Choon-Kil-Tez Choon-Tro-Pel choongary
Choortetev Choot-God-Litanical Choozna Chorortdiapan
Chrkhrta-Zoorrt Cinchona cinque-contra-uno clap
cocaine Codeine cossacks Daivibrizkar Darthelhlustnian
Defterocosmos Defteroëhary Degindad Demisakhsakhsa
Dephteropine Desagroanskrad Deskaldino
Dezonakooasanz Dezsoopsentoziroso Dgloz Dglozidzi
Diapharon Diardookin Dimtzoneero Dionosk
Disputekrialnian Djamdjampal Djameechoonatra
Djamtesternokhi Djartklom Djedjims Djerymetly
Djoolfapal Dooczako Doonyasha Dover
Dukhan Dynamoumzoïn Dzedzatzshoon
Dzendvokh Dzi Egoaitoorassnian
Egokoolnatsnarnian Egolionopty Egoplastikoori
Ekbarzerbazia Eknokh El Koona Nassa
Elekilpomagtistzen Elmooarno Elnapara
Emptykralnian Ephrosinia epithalamium
Epodrenekhs Epsi-Noora-Chaka Epsi-Pikan-On
Erkrordiapan Erordiapan Ersatz
Erti-Noora-Chaka Erti-Pikan-On Esperanto
etherogram Etherokrilno
Etzikolnianakhnian Evosikra Evotanas
Exioëhary Fal-Fe-Foof Ferghanian

Centrigravital Love in Gurdjieff's Rhetoric of Time

... Paul Beekman Taylor ...

"The death of a beautiful woman is, unquestionably, the most poetic topic in the world." (Edgar Allan Poe, *Philosophy of Composition*)

There has never been much doubt that some of Gurdjieff's anecdotes and stories in *Beelzebub's Tales* encode or encrypt moral concepts. The story of the Karapet steam whistle blower and of the Kurd who bought and consumed hot peppers have been explicated, most recently by Robin Bloor, as allegorical comments on traits of human behavior.[1] The riddle in the opening pages of *Meetings* challenging the reader to get a goat, a cabbage and a wolf across a river, carrying one at a time without the goat left alone with the cabbage or the wolf with the goat, can be explained easily. But the strange autobiographical scene that Gurdjieff relates in *Life Is Real Only Then, When "I Am"*, is not only far more complex but appears to concern something of greater importance than as a supposed auto-biographical recollection.[2] It is, to begin with, an integral part of the total book.

Were we to trace a putative history of Gurdjieff's sentimentality, no passage in his writing would touch our sensibilities deeper than the description of his wife and mother sitting beside him at a moment when he was painfully conscious of the impending death of both. The scene is recalled in his fictive recapitulation of the period between 7 November 1927, when he decided to rewrite his book, and the first of January 1928 when he set to work revising it (*Life Is Real* 33–43). While on a trip to the Pyrenees as the Christmas holidays were nearing, he considered that rewriting his book would occupy him for the next seven years (*Life Is Real* 34–35). Back at the Prieuré on Christmas Eve, before entering the house, he recalls that he

" ... sat down on the first bench I came to." (*Life Is Real* 36),

... the bench where he frequently sat during his writing in 1925. He then recalls that at that time his mother and wife would join him, and on one occasion from the Paradou his mother came to the bench in the company of two peacocks, a cat and a dog.[3]

"Always the cat would walk in front, the two peacocks at the side and the dog behind." (*Life Is Real* 37–38)

At the same time, invariably, his wife approached the bench from the Prieuré.

"I remembered how it often happened that they would sit by my side, one on the right and then other on my left, almost touching me, as so seated that, although very quiet in order not to hinder me, they would sometimes when I bent forward concentrating on my work whisper to each other behind my back ...

---

1 *To Fathom the Gist*. Vol. I, 193ff, and Vol. II : Gurdjieff, *Beelzebub's Tales*, "The Arch-Absurd," 13–16 and 26–27.
2 The autobiographical story of the loss of a wisdom tooth in *Tales* 33 invites allegorical interpretation.
3 The Russian for "bench" is *ckaméükam*.

> "The fact is that my mother knew not a word of the language which my wife spoke and my wife in turn understood no word of the language which my mother spoke.[4]
>
> "In spite of this, not only did they very freely interchange their ordinary opinions, but they had imparted to each other in a very short time all the peculiar experiences and the full biographies of their lives" (*Life Is Real* 38–39).

After these memories came to him on the bench, he got up to go into the house.

> "After several steps, in my thoughts there suddenly realized itself, and after only a little confrontation there was established for me clearly the following:
>
> "During the period of my greatest occupation with writing, the quality of my labor-ability was always the result of . . . passive-experiencings of suffering proceeding in me concerning these two, for me, nearest women" (*Life Is Real* 39).

The reader is liable to find himself lost in the labyrinth of images in this scene trying to find a path toward to a unified sense. The narrative context is one challenge to understanding. Consider that Gurdjieff is writing at this time on 2 April 1935 (*Life Is Real* 46), when he remembered that on 24 December 1927 the bench he sat on before going to his room in the Prieuré to sleep reminded him of one or more times in 1925 when his mother and wife sat beside him. In other words the backward temporal leap suggests, first of all, the importance of dates and time periods they localize. Since his mother died in June 1925, in Gurdjieff's fictional history of self, the scene must have taken place in the first half of the year. His wife died on 26 June 1926, a year later. His mother, Evdokia, was born on 20 November 1852,[5] so in June 1925, she was seventy-two years of age. Julia, born in 1889, was thirty-seven when she died. Gurdjieff's father, born in 1847, had died in 1918 in his seventy-second year (Gurdjieff himself, born in 1877, died in 1949, a few months before his seventy-second year). So, on the bench sit an old woman, a young woman and a man in his middle age.

Of course, it would be foolhardy to force meaning into such coincidences of dates, since the Gurdjieff family could hardly be programmed into common life spans. Nonetheless, the care with which Gurdjieff correlates the dates of the scenes on the bench with the imminent deaths of two persons he loves correlates time periods in his life as a writer with the life periods of mother and wife. This is made evident in the lines that follow that intrigue and puzzle the reader. From this moment on the bench in 1927 with the phantom presence of his wife, mother and four domestic animals, he approached his writing, he indicates, with feeling of the hopelessness of their health and their imminent deaths (*Life Is Real* 39). So occupied with his thoughts and his fatigue from his journey, Gurdjieff went to bed without removing his clothes (*Life Is Real* 40). As it is said, clothing is what one dons to greet the world.

On the next morning, when the thoughts of the previous night recurred to him, he realized that the three years of his writing (1925, 1926 and 1927), were a period of a "'degree of contact' between my consciousness and the suffering proceeding in me on behalf of my mother and my wife" that "assisted in the increase of my labor-ability" (*Life Is Real* 42). That Christmas evening, noting the children's joy around the Christmas tree, his own being "was filled as if by some singular, never till now experienced, feeling of joy" (*Life Is Real* 42). At this point he resolves to work from 1 January—the day he often claimed to be his birthday as well as the day in 1925 he began his writing–to 23 April, his name

---

4 In fact, both Gurdjieff's mother and wife understood the Russian Ouspensky used in conversing with them.
5 The French death certificate has her birth year 1841, contradicting the Alexandropol municipal record.

day and the feast of Saint George. This bond between Gurdjieff, his mother and his wife he calls "centrigravital love" (*Life Is Real* 39).

The word "centrigravital" is a nonce word, a neologism that parallels and opposes the term "centrifugal" that denotes a force drawing objects outward from a center or axis. "Centrigravital" would, then, denote a force drawing objects from and toward a hub and adding to the weight of the center which is Gurdjieff's inner subjective being. In this passage it connotes the moral force that draws two distinct groups together. One consists of Gurdjieff, his mother and wife, and the other a cat, a dog and two peacocks. It is not difficult to read the three persons as representing man's three centers: mother the physical, wife the higher-being body and Gurdjieff the spiritual body. Why Gurdjieff invented a word rather than employ "centripetal," the standard term for a physical force drawing things inward toward a center, the opposite, if you will, of "centrifugal" is a crucial point. The Greek suffix form –petra and the Latin verb petere have an etymological sense "seek," while the neologism and hapax legomenon gravital, from Latin gravis "heavy," is the origin of English "gravity"[6] and "grave."[7]

In brief, Gurdjieff, concerned with the imminent death of the two women who mean the most to him, regrets that he can do nothing to counter the hopelessness of their health (*Life Is Real* 39). He recognizes the situation as grave for them and conceives of their moral relationship as "gravital." It is difficult to grasp these threads of relationships and discern the fabric of love they weave. The scene in 1925 is an opportune moment recalled at an opportune moment. The date of recollection in 1927—Christmas Eve—the eve of the birthday of the birth of Jesus, conjoins opportune moments, each of which is a kairos.[8] The moments are opportune because the recalled scene of centrigravital love of 1925 informs a triple "labor-ability." The first in 1925 marks the beginning of his dictation of *Beelzebub's Tales* (*Life Is Real* 32) on New Year's Day. The second on Christmas Eve, 1927 sparks the "will-task" of rewriting his book in the one hundred and fourteen days between 1 January and 23 April 1928, between the feast of Circumcision and Saint George's day. One hundred fourteen is the second dollar fine amount mentioned as a fine for not signing the obligation of renouncing Orage (*Life Is Real* 126). He dates the inception of this third "will-task," on 2 April 1935 which will come to its completion twenty-one days later on 23 April, his saint's day and another kairos moment.

There is much more in this scene than meets the eye. To this scene early in 1925, recalled in the Advent season in 1927, Gurdjieff adds four other witnesses: a cat, two peacocks and a dog. Their presence adds to another vital aspect to Gurdjieff's description: outward beauty that complements the inward centrigravital force. In describing his wife's presence beside him, he pictures her eighteen years earlier, 1907, "where the awarding of prizes for beauty was going on in St. Petersburg, the famous Lena Cavalieri, then in the bloom of her youth, was deprived of the first prize" (*Life Is Real* 38). We need consider the import of this fact to the 1925 scene. The Italian-born Natalina "Lina" Cavalieri (1874–1944) was already widely known as the most beautiful woman in the world as well as Opera's greatest beauty when she visited St. Petersburg. That Julia Ostrovska took a prize for beauty from Lina in 1907 contrasts painfully with "this now stooped and sallow-faced woman" only a year before her death.[9]

6 Russian тжесть
7 I am reminded of Mercutio's pun in Shakespeare's Romeo and Juliet (III, i) who, when mortally pierced by Tybalt's sword, responds to Romeo's question about gravity of his wound with "Ask for me tomorrow and you will find me a grave man."
8 In Greek, Kairos refers to a "supreme moment" of time distinct from chronos, or sequence of time. In his poem, "Kairos and Logos," W. H. Auden characterizes it as a moment of truth in a "rhetoric of time."
9 I cannot verify this apparently invented fact.

The significance of her past beauty and present bent body is represented by the pageant procession of four attendant animals. In their silent movement behind Gurdjieff's mother and wife,

> "These four differently natured animals would already know in advance just when my mother was coming out and ... would very 'sedately' accompany her" (*Life Is Real* 37).

All of Gurdjieff's dogs carried the name "Philos," "loving" if you will. It could be said that Gurdjieff's mother reflects her name. Eudoxie signifies "Good Glory" and Eleptherova is a close cognate of Elephteria "Freedom," the motto of Greece. Her mother's name—Sophia—means "wisdom."

The centrigravital love between mother, son and his wife also includes the animals—feline, canine, and avian—who follow in stately calm and silence in a formation that would be hardly imaginable under normal circumstances. The conjoining of different animals with the intricate natural and emotional ties between Gurdjieff, his mother and his wife comprises a cryptic pageant replete with hidden, or obscure significations that challenges deciphering. In Christian iconography as well as a pet and companion, the dog is a figure of loyalty and fidelity. Though the etymology of "dog" is uncertain, Gurdjieff is known to have played with its anagram form "god," notably in the expression "bury the dog deeper."[10] The cat—Russian ко́шка—is a figure of sloth and lust in Christian iconography, and the peacock—павлин—figures immortality in Christian iconography.[11] The four animals form a cross in their procession with the cat in front flanked behind by the two peacocks and trailed by the dog. I have been told that Ouspensky said that a cat symbolizes consciousness, perhaps consciousness without mind. The lion is the chief symbol of the emotional center. The dog is a figure of man's mechanical nature and education.

One can tentatively identify the two peacocks with the two women beside Gurdjieff. Beelzebub remarks that the beautiful peacock contrasts with the dirty crow (*Tales* 599). The peacock is a figure throughout *Tales* of high class. In describing Russians as "turkeys," Beelzebub explains

> " ... that these poor Russian 'crows' cannot ... possibly become peacocks. And what is worst of all, having ceased to be crows and yet having become peacocks, they willy-nilly turn into the bird turkey ..." (*Tales* 601).

In his 1924 New York City lecture at the Neighborhood Playhouse, in a clever rhyme, Gurdjieff exposed his allegory of the carriage, horse and coachman whom he characterizes as

> " ... a type to whom applies perfectly the definition, 'The crows he raced but by peacocks outpaced'" (*Tales* 1194).[12]

Earlier, Beelzebub had remarked to Hassein that those who chew the seed of the poppy take a crow for a peacock. Curiously, he uses the word "Pavaveroon" for poppy (*Tales* 213) which is a play on the etymology of "peacock," for the Russian for peacock is павлин (pavlin). The word derives from

10 The Russian соба́ка is a common insult.
11 See Angelico Fra Filippo Lippi's "Adoration of the Magi" and Biagio d'Antonio da Firenze's "Adoration of the Child", both of which have a peacock on the roof overlooking the nativity scene.
12 Gurdjieff's jingle rhyme seems original. The Russian has от-ворон-остал-а-к-павлинам-не-пристал. German version is close to the English—Fur-ein-Raben-war-er—zu-gut—und-zu-einem-Pfauen-hats-nicht-gelangt—while the French interprets the rhyme: Corneille, corneille, tu perds ton temps, jamais tu ne seras un paon. The 1992 English has "too good for the crow but the peacock won't have him," a banal and dilatory reading of a clever rhyme. The peacock as a figure of immortality in Western art and literature is often thought to derive from its popular association with the Phoenix. In Sean O'Casey's Juno and the Paycock (1924), the peacock figures a rejection of the horrors of the political and moral reality of subjugated Ireland.

Latin pavus and from the grammatical form pava the English language formed "pea-." The word papaveraceae is the botanical name for the poppy plant. In Roman mythology, pavo is Juno's bird and Egyptian mythology, the peacock is the fetish emblem of Heliopolis, city of the sun and seat of the worship of Ra, the Sun God. Though Gurdjieff's peacocks communicate silently, Medieval Latin bestiaries note that the Pavo is so named because of his voice. In De Civitate Dei, Augustine remarks that God has the power of the flesh of peacocks that never decay. More significant in the context of Gurdjieff's experience, is the Yezidi symbol of a peacock in a circle. I am told that the inner-rooted Yezidi is anchored in an inner centrigravitational field.

It is in Egyptian mythology that an appropriate value for the cat can be found in the person of Bast, the Cat goddess. The figure of a cat decorating her images represents protection against contagious diseases. The cat is associated in some Medieval texts as acuteness after Greek catus. Though Gurdjieff's dog Philos, like the peacocks and cat, communicates silently, dog, canis, is often associated with canor "melody" and canere "to sing." I have been told by one who knows that the Egyptian mythic Anubis, the jackal or savage dog-headed god of the dead, represents the fractal iterative structure of reality, leading ever inward. The Chinese Celestial Dog T'ien-kou helps to drive away evil spirits. In the West, priests are referred to as watchdogs."

It is not unlikely that Gurdjieff was familiar with many of these mythological values attached to his Prieuré animals. His reconstructed pageant procession of them enforces his concern for the two dangerously ill women close to him whom he could not help. Their future state of health in immortal form is prefigured by them. The procession of cat, peacocks and dog can be read as a parade of doctors assisting Gurdjieff whose medical skills have not been able to effect cures of mother and wife. They march in sedate manner to join and reinforce centrigravital love. The bench, etymologically appropriate, is a bank of love.

The lost vitality in mother and wife is regained by Gurdjieff when he overcomes his fatigue and, after sleep—like the sleep in death of mother and wife earlier—is re-habilitated to give his book new life. The retracing in 1927 of an incident in 1925 incites a revival of his creative energy, and the retracing in 1935 of the 1927 recollection invigorates the composition of *Life Is Real*. Both re-tracings rehearse the centrigravital love imbedded in his emotions.[13] The truism Ars longa, vita brevis matches the common cultural belief among many peoples that the life of the book supersedes the death of the maker and his subject. This is at least an ancillary function of Gurdjieff's in the *Third Series*, of course, and the two peacocks that are figures of the two women he loves are icons of the immortality that he forges for them and himself in his book.

If the scene Gurdjieff constructs as a panoply of profound ideas is fiction-fact, we must be aware that the title of the *Third Series—Life Is Real Only When "I Am"*—challenges us to discover the gist of what is actually real; and, Gurdjieff's repetitive concern with the scene in 1925, recalled first in 1927 and then, finally, in 1935, is a concern of the *Third Series* with the possibility of the "prolongation of human life" (*Life Is Real* 143, 161) and "longevity" (166, et passim).

Gurdjieff is, once again, playing with numbers. It is important to note that there are eleven precursory numbered paragraphs of the Prologue that begin and end with the exclamation "I AM." Spinoza conjectured that all things strive to be what they are: a stone would be a stone, man a man and God

13 One recalls Wordsworth's assertion in the "Preface" to the 1800 edition of Lyrical Ballads that the creative impulse "takes it origin from emotion recollected in tranquillity."

a God. Here Gurdjieff exclaims that his striving has reached attainment. God searches for the one who searches for Him; that is in this context the searcher Gurdjieff. The coincidence of the number eleven with the ecstatic realization that there is a God of the All as well as a God of the One is significant. I expect Gurdjieff knew the Cabbalistic tradition that counts ninety-nine names for God in the Pentateuch, eleven times nine, if you will. The hundredth name would be equivalent to the tetragrammaton YHVH, the ultimate, ineffable, or unknowable name. Putting Gurdjieff's enneagram into this context, eternity is the ninth attribute of God.

Timeline
1907 Julia Ostrovska wins a beauty contest in St. Petersburg
1925 June 22, Gurdjieff's mother, Eudoxie Kalerof (Evdokia Elephterova in Alexandropol records) dies
1926 July 26, Julia Gurdjieff dies
1927 December 24, on bench in front of the Prieuré, Gurdjieff recalls 1925 and 1927
1935 April 2, Gurdjieff writes his recollection of the bench in the *Third Series*

Bibliography
Bloor, Robin *To Fathom the Gist*. Vol. I, Austin, TX Karnak Press, 2013.
———. *To Fathom the Gist*. Vol. II: The Arch-Absurd. Austin, TX Karnak Press, 2014.

Postscript: Gurdjieff's Mother

Gurdjieff's mother died on 22 June 1925. The death certificate issued by the town of Avon reads, in my translation: No. 42, 22 June Eudoxie Kalerof Gurdjieff, widow.

On 22 June 1925, seven AM, died at home in the Pieuré des Basses Loges, Eudoxie Kalerof, born in Alexandropol (Russia), 20 November 1841, without profession, daughter of Elepter Kalerof and Sophie, without other information, husbands deceased, widow of Ivan Gurdjieff, documented on 22 June 1925, two PM — according to the declaration of Olga de Schumacker, wife of Thomas de Hartmann, thirty-two years of age, without profession, at Avon, who having read this declaration, signed it with us, Christian d'Aleyrac Baron de Coulange, Maire d'Avon.

The signature of "Olga de Hartman" appears beneath the Baron's. There are a number of curious errors in this document, beginning with Olga's signature which omits the second "N" in her married name. Second, she was not Olga de Schumacker, since there was not a particle of nobility in the family name of her parents, Arkady and Lyova Schumacher. A year later, Olga signed the death certificate of Julia Gurdjieff in the same manner. One would assume that her patronymic was the feminine form Kalerova or Kalerovna, not the masculine form Kalerof[f], but it was probably common for French authorities to use the masculine form for women's names. So, Julia was named Ostrowsky, though on her death certificate her mother's name is recorded as Marie Fédérowska Misich. Gurdjieff's death certificate lists his mother as Evdaki Kaleroff.

One might question why Gurdjieff dispatched Olga to furnish essential birth facts of his mother and his wife, rather than himself. It is not unlikely that she is responsible for apparent slips in fact. Whether fact or fiction, she gives 1841 for the birth year of Gurdjieff's mother. Were she was born in 1841, we must add one more question to those still unanswered about Gurdjieff's date of birth. He was a role-player and spinner of fantastic tales. Gurdjieff himself claimed often in public that he was born in 1866, though all official documents he carried, including his Armenian, Russian, German and French passports have 1877 as the year of his birth. Alexandropol municipal records have 1877, although a census report of 1907 has the year 1880 for his birth and 1883 for his brother Dmitri.[14]

People who knew Gurdjieff, having no access to official records, accepted his word that he was born in 1866, as indicated by references to his age at various times. In his biography, Gurdjieff: *Anatomy of a Myth*, James Moore mounts a formidable argument in favor of 1866, and people who knew him well, including myself, assumed by his appearance at the time of his death in 1949 that he looked far older than seventy-one years. Complicating calculating his age are the dates of birth of his parents. His father, born Ivan Gurdjiogli in 1847 according to official records and died in June 1918, married Evdokia Elephtherova, born in 1852, in 1871. Had Gurdjieff been born in 1866, his mother would have been fourteen years of age then and according to his friend Tcheslav Tchechovitch, Gurdjieff said that he was the third child his mother carried, but first surviving.

On the other hand, if 1877 is the correct year of his birth, his father Ivan Ivanovich would have been thirty years of age and his mother twenty-five at the time, an age at which she might well have lost two children already. Curiously, on the announcement of the death of Ivan in 1918, the name of his wife is recorded as M. [?] Kalerovna. That patronymic appears on a document in 1885 as well. I know of no explanation why Ivan Gurdjieff's wife carried two different names, unless he married a second time within a few years of his first marriage, and his second wife carried the same given name. Eudoxie, from the Greek, is the French form of the Russian Evdokia. Since Elepther Elepteroff, was, indeed, the name of Evdokia's father, one wonders where the name Kaler or Kaleroff comes from. Since Kaleroff is a not uncommon Jewish name, it may well be that Gurdjieff's grandmother had Jewish blood coursing through her veins.

Eleven-year time spans are strikingly present in all these age differences. 1866, the year Gurdjieff's claimed for his birth, is eleven years earlier than the 1877 of his official records; and, 1841, the year Olga's deposition has for Evdokia's birth year, is eleven years before the 1852 in the Alexandropol records. From these facts, it would appear that Gurdjieff is attributed with two mothers with different dates of birth and different patronymics. Another supposition is that there are, in effect, two Georgii Gurdjieffs.

Paul Beekman Taylor — Gurdjieff Historian — paulbeekmantaylor.com — paultaylor1930@yahoo.com

---

14 Dmitri's death certificate, 23 August 1937, has the name of his father, Ivan Gurdjieff, but not his mother's name.

··· ∾ ···

QUESTIONS AND ANSWERS

COMMENT: Paul, that was a little too brief for me. Could you speak a little more about centrigravital and what it means to you as opposed to anything else. Thanks.

TAYLOR: It is that sense of communication—in this case, he's talking about love, but he's also suggesting that the only—again, we can take the word love and say "Gurdjieff never meant this word to be understood as the dictionary defines it"—he is saying that for him love is subjective. Okay, that's easy enough. But the love that conveys the truth of one's emotion, the truth also of one's—not only feeling—but thought and of physical presence can be best expressed by a word that is not in the dictionary at all. So it's not centrifugal, moving outward, not centripetal, just being drawn inward. It is being drawn to a center, which is the center, not only of Gurdjieff's being, but of the beings of those who share that feeling with him: his mother and his wife in this case and in July 21, 1949, his two daughters, which he insisted on having them understand that they are his blood. And so it moves, not only from 1925 to 1927 to 1935 but all the way into 1949 and this is what he is telling his two daughters, but he is afraid it is not being heard by the people who sit around the table at Rue des Colonels-Renard, in de salon Rue des Colonels-Renard. It's too bad that Dushka had stopped recording his talk at eleven o'clock when people got up and left. She was left with my sister and Gurdjieff and with Gabo. The relationship of Gabo to Gurdjieff is another case of centripetal love that no one has understood because no one knows who this man is, or was. So I hope this answers you, but that's perhaps the best I can give you.

COMMENT: Thank you.

TAYLOR: By the way, I will add that I was with Gurdjieff so often by accident—I was with him on that night in July on accident because I had no other place to go, except I had to wait for my sister, because she had the key to where we were staying. I will say also something—Gurdjieff insisted on having a silent, or non-verbal contact with me. He broke it now and then, but it was very clear at times when he spoke—when he spoke, I use that in quotation marks—when he communicated with me, he communicated silently, if you can understand that. I could tell you the story but maybe I'd better not.

COMMENT: Hello Paul, I wanted to ask you if you have got any advice to the reader of the *Third Series*. In your description you've strongly evoked imagery of how the reader should actively picture, represent, have these figures living in their minds when reading, but also separately you have the numbers. Do you have any advice on combining these two streams, of the abstractions of the numbers and the concreteness of the imagery?

TAYLOR: Well you made the point. The point that Gurdjieff is making is that all of those numbers converge into one—again I like the Greek word Kairos, because it means a "supreme moment", a supreme moment of understanding one's self as the Christian martyrs did—this is the way the term was first used—Christian martyrs in the Colosseum—all of these dates draw to one moment and to one person. That one person includes all the others he is thinking of, all of the dates center on one moment of time. I call it a rhetoric of time because the rhetoric is the problem of the language and its situating time.

I wish I could understand the book. I've seen recently twenty different descriptions of the title. Twenty different forms of the title of the book. No one seems to be able to write *Life Is Real Only*

Then-comma-When-quote-I am-close quote. No one seems to be able to do it. It's curious. I even made a mistake at one place in my paper. I remember when I asked Roger Lipsey who told me that he edited *Life Is Real* with Lord Pentland, I asked him "why did you reduce all the capital letters to small letters?" and he said "Well Pentland and I decided there were too many bunches of capitals". I love it, bunches is just what Gurdjieff is talking about. Of course he's bunching anything, bunching time, he's bunching sensitivities, sensibilities and thoughts all together. I wish I could read what Gurdjieff is trying to say. Why, for example, he numbers the paragraphs. I have known people who have counted the paragraphs in the whole work, besides the two chapters in which Gurdjieff numbers paragraphs. If I remember correctly, but I don't have the book right in front of me now, that every paragraph of the eleven in the Prologue that are numbered end with the statement "I Am". Emphatic, capitalized. Does that help?

COMMENT: As best one can, but I really adore it when you say you still don't get it. You don't understand it, you can't read it, because I think he's created an opportunity for a new kind of reader. We hardly know how to read this kind of stuff. And so that's the beginning, how to read it. If we discover that, it's going to be quite incredible. It's going to change one's mind.

TAYLOR: Yes and knowing something of your ideas, there's probably a lot of dance and music in *Life Is Real* as well. It's just we don't know how again to understand the score. It's very difficult for me to communicate my own feelings toward Gurdjieff when he read because he read musically and when he talked and when he played—played what Orage use to call "noo music," American pronunciation, noo music—but he was speaking. He ended every seance in Paris, as well as at the Wellington Hotel in New York City, he ended with playing his music. When he stopped, people got up and left. He didn't say "Go". It was over. Again, his music was the final saying goodbye, which also reminds me of something that doesn't make other people very happy, when I say that *Life Is Real* is a finished work. To me there is no doubt about that. And I can play the game of being a literary critic, or being even a music critic with Schubert's "Unfinished Symphony", which is finished and Coleridge's "Kubla Khan", which is finished. There is no such thing as an unfinished work when we're talking about art. All right, get angry, you can't punch me.

COMMENT: What did you mean by saying that Gurdjieff read musically and part of that is did you ever hear Gurdjieff read out loud?

TAYLOR: Oh yes. Often. When he read from *Tales* it was not very often. There were short passages. I remember sitting on the floor at the Wellington Hotel where the only thing Gurdjieff read was "Ashiata Shiemash" and I always wondered why that was the only thing he read. He refused to read "The Holy Planet Purgatory." Someone once asked him to read from it and he wouldn't. But what I mean with he read musically is—the trouble is, what Donald Whitcomb recorded in New York City of Gurdjieff speaking, Gurdjieff was playing a joke by telling jokes and it was not the same thing of him speaking in New York to others and to children especially and in Paris in the salon when he spoke in cadence. Does that make sense? He was very conscious of a cadence of speech.

COMMENT: Is that from his father, do you think?

TAYLOR: I could not say. I wouldn't dare say. I already said too much that can be doubted. I'm always wary of talking about what I heard of Gurdjieff, by Gurdjieff, for Gurdjieff, because I understood so little. I was 18 and 19 years old at the time and what always bothered me, worried me is Gurdjieff knew what I understood when I was not understanding anything. I/you can fathom that.

COMMENT: Could you say just a little more to describe one or more of these sessions in which he read? Did he read merely a paragraph, or would he read something a little longer?

TAYLOR: No, I never heard him read a long passage. It was very often and he did this from memory and I think he always got it right, but I don't know. In New York no one had ever seen the book, unless some people had seen Orage's version, but he would read statements which would illustrate something that was on his mind. And it was usually, if I remember correctly, a single sentence, maybe two.

COMMENT: So in that sense he was reciting from memory.

TAYLOR: Yes. And by the way, Gurdjieff knew and made fun of, in more than one place, the English expression "by heart", from memory, because he knew enough French to know that by heart means by chorus, not by the organ coeur. Because this is the way he learned. He'd mention this: he learned in school "par coeur", that is by coerce, as everyone in Europe did, as I was taught in the Catholic school, by coerce. That was together. I like it the French now say "par coeur", meaning by heart, when they don't understand their own language.

COMMENT: Paul, I hope you can forgive an associative question, but I have been so intrigued by this person Gabo. Can you say anything more?

TAYLOR: Gabo was a body guard, but body and everything else. It's funny, the people, even Michel de Salzmann, Nikolai de Stjernvall,no one knew who he was. Gabo is of course a nickname and it can be a nickname for a number of Russian names. We know he was with Gurdjieff in Constantinople. I don't remember mention of him in St. Petersburg, or Petersburg as it was called or in Essentuki and he was always silent, but there are photographs of him. If you look at some of the photographs of Gurdjieff getting ready to go on a trip, there is Gabo somewhere standing and he was always in the apartment in Paris and after Gurdjieff died, he disappeared. No one knows where he went, what happened to him. I once wrote a novel about Gurdjieff in which Gabo plays a major role but that's another story.

COMMENT: Hello Paul, I'm posing a question from B, in Salt Lake, who is joining us also from Skype and her question is ... well she is very interested that Gurdjieff read out the chapters on Ashiata while in the hotel in New York. Could Paul describe it a bit more, describe the settings, everything about it?

TAYLOR: (Laughs) Well again, you know, I got to know Ashiata Shiemash better than anyone else in Gurdjieff's world, because over and over again, when he asked people to read, it seemed to me he was always asking to read a part of that chapter. Maybe it was consecutive, day after day. I was not there every night in New York City at the Wellington. I cut classes to stay as long as I could, I was there from let's say about the 20th of December until January 6th or 7th and then I came back down in February just before he left, because he left early.

Why he read Ashiata Shiemash? Well I can say, because he saw himself as Ashiata Shiemash. That's what a lot of other people might think. And he was a messenger from above in the sense that Ashiata was. Remember, Ashiata Shiemash was a human being, but a human being who was touched by... or had a message inculcated into him as perhaps—you know the first thing that Sy Ginsburg ever asked me, back in 1996 was did I think Gurdjieff was a messenger from above and I sort of laughed and said no, but of course Gurdjieff was a messenger from above, if we know what we're talking about when we use that phrase. I wish I could tell B more about New York. Again, I wonder where all those tapes are. Donald Whitcomb—I heard a lot of them because Donald Whitcomb lived in Providence, Rhode Island, and I was going to Brown University after I left Gurdjieff and I used to sit with him and listen to those wire recordings. They were in terrible shape. But I think it was Dushka who used to wire record also in Paris. I don't know when the tape recorders started to be used. But I don't know what happened to all those recordings. Apparently, they are extant, but I haven't heard them. So I'm sorry B, I wish I could say more.

COMMENT: Just a tiny question. I was wondering if Gurdjieff's cats had names.

TAYLOR: I never heard them. In fact, I never saw them. I was at the Prieuré, I was only just about three years old the last time I was at the Prieuré and I never saw a cat in Gurdjieff's presence. I was told by others there were peacocks at the Prieuré but cats I'm not sure, I must say.

COMMENT: There is a picture of him with Philos and I think two cats.

TAYLOR: Oh, the one when he's sitting down and Philos is with him. Yes that's right, I've seen that photo too, but I'm saying that my memory goes back when you're three years old. In Paris he didn't have cats. He had no animals in Paris.

COMMENT: Thank you.

TAYLOR: Thank you. Thank you all. I wish I could be there. Have a beer. Because I can never really understand O unless I have a beer.

COMMENT: Hi Paul, I'm just interested—this is a really a minor detail—but I'm just interested as to whether you have a copy of *Life Is Real* which actually retains the capitalization and the numbering.

TAYLOR: No. I do not. In fact the drafts of *Life Is Real* that I have seen in the hands of Muriel Draper, Sherman Manchester do not have the numbered paragraphs.

COMMENT: Do we have any idea or is it your opinion that there was a final form in that and that the final form would have had the capitals and the numbering?

TAYLOR: Yes. Because, well I'm a literary critic and yes it makes sense. In fact there's no part of *Life Is Real* that doesn't make sense to me. Even the ending is so typical of unfinished works. In other words you end at a particular point where what you are about to say is a secret. Therefore you do not say it. And it's over and over again. Chaucer does it when he translates the *Roman de la Rose*. I could go on—I'm not going to go into time to read Schubert, but certainly Coleridge's *Kubla Khan* is clearly a finished work, although he claims... And the trouble is that people like Madame de Salzmann and Michel say "unfinished, unfinished". Twenty-five years of saying it's unfinished and giving Madame de Salzmann the okay to publish it? All this is very, very strange.

And by the way, since I'm on a tangent, when Mr. Grant showed us an authorization, written by Gurdjieff, giving an authorization to Madame de Salzmann to redo his work, I checked with all my local lawyers here. That has no legal power whatsoever. It's not notarized, it's not witnessed and, to show how silly the whole thing is, when Madame de Salzmann had *Beelzebub's Tales* redone, the legal heirs refused to publish it and she even said and admitted they refused, because they had the legal right. She did not have any legal right to redo that work.

COMMENT: Hello Paul, it's wonderful to hear you.

TAYLOR: Well, it's wonderful to hear you. I'm glad you're there.

COMMENT: So please come again next year.

TAYLOR: Thank you very much and I hope I can get to Oslo before then.

COMMENT: Okay thank you.

COMMENT: Hello, you don't know me, I'm from the Netherlands. I was a pupil of Michel de Salzmann for a long time, and just before your lecture I told that he taught us to be a double agent, not just a secret spy. That when you are the double agent, maybe you get where the secret is. So what you told now is really a good addition to his teaching and I thank you very much for it.

TAYLOR: Thank you. And I agree.

COMMENT: Regarding the end of *Life Is Real,* I'll try to raise this question in the most succinct way: what can you tell us about the provenance and sequence of the last seven pages in the 1978 published version, as opposed to the 1975?

TAYLOR: I have no idea. It's very frustrating. Roger Lipsey says he doesn't even know where the copy is that he edited, which to me seems unfathomable. The archives in New York City, every time I ask to go in and see something, they tell me what I can see, but it's never what I asked to see. So I have no idea of what manuscript or typescript he used. So without that I have no idea where those seven pages came from or what draft they came from or why they were missing from the 1975 edition.

It's all so unbelievably frustrating when I look myself at *Life Is Real* to understand "what am I missing?", "what was edited out?" If you edit something, something was changed and I do not know and I cannot figure out what unless I take what drafts are available and then put them against what we have, but we don't have any drafts of the full work that precedes, that is in the papers of Muriel Draper, or Sherman Manchester, or the people who have a number of chapters.

In other words, one problem is that Orage wrote a good deal of *Life Is Real Only Then, When "I Am"* and what he did not write Gurdjieff added. In other words, from the fourth talk on. But Orage had seen everything before then and had edited it.

COMMENT: Alright, so setting aside the ability to proof anything with this section, as an expert in language and in the meaning which you say you understand, are those pages actually Gurdjieff's?

TAYLOR: Oh well, this is difficult to say because those pages are added to something which is even a greater puzzle for me and that is Russky Golos. As much research as I have done and a great deal, there was no Russian newspaper in New York City in 1935 that was called Russky Golos. Now if there was none there — and who is P. Mann?, I do not know — Mechnikov is well-known, he got the Nobel Prize in 1908.

So did Gurdjieff write a review of Mechnikov's work or did he adapt it from somewhere else? Mechnikov's work is about yoghurt, Gurdjieff didn't eat yoghurt, you know we go on and on and on and on. I don't know. The thing is that those seven pages are a buffer. Whether Gurdjieff wrote them or not, I could not say, but I could say if I could see the typescript that Lipsey and Pentland worked with. But I can't.

COMMENT: Hello Paul, we see you with great delight, although I must say I was looking forward to seeing you in person. This year it will have to suffice. Next year we'll see you in person.

TAYLOR: I hope so.

COMMENT: Maybe in between. That's the only thing I wanted to do, say we're here, but you just dropped the bomb. Did you really say that Gurdjieff did not eat any yoghurt? (Laughter)

TAYLOR: He ate sour cream. I never saw him eat yoghurt.

COMMENT: It is so strange that he made all that noise on the train to Chicago about not having yoghurt.

TAYLOR: Yes but what he meant was—this is another problem—what yoghurt was for Gurdjieff and what yoghurt was for an American is still a problem with me. My wife makes yoghurt and I go to the United States and I buy yoghurt and those are two different products completely. So it's probably a question of what you call yoghurt. And in the end the word he never used. He said "yaourt," as you know it's an alternate word. I heard him use the term. I never saw him eat it.

MODERATOR: Well, if there are no more questions, Paul thank you for doing a wonderful job. You were talking to a machine, but it felt to us as if you were here. And I think maybe a loud applause... Thank you very much.

··· ∿ ···

Filnooanzi Foolon Foos foscalia Frianktzanarali Ftofoo
Fulasnitamnian futurists
Gaidoropoolo Gasometronoltooriko
Geneotriamazikamnian Gnoskopine Gob Gobi
Goblandia Goorban Gornahoor
Gornahoor Harharkh Gornahoor Rakhoork
Govorktanis Grabontzi Gulgulian
Gurdjieff
Gynekokhrostiny Hadji-Asvatz-Troov
Hadji-Zephir-Bogga-Eddin Haidia Hamilodox
Hamolinadir Hanbledzoïn Hanja Hanziano Haoorma
Harahrahroohry Harharkh Harhoory Harhrinhrarh
Hariton Harnahoom Harnatoolkpararana Harnel-Aoot
Harnel-miatznel Hasnamuss
Hassein Havatvernoni Heechtvori Helkdonis
Helkgematios Hellenaki Hentralispana
Heptaparaparshinokh Herailaz
Herkission Hernasdjensa Heropass
Hertoonano Heteratogetar Hikhdjnapar Hirr-Hirr Hivintzes
Hlodistomaticules Hoodazbabognari Hooltanpanas Hottentots
Hraprkhabeekhrokhnian Hre-Hree-Hra Hrhaharhtzaha Hrkh-hr-hoo
Hydro-oomiak Hydrokatarnine
Iabolioonosar Ibrkh Ikriltazkakra
Ilnosoparno Impulsakri Inkiranoodel Inkliazanikshanas Inkozarno
Insapalnian Instruarian Iranan Iraniranumange
Irankipaekh Iransamkeep Irodohahoon
Ischmetch Iskoloonizinernly
Isoliazsokhlanness Ispahan
Issi-Noora Itoklanoz Kafirian Kafirians

Two Souls

. . . Ocke de Boer . . .

In the beginning of the book, *Higher Being Bodies*, I speak of two kinds of Souls, namely the Lunar and the Solar Soul. Let us look a little deeper into this enormous concept:

In *The Tales* Gurdjieff speaks about half beings, who dwell on planets which do not have their center of gravity of their functioning in themselves. Rather, the center of gravity of such planets is in their satellites, or their moons. On both the planet Karatas, and on the planet Earth, such half beings appear. Gurdjieff calls them Ketchapmartnian, which means that they reproduce themselves through a male and female principle.[1]

> "From that time onward, in our Universe many such forms were established, which also began to be called souls. They became, indeed, similar to real souls. But their formation as well as their essence, and also their further perfecting were altogether different. Thus from that time, in the World of OUR ENDLESSNESS, there began to exist two kinds of souls, real and similar to real.
>
> "Real souls are those which are formed and perfected by the beings themselves through intentional suffering labors; and 'similar' souls are those which found themselves ready made, thanks to that cosmic lack of foresight. But in spite of all this, this second kind of souls again owing to heredity also had in themselves all the possibilities of attainment of real souls; but the ways to that attainment, as I have already told you, are usually different, and very much more difficult and complicated.[2]

Later in the chapter "Purgatory," Gurdjieff talks about how Beings on a planet called Modiktheo reproduce themselves. There, three beings are needed for reproduction. The result of the reproduction on Modiktheo is that when the process is completed, the result is a Being with already completely coated Higher Being Bodies, which means they have coated Solar Souls, also called "complete Beings" (page 773, "Purgatory").

This situation on Modiktheo is not the case on the planet Karatas or on the planet Earth, where half beings see the light. Here the souls of Beings are not completed, but are in a Lunar state, which means that these Beings have potential Higher Bodies, but these bodies are not coated in a Solar Way. They are not coated by their own efforts. These Souls are in an embryo state and have the possibility to complete their coating themselves. They have to work until they crystallize their own Law of Three, which means that the third factor for their functioning is not depending on outside forces, but depends on a force functioning from the inside. They have to transform themselves from a Lunar to a Solar state, or from a radiating to an emanating state. They need the latter, that is, an emanating state, in order to establish a direct contact with the emanations of our Holy Sun Absolute. Establishing this contact will help them to become servants of our Holy Father.

Actually, these embryo Lunar Souls, if they transform themselves into Solar Souls through their own effort, can become experienced Solar Souls, which is not the case with Solar Souls who are just born that way. There is more joy in heaven for one being, or half soul who completes his/her own

1 Gurdjieff, G. I., *Beelzebub's Tales to His Grandson*, (Aurota: Two Rivers Press, 1993) PP 770-71.
2 Excerpt from: "The Holy Planet 'Purgatory'", 1931 edition.

evolution than for a hundred angels who are born complete. These experienced Solar Souls are highly needed by OUR COMMON FATHER for the government of the World, especially the denying parts of it.

A Solar Soul is a permanent principle of Consciousness, that is, ascending towards the Sun Absolute (the home of our COMMON FATHER ENDLESSNESS). A Lunar Soul is either ascending or descending, depending on whether it is fulfilling its Being duties or not. These duties consist of Conscious Labor and Voluntary, and later Intentional, Suffering. We need these being duties for the transformation of an embryo Lunar Soul into a Solar Soul. Simply put, these duties are efforts consisting of service and sacrifice in order to be able to lighten as much as possible the sorrow of our COMMON FATHER (the fourth obligolnian-striving).

We do not coat for egotistical purposes. We coat because we understand, that if we do not ascend up the ladder of Consciousness, we will disturb the Law of the Equilibration of Vibrations.

In relation to this aim we can only be egotists. This egotism will be of help only in the beginning of our journey, up to the level of man nr 5. From this fifth level we can grow further only with an impersonal aim.

The first aim will be the coating and forming of the Kesdjan Body. This body needs to grow in strength or else the Mental and the Causal body cannot be formed in it. It is of great importance to understand that, if you are really interested in this material, I mean interested on a feeling, hunger level, that there is corresponding understanding data in the Kesdjan Body. If there is no such data, you will not get anything from what I have written above.

To increase this data is very important because this understanding data is the coating material of the Kesdjan Body. This understanding data consists of astro mental and astro feeling matter, or the end results of pondering processes and the end result of feeling processes.

Around the physical body is the etheric body, which is the less material side of the physical body. This etheric body is, on the other hand, the most material side of the Kesdjan Body. It is the skin of the Kesdjan Body, and it has as its sense organs seven accumulators, also called the chakras.

This body is capable of extracting understanding data by using a physical body consciously. This data is extracted from our three dimensional reality. During our lives on Earth, but especially when we die, the fruits of these Conscious Labors are transported to the Kesdjan Body. This is how the Kesdjan Body grows and gets coated. These two bodies, the etheric and the Kesdjan Body, are around you, and they are capable, through their density of atomic weight, to saturate the physical body and to influence it by communicating with it.

This communication goes through the subconscious.

Here a big obstacle arises, because the Ego, which is attached to the physical body, has to learn, and so, to be trained, to listen to the sub conscious. The Ego has to get out of the way. It has to surrender to something higher than itself. This surrender is very difficult for the Ego, which only wants itself to remain as it is. We are completely addicted to the physical body and its Ego, with its cognitive intelligence. We call this Ego our "ordinary I." This "ordinary I" is afraid of losing its influence.

We try to understand our Work not through, but with our ordinary I, or Ego. By working in this way, we get stuck. This Work has to be understood by the understanding data in the Kesdjan Body, also called the body of Conscience. This intelligence of the Kesdjan Body, when aroused, is of a completely different nature and density than the cognitive intelligence of the Ego. They cannot even be compared.

The intelligence of the Kesdjan Body sees directly what is. It sees and knows what is without a conceptualizing ego. This intelligence, its weight, and how far it is developed, is the Real You.

It is the Substance of Real You or I that has to incarnate in the physical body with its Ego; it has to become the Boss.

This potential second body is of another, a higher density of vibrations. The physical body with the Ego has to get used to these vibrations of a higher level. When this happen we are able to grow in Being.

The Ego is used to live in the most outer parts of our Presences, the most outer parts of our three centers, actually the most mechanical parts. This is why we spend most of our time during the day in automatic energies. These automatic energies belong to what is called in our Work the second state of consciousness. This is the ego or personality state.

The state of consciousness that belongs to the Kesdjan Body is called "the third state of consciousness." This is the state of Self Remembering. To give food and breathing space to the second body, it is necessary during the day to come through Self Remembering, into the third state. In this way we also explore this state, and so learn about Self Remembering. This third state can be reached only by applying Work ideas like Self Remembering to ones Being. This separates the boy from the man, or the girl from the woman. It is only through the application of sacred ideas that we can grow in Being.

Many people get stuck in a sort of intellectual curiosity about this Work. By applying Work ideas we can build an energy that will bring us in touch with the inner parts of our centers. This effort is important, because it is here that we shall meet essence, the small child in us. Essence is the bridge to the potential coating of Higher Bodies. It is essence that must have a hunger for this Work.

This potential second body is attached to several parts of the physical body, especially the lower center, or the abdomen. But it is also attached at the collar bones of the neck and to the pathways of the spine, called ida and pingala in the Raja Yoga philosophies. In ancient Egypt the pathways were called the Djed. These pathways have to be filled with sensation, combined with prana.

In the above way the second body gets nourished. This has to be done so that the substances of the big accumulator above the head can enter the physical body. Gurdjieff called these substances, "the substance of I." This has been well explained by Mme de Salzmann in section 113 of her book *The Reality of Being*.

> "For this I first need to establish a relation between my body and the material that Gurdjieff calls the "substance of 'I.'" This substance is scattered in the body. I practice recapturing it through the mind in order to let it melt and be dissolved in the whole organism, so that it is not fixed anywhere. I say "I" to myself, and it is as though I breathe in this material as I see it melt. Then I say "me," letting this more subtle substance spread evenly in the whole organism, so that a second body can be formed. I repeat this a number of times. In order to see that all the material is distributed evenly, I experience a look from above, a sense of "I" above the head. My body then seems a small thing among everything else, like a drop of water in a glass. I see especially that the "I" is really the intelligence, the master of "me," which is content to be under its look. To have two bodies is the greatest luxury."[3]

> "My body needs to open to a force to which it is closed, a force that comes from above, from a little higher than my head."[4]

3 Excerpt from: Jeanne de Salzmann. *The Reality of Being*, p. 237.
4 Ibid., p 232.

>"I begin to feel this Presence almost like another body. I do not try to imagine it, but I do not reject this impression when it comes to me."
>
>...
>
>"This second body is "I" in relation to my body."[5]

It is important to understand that when a second body does get coated, the center of gravity of the functioning of your Presence will shift from the Ego to the Second Body. The Second Body will become Real I for the Ego. It is in this way that the Ego will take its proper place, which is to function as a digestion organ for impressions.

Note that the brains of the second body are of a completely different nature than the brains of the physical body. A coated second body is superior to the physical body and its brains. An uncoated potential second body is not. Its energies go wherever the desires and wants of the Ego go.

The process of the change of the center of gravity from the lower physical body to the Second Body is a process that will find its completion, through entering, by Self Remembering, into Higher states of Consciousness, especially the third state.

The second body is under fewer laws than the Ego and the physical body . As I said before it has a finer density of vibrations. The automatic second state of consciousness is not accustomed to this higher vibration level.

We have to take this Work very practically. The automatic second Being State has to be used consciously. It has to be purified through Conscious Labor and Voluntary Suffering.

The Second Body is also called "The Body of Conscience." Conscience is the inner memory to bring any given situation back in tune with Unity. In the second state we are not in touch with Conscience because in the second state we have only the third being reason.

The reason of the Kesdjan Body is the second Being Reason called in *The Tales* "okiartaaitoksha." This reason is the property of only those Beings in whom the Second Body is completely coated and functions independently. When this is the case, this Reason communicates with the planetary ordinary I through the sub conscious. To listen to the sub conscious, we have to dwell on a regular basis in the inner parts of the centers, which involves Self Remembering.

A major help is to learn to be aware of your atmosphere and what happens to it when it is with other people (also in groups). Either we use our atmospheres more consciously, or our atmospheres are used as food for the Trogoautocratic principle (the household book of the Cosmos). Understand that, if our atmospheres are constantly hooked to phenomena of our three dimensional reality, the energies that should be used for Coating of the Second Body are wasted.

We need meditation, sittings, to get into a condition, somewhat like an athlete does, to be able to become aware of and to observe if our atmospheres are dispersed or more collected. Getting used to this process will help us to let a higher vibration level from above the head enter into our bodies. In making this kind of effort, we will finally become aware of a body with a different density of vibration of energy around our physical bodies. It is this body that has the substance of Real I in it.

To make this development begin to happen, we have to enter the Third State on a daily basis. Above all, however, we have to suffer because it seems that something so obvious is almost impossible to do. Doing this effort daily is Conscious Labor; observing that you can't is Voluntary suffering.

We, our attention especially, are taken all the time by our actions and reactions to the three dimensional world, third force being always from the outside. If we make the effort not to be

---

5 Excerpt From: Jeanne de Salzmann, *The Reality of Being,* p 233.

taken, but to use the friction for coating, third force will be on the inside. We will no longer be blind to it. This is what we have to aim for.

For instance, my body is always in a hurry. It is difficult for my automaton to wait patiently–in line at the supermarket, for example. This, then, becomes a moment for me to work, to create third force in myself. If I am impatient in line, I am identified with the emotional part of my moving center.

The first thing I need for creating third force in myself is to balance the three lower centers: the moving instinct center-- the spine; the feeling center-- the plexus; and the intellectual center–the head. (A person is not balanced when identified with the emotional part of the moving center.)

I do this balancing by sensing a weight in the abdomen. We humans are surrounded by eggs of energy, so to speak. This egg is your atmosphere. When third force is outside this egg, the energy of this egg goes wherever your attention goes. This attention is our tool: through sensing the abdomen, by putting weight there, I can try to use this weight as a basis for sensing simultaneously the spine, especially the pathways, the plexus, and the head area.

I can become aware of an egg of energy with these three centers in it. If I keep a part of the attention in the abdomen, the bottom of the egg, I can make contact with the top of the egg , above the head, where the big accumulator is. Feel the energy coming from the abdomen mingle with an energy coming from the Accumulator above the head. The energies mingle in the area of the plexus. In this way you use the friction of your automaton who mechanically wants to follow your identification (in my case) with the emotional part of the moving center. You go against your nature.

You will also notice that everything around you wants to put you back in your normal identifications, back into the second state of consciousness. But, in the above way, one creates third force in oneself.

You can all find your own examples and situations to practice. If you do, you will find without a doubt that this egg, your atmosphere, is always hooked to whatever, other atmospheres, dreams, situations.

This egg is never centered in itself, in the abdomen. In the second state you are not aware of this egg. This egg is very important because when it has Third Force inside, it will slowly put you in touch with the Second Being Reason, which will only start to function independently when the Second Body is fully coated, which means that it can only be hooked to other atmospheres by its own free will.

It is important to understand that through the application of Work ideas, we will reach a different kind of intelligence. We will enter a different world. This process will start if we are able to allow a higher energy above the head to enter our planetary bodies (so well explained by Mme. de Salzmann). This energy of another higher vibration level will give us flashes of being completely present. This energy will give a feeling of organic independence. This organic independence belongs to the Third State of Consciousness. It is a Presence that will take over when three forces touch, third force being inside, and the outer and inner world being experienced as a unity. This Presence is capable of dominating the three lower centers in order to show the Ego its place, so that the Ego can be used as a digestive organ of impressions again, instead of being identified with itself.

This Presence will give a completely different attitude towards your life, a different attitude towards the time that you spend in a planetary body. This Presence will make you wish for Work.

HAVE FUN
Ocke de Boer — oboer@xs4all.nl

Egyptian Ka Statue

King Salomon

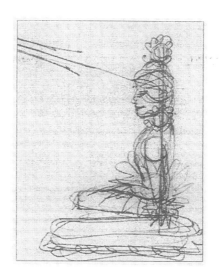

George Adie Drawing

Questions and Answers

COMMENT: The throat, it relates to the emotional center, or what did you say? This part...

DE BOER: I did not say that...

COMMENT: No but you said something...

DE BOER: The throat is the representation of the higher emotional center, according to Mr Adie's drawing. And in the chakra teaching this is called Vishuda, this part of the body and it has to be closed. So if you have an open throat chakra, you will be very easily a victim of internal considering. Which is a big thing in our work. The biggest enemy of the ego and of anything higher, the biggest two of the ego is inner considering and it is an enemy, a dangerous enemy. And it does something to the atmosphere, if you easily innerly consider, your atmosphere goes all over the place, you must learn to keep your atmosphere with yourself.

COMMENT: After the passages from Mme de Salzmann's book you talked about some story, the only thing I got was Tetanus or something? Two words I did not hear, not understand, Tetanus, two names, a story somewhere else in someone else's book. About the change of the center of gravity.

DE BOER: Oh, yeah, the reason of the Kesjdan Body is the second reason called in *The Tales* "Okiartaaitokhsa."

COMMENT: Yeah something like that yeah, (laughing) it was a bit fast.

De Boer: Oh I'm sorry. I've heard that before, you know, in the line of the supermarket I'm always too fast. My body goes too fast, it's ridiculous if you observe it, I mean and it is very interesting because you observe such things later, you know and it seems that you know it already but really you don't.

Comment: So you can read very slowly now for me?

De Boer: Yeah, if I listen to you, I will. (laughter)
Comment: Ocke, what is the significance of the arms?

De Boer: The arms are holding the second, the higher bodies, they represent the higher bodies, they represent an energy that is hold there.

Comment: So why arms, we have seen other things up there before, but why arms in this?

De Boer: I don't know. I don't know.

Comment: Isn't this because it's the accumulator?

De Boer: The accumulator is above the head, that is really true, but I don't know why hands...

Comment: It seems logical to me.

Comment: Maybe the hands are a symbol of doing, in that sense a symbol of will?

De Boer: I don't know.

Comment: Maybe.

De Boer: Might be. Well the Egyptian mythology is full of awesome material, I mean they had three kinds of priests in Egypt. There were the exoteric priests, the mesoteric priests and the esoteric priests. And the esoteric priests they had to be picked, were picked out from the mesoteric and exoteric priests. They picked out the priests that had the ability to become initiated in a knowledge of ancient Egypt and it has a lot to do with our Work.

Comment: So I have seen some statues from Mesopotamia, so as you often see them with two hands touching the ear, big, big, big hands, raising up, so I thought they were some kind of antenna, connecting receptive organs for higher energy, so...

De Boer: I love the word antenna, cause you have the seal of Salomo where the higher, this is what Mme de Salzmann speaks about in her book all the time, the higher level of vibration, if that gets activated, if that gets active again, it becomes an antenna, so we are hooked by the lower level of vibrations to a sort of morfo-genetic field and our atmospheres are hooked to each other in that respect. We call the reactions that we have in the three-dimensional reality we call I, that is not I at all and if this is the only time that we are plugged in to life, we live an Itoklanotz life. So these higher levels of vibrations have to be vivified, so yeah, you become an antenna. I'm sure about that even for other spheres and other planes, like the mental plane, the astral plane, causal plane.

Comment: What is vivified?

De Boer: Belevendigd (answers in Dutch).

Comment: So internal consideration is the enemy because it makes us identified with this state of consciousness (Ocke: Yes) and if we do that, if we are identified we can not make the egg you were talking about (Ocke: No) so when we do a sitting we practice making an egg?

DE BOER: Yes! We practice becoming collected instead of being dispersed.

COMMENT: Ok I think I should do that then! (Laughter)

DE BOER: I have said it to you many years...

COMMENT: Yes...

DE BOER: This is really interesting cause we have the book at home, and many of you will have that book, the Notes of Jane Heap that you can order at the (Two Rivers) Farm, are of such a beautiful quality because in the Notes of Jane Heap, you can feel in that whole book, that this woman really has worked and she called, she talked about being collected and being dispersed in a very beautiful way. I have also written it in my book but it is from her. So you can also read it in my book. (laughter) But Jane Heap, it is amazing how she explains that and Gurdjieff of course has an exercise called the Collected State, which he said you should do ten minutes every day in order to be blessed to live in his name. So, very practical this work.

COMMENT: Ocke, you said something about, there is a lot of information, a lot of words from you...

DE BOER: It is very dense, I know.

COMMENT: It is very dense..

DE BOER: I'm too fast in the line of the supermarket and too dense in my writing.

COMMENT: Yeah but you slowed down a bit, you slowed down a bit but you said something about essence as a bridge (O: Yes), can you explain more because I forget what you said before and after that.

DE BOER: Well, essence is also called the "small little child" in us. And Rodney Collin says about essence that it is the blood that floats through you from conception till death and that is a very good definition of essence. But when we are in inner considering, we are completely a slave of our ego and in personality and every time you really sit, do a sitting you make contact with your essence. And it takes a lot of observation to make a distinction between personality and essence. But essence is the bridge to anything of a higher nature. So not the personality, the personality is a sort of digestion organ for the third being food, for impressions. It is the same with the intellectual center, it's also only sort of an apparatus for receiving impressions. It is way overemphasized in our culture. It is the horse, the emotional and the instinct-moving center that needs to work.

COMMENT: I just wanted to thank you, I find what you said very, very positive, very helpful, very practical and I think in light or in view of all our discussions that were more intellectual and trying to understand difficult formulations and to arrange theories. But your talk was very direct, at least for me to encourage us to work on ourselves in a very practical way and it gave all the notions of soul and a taste of reality and no upper thing and for this I want to thank you.

DE BOER: Thank you, thank you, that was a little too fast... (Laughter)

COMMENT: The word bridge were mentioned here and also you spoke of the importance of having contact with the inner part of centers, and to me that represents also a part of a bridge. Maurice Nicoll refers to it as the steward, which has a permanent center of gravity, knows its same (OCKE: yes) and can use whole centers, including parts of centers. And has conscience awaken? And also this can remember itself at essential moments? And the imagination is lurking around and I think what you point out especially to knowing centers is important, because unless one has an overview what goes on in the different parts, in the different parts of the different parts, including the under-divisions, there is always the danger of making mistakes (OCKE: that's true). And what I'm particularly concerned about, is that when one has conscience awaken at the level of steward and there is still the danger of imagination, one can easily mistake Kesdjan Body for Steward.

DE BOER: I agree. I remember when I got interested in self-remembering I found a paper from Gurdjieff from 1944 and the whole paper is about self-remembering. It is him and Madame de Salzmann who speak in that paper about self-remembering. And I read that paper over and over and over again because in that paper Gurdjieff says, together with Mme de Salzmann, that you should in the beginning learn to remember yourself intensionally in advance, which means to make appointments with yourself at certain times. And you will notice that you cannot remember yourself because you will forget, because the horse dominates you, the emotional and the moving part. But it was very interesting to try and I kept on trying, I did everything strange even stand on one leg, go over my bike in the middle of the city, for making, trying to understand what it was. And how I could reach it or do it, deal with it. I think that paper, it is in the black book, in *Meetings*, is a very important paper and that paper also deals with the centers.

COMMENT: Ocke, I have a message from you from X. She says: Thank you.

DE BOER: Oh, Hi X.

COMMENT: And how do you understand self-remembering now after trying for decades?

DE BOER: Well that's really a good question, because I think that you can only learn to understand self-remembering by trying to do it and than you will find what it is not. And when you really are trying and trying, you will suddenly get results that you did not expect at all or results, I will say in between quotation marks, but you will suddenly be completely there. And I did with this times and appointments, I did for many years, I now do it in line of the supermarket. I'm trying to be patient in the line of the supermarket, or wherever, I try to not go to fast. I tell you a story, I'm a member of a dog school, I train dogs for the police. And the dog I have, I have two dogs, but the German Shepherd, it has to follow you on your left knee and it has to look at you all the time. And my dog never looked at me, never! I could not make her look at me, she would look at me like this (laughter) until I suddenly observed that I do that too, if I walk I do like this (laughter) so my dog just copied me and that was why, that was a moment of pure self observation, that is why she never looked at me, you can learn an awful lot of dogs, because dogs read your body like you cannot read a body, so...

COMMENT: In reference to self-remembering, I for many years tried many attempts of experiencing self-remembering and when you sent me those sittings, they were very, very beneficial in that I was able to determine and see the difference between the physical center and the emotional center. Because you say: oh I feel, you feel with your center physically but to feel with your emotional center is different and with those sittings and being in a collected state, and if you do it every morning, you find yourself in a state of self-remembering and you can continue it throughout the day. And I thank you for those.

DE BOER: I agree with the sittings, the sittings are of great importance, the exercises Gurdjieff gave and also the exercises in Mme de Salzmann's book. One of our group members wrote out for us on paper, an exercise about the distinction between sensing and feeling, which John Bennett had a paper about from 1949. And Wim Nyland had an exercise about that, that he gave on a tape and we wrote it out and that is a very, very important exercise and I found exactly the same exercise in Mme de Salzmann's book *Reality of Being*, it think it is on page 34, I don't know. Only she does it the other way around. But I think these exercises and especially also the exercises I got from the Farm, the collected state and whatever are very important! For us to start the day, to be able to build an energy that keeps you in contact with the wish for work. So, I agree the sittings are very important.

COMMENT: The last thing that came up here, reminds me of something coming from Rodney Collin, because he speaks of sensations as reading the physio-psychological weather. So I think that's a very good description, the physio is of course related to the physical sensations, and the psychological is this sensation of emotions. Emotions are really a physical thing but he calls it a physio-psychological weather.

DE BOER: In *Celestial Influences*, his book he has a beautiful part about self-remembering, there is even a drawing there from the sun, it is a very good book, *Theory of Celestial Influence* by Rodney Collin.

COMMENT: Ocke, more X for you: The efforts you've made, Ocke, to understand the work of higher bodies is helpful for all, I especially value the relationships you've made throughout this teaching and other esoteric knowledge, another thank you.

DE BOER: Okay, that's great. Are we going to have coffee now?

··· ∿ ···

Kafiristan Kahketeenian Kaialana Kaimon
Kalianjesh Kalkali Kalkians Kalman Kalmanuior
Kalnokranonis Kaltaan Kaltusara Kalunom Kalyan Kalzanooarnian
Kanil-El-Norkel Karabaghian Karakoom
Karapet Karatas Karatsiag Karnak karoona
Kartotakhnian Kashiman Kashireitleer Kashmanoon Kasnik
Kasoaadjy Katarnine Katoshkihydooraki kazi
Kaznookizkernian Keesookesschoor Keeziak Kelli-E-Ofoo
Kelnuanian Kelnuk Kerbalai-Azis-Nuaran Keria-chi
Kerkoolnonarnian Kesbaadji
Keschapmartnian Kesdjan
Keskestasantnian Kesshah Keva Kezmaral
Khaboor-Chooboor Khaivansanansaks Khaivatine
Khalmian Khanate Khenionian Khevsoory Khlarfogo
Khooti-Noora-Chaka Khooti-Pikan-On Khorassanian Khrh
Khritofalmonofarab Kilmantooshian Kilpreno
Kimespai King-Too-Toz Kirkistcheri Kirmankshana
Kirmininasha Kishmenhof Klananoizufarab kldazacht
Klian-of-the-mountains Klians Klintrana
Kmalkanatonashachermacher Knaneomeny Kodomine
Kofensharnian Koilononine Kolbana Kolenian Loots
Kolhidious Kolhidshissi Kolomonine Kolotine Kondoor
Konuzion Koorfooristanian Koorkalai
Koritesnokhnian Korkaptilnian Korkolans
Kreemboolazoomara Krentonalnian Krhrrhihirhi
Krikhrakhri Krilnomolnifarab Krintonine
Krishnatkharna kroahn Kronbookhon
Ksheltarna Ksherknara kshtatsavacht Ksvaznell
Ktulnotz Kulnabo Kundabuffer
Kundalina Kupaitarian Kurlandtech
Kusma Proutkoff Lanthopine Latinaki

Understanding Cosmic Laws in ALL and Everything

... Anthony Blake ...

We can look at Gurdjieff as a 'cosmic journalist' and *Beelzebub's Tales* as 'cosmic journalism', as opposed to the softer option of treating it as a sacred book.

By the word Akhaldan the following conception was then expressed:

"The striving to become aware of the sense and aim of the Being of beings."[1]

To bring it more into the theme:

"The third: the conscious striving to know ever more and more concerning the laws of world- creation and world-maintenance."[2]

1 Gurdjieff, *Beelzebub's Tales*, p 297.
2 Ibid., p 386.

This address will be in three parts, beginning with...

Meanings of Law

The "conscious striving" of this third Obligolnian principle influences me to think of the notion of the spiritualization of the centers, which plays such an important part in All and Everything right up through the Third Series. It is in this context that I take the meaning of the word "striving" as being always in progress and I think of this conscious striving as the 'breathing' of the Thinking Center. How it can assimilate from all possible sorts of information available the finer impressions which are 'to know ever more'. This is to draw attention to striving as a dynamic and not as an acquisition; attuned to know what is happening. To 'know' here means to see in what is happening in me and through me as well as in everything I see around me, the same laws. John Bennett in the appendix to his book *Gurdjieff–Making a New World* seemed to be saying–but these are my words–that the laws see the world through us. They are not models of how things work which we can use as concepts. In some way they operate before we have even begun to think, to measure and compare. This we may associate with the early idea Gurdjieff had of the Higher Intellectual Center, which is always working.

Aphorism: *The spiritualised thinking centre sees connections between things that appear unconnected.*

(Mr. Bennett had a lovely term to describe that which was not just mechanical–this bit connected to that bit. He talked about mutual relevance: everything in the Universe as mutually relevant with everything else and that is, itself, an expression of one of the laws.)

Gurdjieff indicates just two categories of law, related to creation and maintenance. This seems strange to me, because if ever there could be a valid generalization about Gurdjieff 's thinking it would be: whenever there is a two, look for a third. It also occurs to me that creation and maintenance correspond to Brahma and Vishnu in the Hindu Trimurti in which there is a third, Shiva, combining destruction and creation. I believe we can find echoes of Shiva in the action of djartklom and we will come to this later.

As far as I know, the sense of the word zakon in Russian, which Gurdjieff originally used, is much the same as that of the word 'law' in the English *Beelzebub's Tales To His Grandson* and English usage. I want to consider its overtones. There is a sense in which it implies strict mechanism, causality, determinism and blindness; corresponding to the most reductionist view of the world. (Rather close in feeling to what Gurdjieff expressed as the 'hydrogen without the Holy Ghost'.) There is another sense–which is both close to and also the opposite of the former–of belonging to 'God's Will' or Divine purpose. I skate over issues of profound complexity here. We can think of laws as expressions of the mind of God, or of the Demiurge only (the maker of the world who is really the secondary creator denounced as evil by many Gnostics). The laws enslave us yet enable us to realize God. How is this possible? But law mostly suggests human law–the setting up of regulations connected with force to constrain behaviour and enable people to coexist in large numbers without always killing and stealing from each other. Human laws are for the maintenance of society. (It is then always an issue of how evenly-handed such laws are, that is free from the exercise of privilege and exploitation.)

I'll pick out from the complex diversity of overtones of meaning of the word "law" just three aspects and speak of Divine law, Human Law and Natural law as a convenient summary. I need to add something else, another threefold summary: that of the mechanical, the intentional and the cosmic. I cannot spend time on defining these terms closely nor would I wish to. I hope their meaning will emerge as I go on (and as you participate in the enquiry that is proceeding. They are ciphers in the game of meaning we are now playing.)

Divine law can appear mechanical. This was Gurdjieff's original picture: God in his freedom initiates the creation but then it proceeds mechanically. Looked at literally, we are in a machine that was freely created but we are separated from the freedom. Later, in the first version of *Beelzebub's Tales,* Gurdjieff had God's Will participate in all triads of all worlds to guarantee some touch of freedom throughout creation but this was cut out later as he explored other formulations to cope with the mystery of 'freedom through laws'.

Another expression of this which you will find among 'fourth way' thinkers is the 'terror of recurrence'; how to be free of 'recurrence', because recurrence is the natural expression of mechanical law. I'm sure all of us experience this personally, as we year after year do the same things over and over. This was a particular obsession of Ouspensky's who got it from Nietzsche who got it from Pythagoras; that willy-nilly we do the same things over and over and that this is law-conformable.

When it comes to the idea of natural laws we can find soft and hard options: the first gives scope to factors such as 'self-organization' which supports belief in autonomy; that everything that lives has its own laws and some measure of freedom–while the second does not.

(Mr. Bennett used to misquote William Blake when he said that "everything that lives has meaning and needs neither suckling nor weaning." Blake actually said that, in respect to a poem, "every line has meaning and needs neither suckling nor weaning." But the idea is clear: that everything that lives has meaning of its own self; its autonomy. This self-creation has become a major theme in certain lines of 20th Century thought.)

In the context of modern paganism, nature becomes endowed with characteristics of creativity and compassion that are taken as emergent rather than as implanted from some external higher source. But there is also a peculiar populist sense of what is 'natural' that implies or is concomitant with the view that man and current civilization are un-natural! Here I will cite one of my favourite Nietzschean sayings: "It is the nature of man to be un-natural." I invite you to keep this provocative idea in mind as we journey on.

The three elements Divine, Human and Natural have ambiguous interfaces. Think of the Trinity as where the Divine and the Human meet: sometimes the Trinity is treated as a Revelation given to mankind to enable it to find an understanding of the workings of God's Will. On the side of the Natural and the Human we find the question of whether the laws of nature we discover are at least to some degree an expression of us and our specific nature, as rooted in the way we perceive what is around us, due to the way we are constructed.

At this juncture I am going to quote from *Beelzebub's Tales* a passage that emphasizes on the one hand the inevitable incompleteness of our grasp of natural law but also suggests that we have an essential role in rendering the world intelligible.

> I repeat, my boy: Try very hard to understand everything that will relate to both these fundamental cosmic sacred laws, since knowledge of these sacred laws, particularly knowledge relating to the particularities of the sacred Heptaparaparshinokh, will help you in the future to understand very easily and very well all the second-grade and third-grade laws of World-creation and World-existence. Likewise, an all-round awareness of everything concerning these sacred laws also conduces, in general, to this, that three-brained beings irrespective of the form of their exterior coating, by becoming capable in the presence of all cosmic factors not depending on them and arising round about them–both the personally favorable as well as the unfavorable–of pondering on the sense of existence, acquire data for the elucidation

and reconciliation in themselves of that, what is called, 'individual collision' which often arises, in general, in three-brained beings from the contradiction between the concrete results flowing from the processes of all the cosmic laws and the results presupposed and even quite surely expected by their what is called 'sane-logic'; and thus, correctly evaluating the essential significance of their own presence, they become capable of becoming aware of the genuine corresponding place for themselves in these common-cosmic actualizations.[3]

Aphorism: *To understand is to understand that one does not understand.*

The suggestion I propose is that Gurdjieff's cosmic laws are themselves the intelligibility of the world and we are the imperfect organisms that seek some approximate understanding of them, but I believe there is a deeper possibility – that we are engaged in making the world intelligible. In the cosmic drama that Gurdjieff writes, God modifies laws rather than creating them and sacred individuals intervene to make them work out in practice. It's not generally understood that science and technology are not identical and making things work does not derive from science. Theory is never enough.

It's convenient to consider the laws as something in themselves even though this is probably quite false. We never know the laws apart from instantiations of them. Here I appeal to the views of Jung on something similar, his Archetypes, of which he said that we cannot know them as they are only entertain images of them. There are however many reports of people receiving or realizing the intrinsic reality of what is usually only imagined, often couched in geometric or mathematical form, indicative of what Gurdjieff describes in terms of communicating with Higher Intellectual Centre. Let me go on by treating the laws as symbols. This does not mean they are artificial.

We can treat the laws as 'out there' in a pure Platonic sense or as 'in here' in the way we are put together or work. I want to do both at the same time. A possible justification for doing this is, I believe, given by Gurdjieff's treatment of sacred individuals. I think it reasonable to say that *Beelzebub's Tales* contains two main kinds of 'character' or 'agency': one is that of the laws and the other that of sacred individuals. I am immediately led to think of them both as archetypes of Will. The laws determine what can and what cannot be done–the division between the possible and the impossible as Bennett understood it–while the sacred individuals and other higher beings play the game so to say between the two sides. While God alone could alter the laws, the particles of his divinity were free to intervene in how they worked out in existence.

"'For our COMMON CREATOR all beings are only parts of the existence of a whole essence spiritualized by Himself.[4]

I have just referred to existence. In my frame of reference, though maybe not yours, Existence is less than Being. What exists longs to be. To exist is to stand out, to be in some state of separation. In ancient cosmogonies the original state is one of unlimitation, hence chaos. Cosmos is a restriction on chaos. I use the familiar word 'chaos' here in spite of the fact that its original meaning was not confusion but something like 'yawning gap', the condition necessary for creation to take place. In ancient Greece it was called "apeiron," the unbounded. It is easy to see then that people would come up with such ideas as the logos as the intelligible fire that would become the Word later in Christianity and 'number; as the universal principle of both understanding and the structure of the world as in

3 Gurdjieff, *Beelzebub's Tales*, PP 755-56.
4 Ibid., P 197.

Pythagoras and modern mathematical physics. In *Beelzebub's Tales*, we find the "Word-God," the "theomertmalogos" and also the numerical laws, the 'laws' of three and seven.

But, before we get into number and understanding I need to point out that existence can be understood as the stage for the cosmic drama that Gurdjieff describes in his book. Having such a stage came in all probability from the Zoroastrian tradition. This tradition had two cosmic powers, Ahriman and Ahura Mazda, at loggerheads; they are so balanced that neither could ever win. Ahura Mazda then made the world and enticed Ahriman into it to battle in finite time. The existence of the world makes it possible for the 'good guy', Ahura, to win over the 'bad guy', Ahriman. I am sure you can pick up on how this Zoroastrian myth–though not the same–resonates with the story in *Beelzebub's Tales*.

Harmonic Theory and Systematics

Since I have mentioned the ancient Greeks and Zoroastrianism I might as well speak about the way in which all three facets of law–divine (or cosmic), human and natural–were treated as one in the earliest known harmonic theories. Let me speak of the natural aspect first:

It is useful to know that all melodic scales derive from the physical phenomena of overtones. If a string for example is struck and vibrates according to its length, tension, material and so on at a certain rate called its frequency, it is also vibrating at twice the rate or double the frequency and three times the rate or triple the frequency and so on. These higher frequencies operate with lesser and lesser energy than the fundamental one. Sensitive people can still hear many of them. They can hear how two or more of them are sounding together. The sounding together of two different frequencies or 'notes' manifests the musical interval between them. Some musical intervals sound pleasant to most people and others sound unpleasant to many. If we picture the series of overtones as the series of integral numbers, what could be simpler? Just imagine, artificially, early people getting together and saying 'how can we start?' And they say, 'well, we can start from 1, 2, 3, 4, 5, ... and that can be the basis from which we get everything:

$$1\ 2\ 3\ 4\ 5\ 6\ 7\ 8\ 9\ ...$$

It is easy to see we can find relations between them, simple ratios on which early peoples constructed their theories of music, such as...

$$2{:}1\quad 3{:}2\quad 4{:}3\quad 5{:}4\quad 6{:}5\ \text{etc.}$$

Applied to musical frequencies, the first of these ratios, the diapason, is known as the "octave interval," because it is eight major scale steps above the fundamental. Typically men and women have voices pitched an octave apart and it is intriguing how the two notes–a DO and a high DO–sound as both the same and different. The next simple relation is 3:2 and creates the "fifth interval." People in all cultures find this pleasing. After that, comes 4:3, the "fourth interval," which is the basis of tuning the lyre in ancient Greece but which some cultures reject.

The few numbers 1, 2 and 3 suffice to create what is called Pythagorean tuning based on making a succession of twelve fifths across seven octaves. The details do not concern us here besides the fact that 12 fifths do not exactly equal 7 octaves; there is a difference called the Pythagorean comma which exemplifies how the archetypal laws based on small integers can never be exact, which I find intriguing. This note that something has to be periodically and artificially put to make things work has enormous resonance allowing, for example, there to be hazard and hence conscious intervention. Isaac Newton, who made a special study of what we now call the "chaos" inherent in the solar system, firmly believed that the solar system was possibly unstable and required God or some higher power to intervene and keep it going, to keep it from destroying itself. This is still unsettled in physics; whether the solar system is stable or not. Some people think that radical changes are inherent in the possibility.

And the role of the moon in the formation of the solar system is extraordinary in that the way in which the earth is situated among the planets may depend on the origins of the moon, which changed the orbit of the earth. Newton talked about the way in which the planet earth is sitting, with the outer planets orbiting on simple ratios, while the inner planets do not, but I go off with these implications into astronomy.

In the famous fresco by Raphael, The Academy (The School), there is represented a summary of the ideas of ancient wisdom, "ancient" being only 2000 years, since the origins of Greek knowledge were not known at his time, in particular, the wonderful contributions of the Sumerians 5000 years ago, with whom Gurdjieff had his initial contact through his father.

The School of Athens by Raphael. Plato and Aristotle are centre, Socrates on the steps and Pythagoras to the left foreground. Below is a detail showing Pythagoras, center foreground is the symbol signifying the whole tone ratio 9:8

So here is Pythagoras and held at his feet the Epogdoon (a summary of Pythagorean ideas), meaning 'one eighth in addition'; signifying the fifth interval going down and the 4th going up, the whole tone ratio 9:8, it has a beautiful form to it; all showing how they were interested in creating meaning and structure from the simplest ideas. The diagram shows a Pythagorean tuning based on fifths which separates two tetrachords to make eight notes, each composed of four notes spanning what we now regard as two and a half whole tones. The pyramid of four numbers beneath is the tetraktys which adds to ten giving all the Pythagorean numbers. The aesthetic symmetry contrasts, of course, with the complexities of the physical world. Actual tuning systems could be very different and varied.

There is a story about ancient practices described in the writings of a 2nd Century Roman, at a time when people did things Gurdjieff reports about in which they danced ideas. They danced the ideas of Pythagoras and the audience would know if the dancers made a mistake but neither the audience nor the dancers would not necessarily know the laws being depicted in the dance. So much has been lost and covered over due to the Renaissance which eschewed ancient ideas, but Gurdjieff was familiar with Pythagorean ideas and assimilated them.

The patterns analyzed in theoretical music were also found in the heavens, in the movements of celestial bodies, such as the mythical roles of Jupiter, Saturn and the notion of Old Father Time and the changes of epoch from one historical period to another related to the outer planets. The workability of using the simplest integers to such effect gave credence to the sense of the heavens as divine as part and parcel of the view that the higher was bound to be simpler, one rather than many and that bias comes in at the very beginning of the harmonic sequence.

But musical tuning systems and number-based cosmogonies and cosmologies were not the whole story; the human world of morality, governance and society was also involved. In ancient China, when the ruling powers changed, attention was paid to establishing a new musical tuning. (They believed that if they did not do this, the governance would not work.) The various combinations of numbers generated many kinds of musical scales giving rise to the Greek modes (the names of which correspond to regions of Greece). In Plato's writings you can find them described in moral terms and each of the basic six was associated with a particular location and ethos. They ascribed to each certain moral qualities: 'use this mode for warriors', 'this one for guardians', 'avoid this mode, because it would create conflict', etc. This kind of thinking was universal in the ancient world. The musical scale used would contain factors which would structure the human psyche.

Starting with the simplest numbers which appear in Genesis as the six days of creation and continuing to the possible forms of the musical scales, hearing the modes is almost a universal way of understanding things.

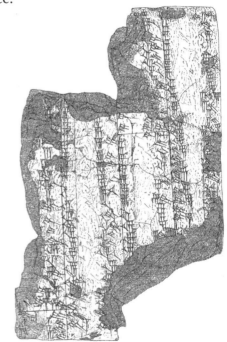

One of four cuneiform tablets from the Temple Library of Nippur c. 2200 BC showing number sequences; it's found to be curious because of the numbers left out (7, 11, 13).

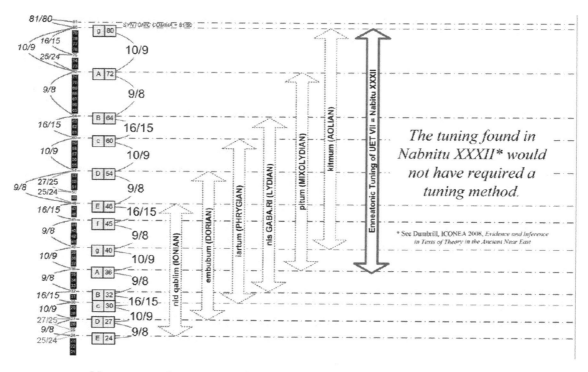

The tuning found in
Nabnitu XXXII would
not have required a
tuning method.

* See Dumbrill, ICONEA 2008, *Evidence and Inference
in Texts of Theory in the Ancient Near East*

HARMONIC ANALYSIS OF NUMBER SEQUENCE – BY RICHARD HEATH

Much harmonic theory goes back at least to the Sumerians 5,000 years ago. It seems it served as a 'lingua franca' of reasoning about the intelligible in whatever domain across the whole of Eurasia. Musical structures were based on the number 2, the female number, the number of the octave, and the prime male numbers 3, 5, 7, 11 and so on. Plato uses variously numbered octaves to distinguish the character of different city states such as Atlantis, Athens and Magnesia and scholar Ernest McClain showed how musical structures based just on the numbers 2, 3 and 5 underlay scriptural and mythical narratives throughout the civilized world.

It seems reasonable to me that we could make use of any set of integers to think about the way things are organized or come about. Even a cursory study of cultures and philosophies will turn up various instances. Just think of Celts with their triads, or Amerindians with their tetrads and so on.

Concerning philosophies and numbers, the great American thinker, Charles Sanders Peirce famously said:

> Perhaps I might begin by noticing how different numbers have found their champions. Two were extolled by Peter Ramus, Four by Pythagoras, Five by Sir Thomas Browne, and so on. For my part, I am a determined foe of no innocent number; I respect and esteem them all in their several ways; but I am forced to confess to a leaning to the number Three in philosophy. In fact, I make so much use of threefold divisions in my speculations, that it seems best to commence by making a slight preliminary study of the conceptions upon which all such divisions must rest. I mean no more than the ideas of first, second, third—ideas so broad that they may be looked upon rather as moods or tones of thought, than as definite notions, but which have great significance for all that. Viewed as numerals, to be applied to what objects we like, they are indeed thin skeletons of thought, if not mere words. If we only wanted to make enumerations, it would be out of place to ask for the significations of the numbers we should have to use; but then the distinctions of philosophy are supposed to attempt something far more than that; they are intended to go down to the very essence of things, and if we are to make one single threefold philosophical distinction, it behooves us to ask beforehand what are the kinds of objects that are first, second, and third, not as being so counted, but in their own true characters. That there are such ideas of the really First, Second, and Third, we shall presently find reason to admit.[5]

Peirce was one of the main influences on John Bennett, who I think encountered him through Bertrand Russell's *Principles of Mathematics*. Once you have the idea of a sense of numbers in which they are symbolic indicators of structure and organization there is no reason to reject any number as incapable of serving intelligibility. Bennett developed a scheme he called "Systematics" based on the first twelve integers (he himself was very fond of the number 12!) which rather relieves the pressure of trying to deal with everything in the universe in terms of just one or two numbers–as of course Gurdjieff did.

But Gurdjieff's choice of the two numbers 3 and 7 is undoubtedly smart. We can look at them in various ways such as considering 3 as the basis for the arising of something new and 7 for the transformation of one thing into another. In the enneagram where they are combined,7 goes around the circle while 3 defines the inner form. The two are related in the meaning of form and sequence (which was as you know the title of one of his chapters); in this case 3 corresponding to form (I call it the logos) and 7 to sequence. These are mere suggestions. The important operational part is that we are called upon to generate a stereoscopic picture in depth, a third dimension, by combining the two. This is where we come into the picture. These things are then no longer 'out there' but we are in a depth with them.

I must add, even though it is somewhat of a distraction, that the form of the enneagram in its combination of two laws derives from the progression of square numbers: 1, 4, 9, 16, 25, 36, etc. If A is the number squared it is the 'informing number' or logos and from it we derive another law or number B: $A2 + 1 = A + B$ = the number base. In the case of the enneagram A is 3 and B is 7 ($32=9$, $9+1=10$, $3+7=10$ = decimal). As we know, the number base of the enneagram is 10 but we can have any number base.

---

5 Peirce, C. S., "Peirce on Signs," *Stanford Encyclopedia of Philosophy,* November 2010.

For example, if A is 4 then B is 13 and the number base is 17. This creates a hexdecimagram that combines two inner hexadic sequences. The following diagram is based on the law of four (a square is inscribed in a circle, with 17 points around the circle). The inner sequences are the familiarly-shaped hexad 153FBD and the less-familiarly-shaped hexad 92A7E6.

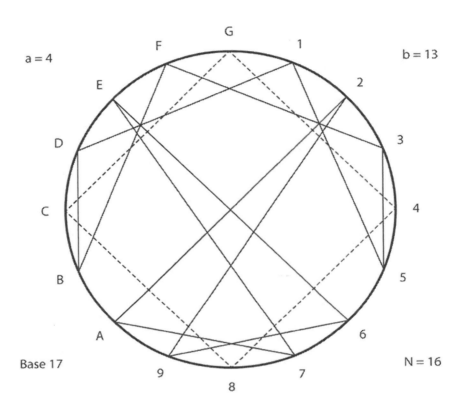

HEXDECIMAGRAM

My indulgence in such mathematizing is only justified to raise the question of why two basic cosmic laws together with the question of why just these particular cosmic laws?

Before going further into our involvement with the laws I want to indicate briefly ways in which 3 and 7 are related mathematically. Later on I'll briefly show how all possible laws might unfold from a unity and fit together in a boundless mosaic.

It's a fairly common thing to seek to derive the sevenfold from the threefold, even though Gurdjieff calls the law of seven the first common cosmic law and the law of three the second. In the approach of what is called combinatorial hierarchy—an exciting branch of abstract mathematical physics—there are four levels of reality based on primary acts of discrimination. It will probably appear to you as ridiculously simplistic but bear with me.

Just imagine something—call it A—and then think of another thing and call it B. Put A and B together in combinations. Now, if B is the same as A, there is only A (one element) but if there is a difference then not only is there A and B but also what distinguishes them, so there are three combinations;

this is written as A, B and AB—the first level is threefold. Once you have three elements, to make the next level we look at the possible (dual) combinations of the three elements. These turn out to be seven in number.

A   B   AB   A,B   B,AB   AB,A   A,B,AB

So, spontaneously, 7 comes out of 3! The next level produces 127 elements! The next after that has 2 raised to the power 127 minus 1 elements and is where the hierarchy stops. Many important physical constants come out of this scheme including the cosmic number 137 which determines the structure of matter as we know it. This has ramifications in physics that don't concern us except to say that there is this understanding of how structure emerges from very little.

In the figure, a simpler picture of the making of 7 from 3 is given by a triplet of overlapping circles which shows seven distinct spaces.

Now, there is an intriguing thing, an insight which the Irish mathematician Hamilton inscribed on a bridge he had to cross, about 3 and 7 related to "quaternions," which we might be able to relate to Gurdjieff's ideas. This important vista of 3 and 7 is provided by what are since called Hamiltonians; special combinations of real and imaginary numbers. A quaternion has one real number and three imaginary ones (recall that imaginary numbers involve the infinite set of the square roots of minus 1) and that this set of numbers can form what is called a group in which the numbers can combine in consistent ways to operate an arithmetic. (Sets with two or four imaginary numbers will not work like this. The next set that works is the octonian having no less than seven imaginary numbers.) Hamilton wrote in 1844 these lines that are strikingly resonant with our discussion:

> And here there dawned on me the notion that we must admit, in some sense, a fourth dimension of space for the purpose of calculating with triples ... An electric circuit seemed to close, and a spark flashed forth.[6]

Those of you who have studied the Gurdjieff teaching in the Russian period will recognise the similarity of quaternions with Gurdjieff's Carbon, Oxygen, Nitrogen on the one hand (as the imaginary numbers) and Hydrogen (as the real number) on the other. The seemingly trivial abstraction of having a coherent set of four elements in the form $4 = 3 + 1$ has immense significance. Throughout Gurdjieff's teaching but particularly in the Third Series the question of real 'I' revolves around the unification of three. Also, the law of three is both disintegration and unification. Here is the promise of a new Heaven and a new Earth, suggested a little in Gurdjieff's idea of harnel-miatznel, the image of a moving equilibrium.

These seemingly silly little numbers and silly little forms are actually incarnating or materializing immense forces directly dealing with creation.

This form comes out to be rather the impossible $3 = 1$, akin to the Christian Trinity. The form $7=1$ is more unusual; it reflects the feeling of such expressions as Eliot's 'In my end is my beginning' and the myth of 'eternal return' that so obsessed Ouspensky, originating in Pythagoras and re-emerging in Nietzsche. There is a logic that has the general form $N = 1$ that implies all integers share in a universal characteristic.

I return to the question of why just two cosmic laws? There is no sufficient reason for denying the other numbers. Nor is there sufficient reason for having just two or any specific numbers of laws. This became apparent to Bennett through his work of rendering Gurdjieff's cosmology intelligible; the work that culminated eventually in his four volume masterwork *The Dramatic Universe.*

6 Hamilton, W. R., *Quaternian* (re: Wikipedia)

He called his magnum opus a series of footnotes to *Beelzebub* but I regard it as a rewriting of *Beelzebub's Tales*. If one is to understand anything one must in the end rewrite it in one's own terms, one cannot just repeat the words of the original.

One of the features of having more than one cosmic law–I must emphasise that 'cosmic' means operable in every possible instance–is that they mutually interfere. We have seen a little of this in discussing harmonic theory–the different primes must at certain points clash with each other. But also, to use the analogy of Moire patterns, when they overlap they may produce unexpected and interesting patterns.

There might be an indefinite series of laws coming out of the world of all possibilities, such as were codified by Bennett in his *Systematics* of a series of systems which, at least up to twelve, could be exemplified by aspects of world cultures. But there are also then their combinations. Harmonic theory points to a few of the simpler relations. I mentioned that the series of patterns akin to the enneagram go further, showing how one law could intervene into another at transitions–Gurdjieff described these as 'shocks' in respect of the enneagram but they have many nuances and implications. I myself tend to favour looking at them as regions of hazard.

I count monad, diad, triad, tetrad, ... all the way down, and it has three main streams in the Christian tradition. Each level cascades down into the others. These are the series of central pivots reconciling 'suchness', 'the present moment of the soul', and so on. The pattern picked up on in a lot of cultures is threefold.

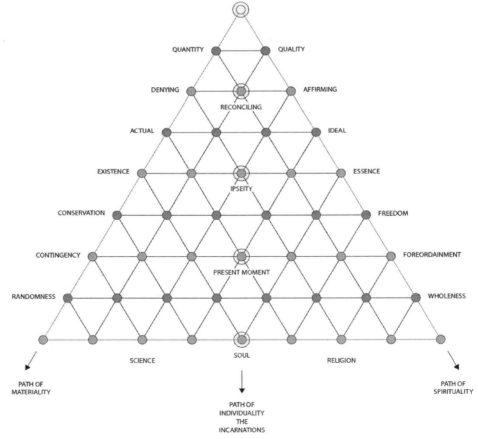

LATTICE OF UNDERSTANDING

I have visualized a cascade of the totality of all possible laws in what I call a "lattice of understanding."

The lattice contains multiple lines of meaning but particularly a threefold structure that echoes the Celtic symbol of Awen which, amongst other things, symbolizes the inspiration of the bards, who were equivalent to the ashoks of the near east, such as Gurdjieff's father.

One can also adopt the enneagram format to give a general picture of laws overlapping and mutually impinging on each other. The diagram here is deliberately casual and roughly made.

The point at the top is like the 0/9 point of the enneagram. In N-grams based on squares the two laws have a common point at the top. The coloured lines are just to suggest two laws that intersect in some way and structure the process designated by the circumference. The green point at the bottom signifies any equivalent to the tritone of the octave, the midpoint of greatest tension, referred to in earlier times as diabolus in musica, the devil in music, which we might reasonably associate with Beelzebub, the old devil. (In India it's Agni, the god of fire; in mathematics it's the square root of 2, an irrational number.) If the top point can be seen as the Holy Sun Absolute then this bottom point is symbolic of free intelligence within the created universe. Which always causes trouble. And here we are. The angels fixed it like that.

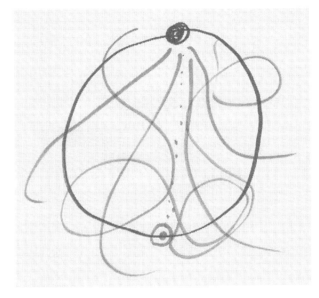

The Universe is always becoming One

The Universe is not one; it is becoming One. We return to G's coupling of sacred individuals with cosmic laws. In Bennett's terms, laws are self-limitations of Will, whereas individuals are particles of Will. Such a complementarity is a twofold cosmic principle somewhat reflected in quantum mechanics. According to theory the actualizations of the universe necessitate the presence of observers (called "Boltzman observers" after the nineteenth century physicist) since actualizations must be observed in order to happen. Such observers might not be like humans at all in appearance but some might nevertheless be three-brained or have the potential of their own law of three inside them. These ideas are conjectures but it is appealing to think of myriads of observers in the universe as undetectable by us as dark matter currently is.

St. Paul to the Hebrews: 12:1

> Wherefore seeing we also are compassed about with so great a cloud of witnesses,
> let us lay aside every weight, and the sin which doth so easily beset us, and let us run
> with patience the race that is set before us,

I have already implied that observation is not some passive by standing of phenomena and want to go further to suggest that the way phenomena are seen transforms what they are. This comes out to some degree in Gurdjieff's neologism triamazikamno roughly translating into 'I put three together and do'. The 'put' is rather a seeing than what we might think of as doing something. By seeing the triad something is possible that was not before. Obviously, I speak of perception as an agency of reality, akin in meaning to the idea of the 'ayn' or 'eye' in Sufism. This is a deeper take on the concept that how we think is superordinate to how we act.

There is a mysterious aside in *Beelzebub's Tales* when Beelzebub speaks of beings as 'two-natured' and goes on to explain the inner bodies possible for man. These inner bodies seem related to perception. The role of perception as I am trying to explore now is, I feel, intimately linked to Gurdjieff's remarkable concept of djartklom, a word implying sudden death. In the moment of the arising of a cosmic concentration the three forces of the triad are split asunder, thereafter seeking to reblend; an idea that may have been stimulated by the myth recounted in Plato's *Symposium* of how primordial man was originally a sphere divided by the gods into two halves that then have to seek each other. When there is djartklom, it is a kind of darkness and when the three unite it is more than day. Between, there is light, energy, action and feeling. Such labels and metaphors may not be helpful to you. The point to grasp is that the world is in process, is incomplete and our lifeblood of vision may serve its unfolding and realization. The physicist Richard Feynman magnificently said: "I cannot understand anything that I cannot make."

I'd like to end with a conjecture about the Law of Seven. I believe it is about uniting things on different levels. The metaphor afforded by music dominates my thinking. The higher DO is 'already sounded' in the lower DO; and though they may belong in different worlds they are the same. That is why, I believe, our search for transformation of ourselves is to become more what we already are. However convoluted is the path between, we must return home and know that we have and understand what home really is. Along the path there are hazards, which is maybe why Gurdjieff put his two intervals in the octave (though why he did this according to the Major Scale is a total mystery to me). It has seemed to me that my path such as it has been has mostly consisted in disillusionment because I had a wrong idea of my purpose and what was possible. G's final SI-DO step came to symbolise for me the giving up of all the pretensions, the surrender of the pretence for the reality. I believe Gurdjieff implies that what we have to sacrifice is what is unreal. I have to go through 'hell and high water' to arrive at what was and is always there.

The line from God to me is not a continuity. At one end I am not God, whereas at the other I am God. In this sacred octave we have the basis for the music of our becoming. The word 'universe' usually makes us think of something already there, brought into existence and waiting for us to run into it or fall over! But what if it is essentially a work in progress? The real work of the universe is to make meaning and we are part of it to the degree we wish and can be. Then who we are and what there is cross over into each other. They do this or can do this by reason of the kind of laws Gurdjieff writes about.

The crossing over of individual intelligence with general processes–Immanuel Kant defined understanding as the relation between my will and general laws–leads me to suggest a third kind of law to be added to the two named in Gurdjieff's third striving: laws of world meaning–making. I see a correspondence with the role of Shiva whom I referred to at the beginning of my talk. The idea of djartklom is crucial. We find it reflected in the practice of the yogi who disintegrates his limbs in order to re-assemble his being, and in the writings of Steiner who explained the tortures of Hypatia in being torn apart as symbolic of the transformation of her being.

I related the law of seven to sequence, which implies narrative. Narrative is how we compose our minds. It is also how we grapple with the meaning of the universe, the earth and our place in it.

HADJI-ASVATZ-TROOV
DRAWING BY BOB JEFFERSON

If God writes the Universe our science and art rewrite it. First of all to create a place for ourselves in the Universe and secondly to contribute towards its ongoing creation.

Aphorism: *This approach constitutes the universe as a sacred text that we are involved in writing.*

The Universe I liken to a Koran or equivalent. It can be read and in reading it we enter into another level of creation. Gabriel means "messenger" but he commands Muhammad to read, that is, to say or proclaim:

> Read! in the name of thy Lord and Cherisher, Who created man, out of a (mere) clot of congealed blood: Proclaim! And thy Lord is Most Bountiful, He Who taught (the use of) the pen, Taught men that which he knew not.[7]

I am well aware that I have done little to unravel in articulate explanations the profound implications of Gurdjieff's laws to which I have alluded. I am reduced to ending with a passage from the Third Series, one of the most inspiring and enigmatic.

> For the definition of this property in man, which is called "attention," there is, by the way, found also in ancient science the following verbal formulation:
> "THE DEGREE OF BLENDING OF THAT WHICH IS THE SAME IN THE IMPULSE OF OBSERVATION AND CONSTATATION IN ON TOTALITY'S PROCESSES WITH THAT OCCURRING IN OTHER TOTALITIES."[8]

Especially was I intrigued by the words, "that which is the same." What is "sameness"? Why "sameness"? For what purpose this peculiar "sameness"?

Anthony Blake — tony@toutley.demon.co.uk

7 Sura 96:1-2
8 Gurdjieff, *Life Is Real Only Then, When "I Am"* (New York: Triangle Editions, 1978) P 147

References:

Bennett, J. G., *The Dramatic Universe* Vol 3, (Coomb Springs: Claymont Communications, 1987)
Gurdjieff: Making a New World (New York: Harper & Row, 1973)

Blake, A. G. E. *The Intelligent Enneagram*

Gurdjieff, G. I., *Beelzebub's Tales to His Grandson* (Aurora: Two Rivers Press, 1993)
Life Is Real Only Then When, "I Am," (New York: Triangle Editions, 1978)

Hamilton, W. R. *Quaternion* in Wikipedia

McClain, Ernest, *Myth of Invariance* (York Beach: Samuel Weiser, 1976)

Peirce, C. S., *Peirce's Theory of Signs* (First published Fri Oct 13, 2006; substantive revision Mon Nov 15, 2010)

Steinhart, Eric, *More Precisely: The Math You Need to Know to do Philosophy* Supplement: Combinatorial Hierarchies (Broadview Press, 2009)

QUESTIONS AND ANSWERS

COMMENT: Is the number representing seven things just as special in other base systems as it is in decimal? For example, does it lead to an elaborate repeating series such as 142857 in decimal?

ANTHONY: In 5-base 1/7 is 0.7777777... In 12-base it is 0.171717..... etc. (if my maths is correct – why not try it yourself?)

One of my purposes is to try to make you aware of the vast stuff in ancient thinking and modern mathematics which is an original ongoing exploration. There is so much rich stuff out there. One of the things Gurdjieff was doing, I believe, was a function of the time when he arrived at the beginning of the 20th Century: to at least make a contribution to some global awareness in terms of the East an also in terms of the past. When he wrote "Who cares what ancient savages thought?" the idea was prevalent but not so much now. There is a growing appreciation of ancient peoples.

The feeling of *All & Everything* is to appreciate everything and to find a place for everything. It is that attitude, I feel I am going along with when I talk about things. Unfortunately, a lot of people who come across Gurdjieff's ideas have no background in ancient knowledge so they think that Gurdjieff invented it all. But he was a very educated chap; he read widely at a certain time; he was a voracious learner and that was one of his joys.

COMMENT: I would rather say that two laws interact rather than interfere.

ANTHONY: Okay.

COMMENT: We do have three laws, rather than two: the third is that everything is One.

ANTHONY: Of course.

COMMENT: Would you be bothered by the idea that the primordial laws concern perception?

ANTHONY: No

COMMENT: Do the laws exist as a result of human perception? Or are they outside human perception? Or even more, are humans creating this perception?

ANTHONY: I didn't resolve this very good question because I can't. Each of these three views can be a point of departure for looking at the three. People look at these systems as if they were gods looking down at them but actually you can only observe a system if you are playing a part in it and you are standing in a certain position in the system. You can only enter and say "From this point of view, what can I do?" In the way you have asked the question there is no answer because where is the standpoint from which you could make that judgement? We don't have it; then we pretend God has got it; then we pretend somebody knew God and God told him the secret and if we pay him money he might tell us of it.

COMMENT: You can cut an egg in various ways and all the ways are right, if you want to eat it.

ANTHONY: That's a wonderful saying; precisely right.

••• ∿ •••

Laudanine Laudanosine Lav-Merz-Nokh
Legominism Leitoochanbros
Lentrohamsanin Leonardo da Vinci Lifechakan
Liktonozine
Litsvrtsi logicnestarian London-Phu-Phu-Klé
Looisos Lookosikra Lookotanas
Loonderperzooonias Loosochepana lounging
Maikitanis Maikosikra Majestic
Makanidine Makary Kronbernkzion Makhokh
makhokhitchne Makkar Mal-el-Lel Malmanash
Mamzolin Maralpleicie Margelan Martaadamlik
Martfotai Martna
Mdnel-In Mdnel-outian
Megalocosmos Mekonoiozine Mendelejeff Menitkel
Mentekithzoïn Meshed Mesmer
Messaine Metamorphine Microcosmos
Microparaine Microtebaine Midosikra Midotanis Mindari
Mirozinoo Modiktheo Mohammedans Momonodooar
Mongolplanzura Monoenithits
Mont-Saint-Michel Moordoorten Morkrokh Morphine
Mosulopolis Moyasul Mukransky Mullah
Mullah Nassr Eddin
Mungull Naloo-osnian Nammus
Nammuslik Naoolan El Aool Nar-Khra-Noora narcotine
Naria-Chi Nartzeine Neomothists Nerhitrogool Nilia
Nipilhooatchi Nirioonossian Nokhan Nolniolnian
Noorfooftafaf Nooxhomists Noughtounichtono
Oblekioonerish Oduristelnian Oilopine Okaniaki

The Diagram of Everything Living

... Robin Bloor ...

The Apes of Objective Science

"For the kingdom of heaven is as a man travelling into a far country, who called his own servants, and delivered unto them his goods. And unto one he gave five talents, to another two, and to another one; to every man according to his several abilities; and straightway took his journey.

Then he that had received the five talents went and traded with the same, and made them other five talents. And likewise he that had received two, he also gained other two. But he that had received one went and digged in the earth, and hid his lord's money.

After a long time the lord of those servants cometh, and reckoneth with them. And so he that had received five talents came and brought another five talents, saying, Lord, thou deliverest unto me five talents: behold, I have gained beside them five talents more. His lord said unto him, Well done, thou good and faithful servant: thou hast been faithful over a few things, I will make thee ruler over many things: enter thou into the joy of thy lord. He also that had received two talents came and said, Lord, thou deliveredst unto me two talents: behold, I have gained two other talents beside them. His lord said unto him, Well done, good and faithful servant; thou hast been faithful over a few things, I will make thee ruler over many things: enter thou into the joy of thy lord.

Then he which had received the one talent came and said, Lord, I knew thee that thou art an hard man, reaping where thou hast not sown, and gathering where thou hast not strawed: And I was afraid, and went and hid thy talent in the earth: lo, there thou hast that is thine.

His lord answered and said unto him, Thou wicked and slothful servant, thou knewest that I reap where I sowed not, and gather where I have not strawed: Thou oughtest therefore to have put my money to the exchangers, and then at my coming I should have received mine own with usury. Take therefore the talent from him, and give it unto him which hath ten talents.

For unto every one that hath shall be given, and he shall have abundance: but from him that hath not shall be taken away even that which he hath. And cast ye the un-profitable servant into outer darkness: there shall be weeping and gnashing of teeth.
Matthew 25:14-30

A proportion of the abundant legacy bequeathed by Gurdjieff has, like the talent of the wicked and slothful servant, been left buried in the ground. While followers of Gurdjieff may have merely "scratched the surface" of his writings, it can at least be said that a good deal of effort has been devoted to this by a fairly substantial number of people. By contrast there seems to have been little effort made to delve into and pursue the many indications and "explanations" Gurdjieff provided concerning Objective Science - including, of course, the excellently documented information furnished by Ouspensky in *In Search of the Miraculous.*

It would be inaccurate to say that no effort has been put in at all. Both Rodney Collin and Keith Buzzell have made useful and substantial intellectual contributions - they are welcome exceptions that test the rule. Otherwise, it seems that most people in The Work have paid only lip service to the Third Obligolnian Striving:

> "The third: the conscious striving to know ever more and more concerning the laws of World-creation and World-maintenance." (*Beelzebub's Tales*, p 386)

In general it can be said, quite fairly, that very few people in The Work have any grasp whatsoever of Objective Science at even a very basic level. As a consequence there is an unfortunate tendency for many people in The Work to believe, almost without question, many of the assertions of modern science; that "science of new formation" that Gurdjieff decried so artfully.

So, before setting out to consider the Hydrogens and the Step Diagram (The Diagram of Everything Living), we will first turn our attention to a discussion of modern science–Gurdjieff's "science of new formation."

Subjective and Objective Science

Both Subjective and Objective Science demand an intellectual posture of skepticism, which assumes that the scientist does not know, but seeks to know.

Subjective Science operates roughly as follows: The scientist begins with a hypothesis that is most likely based on some already existing "accepted truths." He proceeds by formulating experiments, analyzes the results of those experiments and then either proclaims that the hypothesis has been wholly or partly confirmed, or if that is not the case, alters the hypothesis to conform with the experimental results. Results and theories are subjected to peer review. Thus the scientific community decides what is accepted as proven and what is accepted as a credible theory. This process is repeated time and again. This is how contemporary science evolves or involves.

Modern science works from the bottom up. It starts from some basic assumptions about reality and, via "provably repeatable" experimentation, it builds a "tower of knowledge." Occasionally some of the basic assumptions of this science are challenged and proven to be wrong. As a consequence the "tower of knowledge" is periodically remodelled.

In Objective Science, we are given formulations of fundamental laws and information about them. It is suggested to us that these laws come from "higher mind" and can only be thoroughly understood by higher mind. Our goal, as Objective Scientists, is to attempt to comprehend these laws and how they operate. We are expected to adopt an attitude of skepticism as we investigate them. We do not formulate original hypotheses and investigate them, but we do formulate personal hypotheses about what these laws may mean or imply in our attempts to understand them. We carry out experiments to gather information. As such we confirm or refute the formulations we have been given or invented.

Objective Science can thus be characterized as "top-down," coming (in theory) from higher mind, with the possibility that by our efforts we may ascend step by step to that level. If the formulations of Objective Science that we have been given are wrong, then we will never get anywhere close to the truth by our activity.

As individuals in The Work, we give credence to the formulations of Objective Science mainly because we have personally verified some of the formulations and information passed to us. Most, if not all of us, have done this through internally testing the psychological formulations of The Work, such as inner considering, identification, keeping accounts, formatory thinking and so on. We have personally proven the description of these activities to be accurate.

Objective Science and Subjective Science share the attitude of skepticism and the activity of experimentation. They are also both completely materialistic. Aside from that they have little in common. Subjective Science tends to be agnostic or atheistic. Objective Science is not atheistic—it asserts an Absolute being.

Assertions of Objective Science

Here, we prefer not to discuss the differences between subjective and objective science in detail. The topic is dissected thoroughly in *To Fathom The Gist*, Volume 1. What we intend to do is develop some narratives for objective science that may make its assertions more comprehensible to the reader.

On the next page we provide a table that contrasts the assertion of Objective Science with corresponding assertions from modern science for the sake of comparison. Perusal of this table ought to convince the reader that the two "world views" have almost nothing in common whatsoever and are in complete disagreement on many fundamental points.

Objective Science	Science of New Formation
There is an ether. [1]	There is no ether, but space is permeated by a "Higgs Field," which acts a little like an ether.
Time is subjective, but the flow of time is Objective in a given location, experienced by a single observer. [2]	Time is a fundamental dimension of the universe, equivalent to the three dimensions of length in every respect.
The whole Megalocosmos operates according to two laws: Heptaparaparshinokh and Triamazikamno, assisted by Theomertmalogos (the manifestation of the by Theomertmalogos (the manifestation of the will of the Absolute).[3]	There are a number of immutable Physical Laws including the Three Laws of Thermodynamics, Law of Gravity etc. Others may yet be discovered.
The creation is a consequence of a change to these two laws which was initiated by the Absolute. [4]	The creation is a consequence of the (unexplained) emergence of a vast amount of energy from a single point in the universe.
Elements (insofar as the concept exists in Objective Science) are defined to be substances that have different properties. The atom of an element is the smallest quantity of thatelement which retains all its properties including its cosmic properties.[5]	Elements are defined by the number of protons in the nucleus of an atom of that specific element. Elements can have isotopes.
The Sun grows of its own accord and is not running down. This does not preclude nuclear fusion being one of the causes of the Sun's heat and light. [6]	The Sun is powered entirely by nuclear fusion and is slowly running down.
The planets grow of their own accord, from within. [7]	Planets grow only as a result of collision with other solar system bodies (comets and meteors).
The Moon is a "child" of the Earth and it is growing/evolving. [8]	The Moon may be a child of the Earth, thrown out after planetary collision. But it is not evolving. It is an inanimate aggregation of rocks.
Life on Earth formed because of the need to fill the interval in the Lateral Octave from the Sun. [9]	Life on Earth formed accidentally via chemical and electrical reaction.
The evolution of life on Earth in governed by the influence of the planets. Great Nature transmits the influence of other planets directly to the Earth.[10]	Evolution of life occurred and continues to occur by "Natural Selection."

Objective Science (continued)	Science of New Formation (continued)
Everything is material. Even knowledge is material. [11]	There is a distinction between matter and energy although they can convert one to another. Science doesn't recognise the material nature of knowledge and has no theory as to the substance from which it is formed.
Everything is alive or is a substance within something that is alive.[12]	Some things are definably inert and do not have the qualities of life in any conceivable way.
Living things, at every level, from the whole of the universe itself through suns and planets down to (Objective) atoms form cosmoses. Each cosmos is a unit that ingests three foods.[13]	There is no discernible commonality between the higher (astronomical things) and the lower (biological things).
All laws are the same at every level.[14]	Different laws apply below the atomic level.
There is a Supreme Being, God. [15]	There may or may not be a God. A God is not necessary to explain anything. **1** continued

The Scientific Narrative

We define the scientific narrative to be the narrative that is crafted by members of the scientific media who attempt to convey scientific theories and ideas–which in general are presented as truths rather than hypotheses. Most of us are vulnerable to repeated suggestion and thus by this mechanism we can come to accept all or part of the scientific narrative, as though it were true. The narrative is, in practice, a far more powerful persuader than the scientific explanation.

Consider for example, the scientific creation theory; the "big bang." It was born from the assumption that the movement of galaxies observed through telescopes is utterly predictable. The telescopic evidence strongly suggests that the universe is expanding. So scientists extrapolate the observed movement backwards about 13.8 billion years and conclude that the whole universe must have originated from a single point. Since cramming the whole of the universe into a space smaller than a tennis ball would create a "black hole" (another scientific idea that is taken to be a reality, but for which there is not an ounce of evidence) from which nothing could escape, because of the force of gravity, they wiseacre furiously to invent explanations of how, in that particular instance, energy could escape. When their cherished theories create contradictions, they wiseacre.

The obvious alternative idea (one which, incidentally accords with Objective Science in a minor way) that the universe was once not expanding, but still very large, and then suddenly began to expand, is not acceptable to science because no-one has floated a clever theory as to why expansion would suddenly begin.

From the perspective of Objective Science, all this chatter is irrelevant, because it does not view the universe that way. Objective Science cannot accept, for example, that anything can be extrapolated "in a straight line" backwards for billions of years. This would be counter to the Law of Heptaparaparshinokh which insists that everything progresses in the manner of an octave and that at certain points, where the intervals occur, there are deflections. So even in a Megalocosmos that posited galaxies and suns as dead things incapable of independent action of any kind, it is not logical to draw straight lines back in time, because there would have been deflections. In a Megalocosmos where galaxies are considered to be living things, then a galaxy's behavior in any manner could change simply because the galaxy decided to change.

As regards the movements of galaxies, we can collect so little data in even several hundred years that has any meaning in the lifetime of a galaxy (billions of years it seems) that we are only ever likely

A gift for you

Send a Thank You Note
You can learn more about your gift or
start a return here too.

Scan using the Amazon app or visit
http://a.co/dj14OAP

The Proceedings of the 20th International Humani
Conference: ALL and Everything 2015
Order ID: 111-0771891-7619422   Ordered on May 11,

to observe straight lines. Even were we to have measurements from the whole 15-20,000 years that mankind seems to have existed we would not have any useful data.

Objective Science has little need of such data, although it is intellectually affirming at times to reconcile such observations with the tenets of Objective Science. Objective Science sees the same "pattern" of laws everywhere at every scale. As Gurdjieff says: God, Man and Microbe are all the same system.

In looking at the Aristotelian division of fields of study, that was adopted by our education systems and has held sway for millennia, we see the origins of the fracturing of modern science and its parallel fracturing of modern education. Modern science is bewilderingly diverse. It has "different laws in different fields"–even "different laws in the same field." The lack of a GUT (Grand Universal Theory) in physics arises from the use of fundamentally different frames between quantum mechanics and astrophysics. The lack of coherence between many different fields of science comes from the lack of an overriding universal view. This results in clear absurdities (black holes, 11 dimensional spaces, evolution by natural selection, parallel universes, etc.) that are accorded credibility and presented as knowledge.

The point here is not to engage in debate with the current theories proffered by modern science, but to reject all of its viewpoints, so that they do not infect our attempts to formulate Objective Science viewpoints. In doing this we do not reject data honestly gathered by modern science, we simply choose to ignore its theories and provide alternatives to their narratives.

The Megalocosmos — An Objective Science Narrative

Let us begin with material. The Megalocosmos is awash with material. Some material is very common; other material is less common. Observing the universe we see that there are points of concentration where heavier material (material which has a low frequency of vibration) gathers and exists and is transformed. Such material is rare. It is found on moons; small aggregations of material that spin around planets. The planets are larger concentrations of materials that have higher frequencies of vibration than moons. These planets in turn revolve around suns that are larger concentrations of materials that have higher frequencies of vibration than planets or moons. They in turn are parts of galaxies and the collection of all galaxies lie within, are contained within the domain of the Absolute.

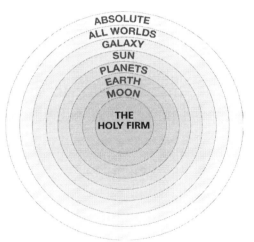

WHAT EACH LEVEL CONTAINS   2

The suns, planets and moons are cosmic units: living beings, complex growing entities and apparatuses for the transformation of substances. In propitious circumstances a moon will, in time, grow to become a planet. A planet will grow and may even reach a point where it supports multiple moons and becomes incandescent and forms a solar system of its own. None of this is guaranteed. If a moon fails it will simply become food for something else, possibly to be absorbed in time by a planet or a sun or even to disintegrate into asteroids to be consumed little by little by other cosmic units.

It may appear that the space between planets and the space between solar systems is "empty space." However, this is not the case. It is full of various materials that have very high frequencies of vibration. Modern science conceives of these materials as energy in the form of magnetism and electromagnetism and streams of particles. They are what Gurdjieff described as high hydrogens. We have very little knowledge of these substances as they occupy spaces that we cannot observe well, even with the most powerful telescopes, and which contain no suitable lower hydrogens with which they can interact. It may even be that our range of scientific mechanical viewing devices do no detect these hydrogens. It is not difficult for modern science to believe that the space they occupy is empty. However, at times it is possible to observe these substances simply by experiencing them personally –for they exist in our presence too as well as in "empty" space.

From the perspective of Objective Science, the Absolute is omnipresent, since the substance of the Absolute, HIS individual atoms pervade the whole of the Megalocosmos, just as the substance of "I" pervades the whole of my body. This is illustrated simply in figure 2 on page 87, indicating each level of vibration fully contains the levels below it–levels of less vivifying vibration. To understand this we need to consider atoms as defined by Objective Science. There are atoms at each level. Atoms at one level interpenetrate atoms at levels below them, just as water can penetrate a solid object, and gases can penetrate water. The same principle applies at every level. Thus atoms of the Absolute penetrate collections of atoms of All Worlds, which in turn penetrate atoms of a galaxy. These in turn inter-penetrate atoms of suns and so on. The points of concentration: suns, planets and moons, contain all levels, interpenetrating one another, but not in equal amounts.

Life - An Objective Science Narrative

What is life? The Megalocosmos itself is life. It was forged in the moment of creation and gov-erned by the will of Our ENDLESSNESS. It is HIS intention and continues to be HIS intention. It is the playground of Time. The Heropass, its power vanquished within the Sun Absolute, yet has dominion over the Megalocosmos and every cosmic unit (cosmos) within it. It measures out the lives of every-thing living. It is a demigod. (*Beelzebub's Tales*, p 124)

> "[it] has no source from which its arising should depend, but like 'Divine-Love' flows always independently by itself, and blends proportionately with all the phe-nomena present in the given place and in the given arisings of our Great Universe."

The Megalocosmos manifests as Trogoautoegocrat. Each cosmic unit (or cosmos) that exists with-in it depends upon other cosmic units for its food. For many life forms, their feeding necessitates the destruction of other life forms.

Life forms are recursive in a remarkable fashion. While they may manifest an individuality, yet they are formed from aggregations of other life forms with far shorter life spans. We are aggregations of diverse cells, including many life forms (bacteria) that are not of our life pattern (our DNA) but are symbiotes or parasites. Cells themselves are aggregations of diverse molecules, which are alive within their own context. And these molecules are composed of atoms and particles that are also imbued with life.

When we consider the larger worlds, we also encounter life. We, ourselves, are merely insignifi-cant particles in the life of humanity, and humanity itself is merely one of the many life forms that constitute Great Nature which is itself vibrant and alive. And yet it is merely an organ on a single planet digesting influences from other planets within the solar system. The solar system itself is alive, and yet it is merely one of billions of such systems which form atoms in the living body of the Milky Way. And it too is just an atom in the totality of the living and breathing Megalocosmos.

And we may note, as we peer down into microscopic worlds or gaze up into macroscopic worlds, that life appears to lose its form as our scale expands or contracts. Thus we conceive of nature as a skin on the surface of our spherical planet and while we see our solar system as having a family of spherical planets, distant solar systems if visible to us at all, are seen as points of light. At the same scale, near galaxies may be seen as spheres of light but more distant ones are seen only as points of light.

Going down in scale we see cells as spheres, similar to planets and we see the traces of atoms simply as lines, or when they emit photons as points of light. On their scale, these living things may have utterly different forms than the ones we intellectually project on to them, for we live at completely different time scales and we are a completely different size. We cannot see these things as they see themselves. No doubt the Earth conceives of us human beings as mere cells, or perhaps something even less defined than that.

So while modern science chooses to view what is higher or lower in scale as inanimate, they are not. Not only are such things alive, but they eat and breath and perceive.

The Step Diagram

Gurdjieff gave very few details about The Step Diagram (also called The Diagram of Everything Living). He introduced it as a "different" kind of classification of living things. In *In Search of the Miraculous* (page 322) we read:

> "The diagram of this classification is called the 'Diagram of Everything Living.'
>
> "According to this diagram every kind of creature, every degree of being, is defined by what serves as food for this kind of creature or being of a given level and for what they themselves serve as food, because in the cosmic order each class of creature feeds on a definite class of lower creature and is food for a definite class of higher creatures."
>
> G. drew a diagram in the form of a ladder with eleven squares. And in each square excepting the two higher he put three circles with numbers.
>
> "Each square denotes a level of being," he said. "The 'hydrogen' in the lower circle shows what the given class of creatures feeds on. The 'hydrogen' in the upper circle shows the class which feeds on these features. And the 'hydrogen' in the middle circle is the average 'hydrogen' of this class showing what these creatures are.
>
> "The place of man is the seventh square from the bottom or the fifth square from the top. According to

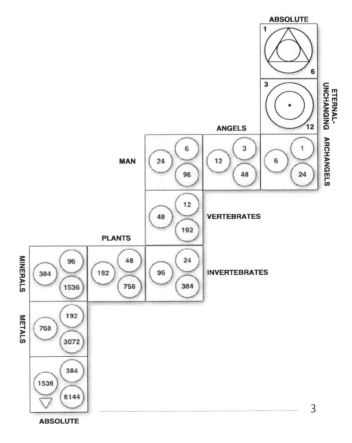

this diagram man is 'hydrogen' 24, he feeds on 'hydrogen' 96, and is himself food for 'hydrogen' 6. The square next below man will be 'vertebrates'; the next 'invertebrates.' Invertebrates are 'hydrogen' 96. Consequently man feeds on 'invertebrates.'

This diagram cannot be discussed clearly without our first discussing the Hydrogens. As we are surely all aware the Hydrogens are a classification of substances based on how Objective Science views the Universe/Megalocosmos. The list of Hydrogens is deduced from the Law of 3 and the Law of 7.

The integers following each "H" refer to the sum of the three forces (Carbon, Oxygen and Nitrogen) which create the Hydrogen. Carbon, Oxygen and Nitrogen designate substances through which one of the three fundamental forces (Active, Passive, Neutralizing) is acting. So when Hydrogen 12 has the Active force acting through it or within it, it is called Carbon 12. With the Passive force acting through it, it is Oxygen 12 and with the Neutralizing force acting through, it is Nitrogen 12.

The Four Elements

It has been suggested that Hydrogen, Carbon, Oxygen and Nitrogen correspond to the traditional idea of The Four Elements: Earth, Water, Air and Fire. We do not see how this can be correct, except symbolically, nevertheless we believe the concept of Earth, Water, Air and Fire to be important in this study.

The idea that we could classify substances into the groupings of Earth, Water, Fire and Air tends to be derided by science, since these were designations that the disparaged Alchemists made and, they appear in the also disparaged Astrology, where signs of the Zodiac are classified as Earth, Water, Fire or Air. The origin of this idea is, as far as we can tell, from the Pythagoreans. Ignoring this tradition entirely, modern science started with the idea that substances could be classified as: solid, liquid or gas - and also, of course, that the same substance might, depending upon temperature (i.e. rate of vibration), move between these states. It wasn't until 1928 that modern science realized that there was definitely a fourth state of matter, which they named "plasma"–the term was coined by Irving Langmuir. Experiments with plasma began much earlier, with the discovery of the cathode ray tube.

So, in time, modern science arrived at a similar set of classifications. Since then, modern science has uncovered other synthetic states of matter (Bose-Einstein condensates and neutron degenerate matter) at extremely low temperatures, and there are yet other theoretical states that have yet to be synthesized or are possibly imaginary. In general, modern science thinks in terms of four main states of matter.

As regards Earth, Water, Fire and Air, Pythagorean tradition also asserts another, a fifth state, which it designates Ether.

The Hydrogens

Gurdjieff described the Hydrogens (categories of substances) as produced by three internal Octaves of the Ray of Creation: the first from the Absolute (Do) to the Sun (Sol); the second from the SUN (Sol) to the Earth (Mi) and the third from the Earth (Mi) to the Moon (Re). If we begin with Do in the Moon-Earth Octave, we note that it spans one eighth of the Ray of Creation (the Re-Mi "distance" is always one eighth of a whole octave). The Earth-Sun Octave spans one quarter of the Ray of Creation (the Mi-Sol "distance" is always one quarter of a whole octave) and the Sun-Absolute Octave spans one half of the Ray of Creation (the Sol-Do "distance" is always one half of a whole octave). So each of these Octaves doubles the lower one.

In the adjacent diagram (4) we show Gurdjieff's derivation scheme. Rather than use the original numbers (shown in the first column) Gurdjieff "steps them down" twice because the top level (H6 ▶

H1 ▸ H0) did not participate at all in the life of man. We have slightly changed the diagram shown in *In Search of the Miraculous* by adding in H0 in a space that Gurdjieff left blank.

Why we have done this will become clear later. In the third column, then, the Hydrogens have the numbers that Gurdjieff later uses in the Food Diagram, which shows all the Hydrogens from H6 to H768 that participate in the transformation of substances by man –the cycle of food.

To get a better idea of what each of these Hydrogens represent it helps to have examples. We provide these in figure 5, next page. This table combines information from *In Search of the Miraculous, Perspectives on Beelzebub's Tales* by Keith Buzzell and *The Theory of Celestial Influence* by Rodney Collin. We are not sure of all details, so the reader is warned to beware of taking it as 'gospel.' The columns adjacent to the Hydrogens show entirely separate views that are not easy to reconcile.

First let us consider the first of these columns: Example Substances. Everything up to H96 is fairly clear and needs little discussion. With H48, H24 and H12 we are dealing with mental processes some of which are relatively slow (thinking), some which are

THE HYDROGENS
(Reduced for The Study of Man)

	1st Step Down	2nd Step Down
H6	H1	H0
H12	H6	H1
H24	H12	H6
H48	H24	H12
H96	H48	H24
H192	H96	H48
H384	H192	H96
H768	H384	H192
H1536	H768	H384
H3072	H1536	H768
H6144	H3072	H1536
H12288	H6144	H3072

4

faster (normal emotional response and moving center "thinking") and some which are faster still. These take place within the body using the energies of the body.

In reference to the chart on the following page, the mechanisms are most probably the mechanisms of the nervous system, which at the lowest level work via ionic waves but at the H12 level, most probably, work via electromagnetism. We have equated H6 with photonic activity (light) and the electromagnetic force which are presumed not to exceed light speeds, but may be slowed by the medium they pass through. We know very little about the action of H6, which Gurdjieff equated with the highest intellectual activity (higher intellectual center) of the "master in the carriage."

The second of these columns: Relative Speeds, is derived from a table provided by Rodney Collin in *The Theory of Celestial Influence*. We have tallied this with the Example Substances column. The speed ranges span a factor of one hundred, and it generally appears that we can indeed match this to the Example Substances. Bearing this in mind, it would seem that we need to consider a cosmos' speed. Clearly metals, minerals, plants and invertebrates are, generally, slower than man. Animals could be considers as having equivalent physical speed (with one or two being faster). However, through the use of invention, Man can move faster than animals (in recent times much faster).

At higher levels we are dealing with the speed of the nervous system and other inner processes. Their speed equates to that of the speed of sound in air and at a higher level, the speed of magnetic storms or the speed of the sun itself. Beyond the speed of light we have no real knowledge. However, recent physics experiments suggest that the "speed of communication between particles that are entangled" (a quantum effect) is 10,000 faster than light. Tachyons (theoretical particles proposed by

Hydrogen	Example Substances	Relative Speeds	Halogens
H0	Quantum material (subatomic) communications	Speed of quantum entanglement 2 light yrs/week - 1 light yr/hr)	-
H1	Tachyons	Unknown 300000 km/sec - 2 light yrs/wk	-
H6	Photonic activity (light) and the electromagnetic force.	Speed of light, electricity 3000 - 300000 km/sec	-
H12	Electromagnetic fields	Speed of solar magnetism and of solar system 30-3000 km/sec	Hydrogen
H24	Ionic acoustic waves	Speed of sound in air 300 m/sec - 30 km/sec	Fluorine
H48	Ionic wave forms	Speed of nervous system 3 m/sec - 300 m/sec	Chlorine
H96	Hormones, Vitamins (ionic molecules)	Speed of animal motion, gaseous diffusion 3 cm/sec - 3 m/sec	Bromine
H192	Air, atmospheric and other gases	Speed of worms, ants, liquid diffusion 1 m/hr - 3 cm/sec	Iodine
H384	Water, most liquids especially organic liquids	Speed of osmosis 1 cm/hr - 1 m/hr	Astatine
H768	Food, cellular material (often cooked)	Speed of plant growth 1 m/yr - 1 cm/hr	Ununseptium
H1536	Wood, lignin, cellulose	Growth of wood, hair, bone 1 cm/yr - 1 m/yr	-
H3072	Iron, minerals in crystalline form	Mineral erosion 1 cm/100yr - 1 cm/yr	-

5

Richard Feynman) are defined to be faster than light, but their existence is not proven and they may in fact be imaginary rather than real.

In the third column we show the Halogens, including Hydrogen as a Halogen, which is not normal in the terms of modern science, but aligns with Gurdjieff's description both in *In Search of the Miraculous*, and in *The Tales*, where it is called the Inner Ansapalnian Octave. This octave may seem to contradict the entries in the two previous columns if we view it in the normal manner. In *In Search of the Miraculous* Gurdjieff draws attention to the approximate doubling in atomic weight between fluorine (atomic weight 19), chlorine (atomic weight 35.5), and bromine (atomic weight 80). The inexactitude of iodine's atomic weight (127) being only about 50 percent more than bromine, is repeated with astatine (atomic weight 210), which is about 65 percent greater than iodine. Although the atomic weight of the undiscovered "ununseptium" is unknown, the estimated atomic weight of the adjacent element Livermorium at 298, suggests that the atomic weight of "ununseptium" will be at most 50 percent greater than astatine.

This octave seems to confuse everything. If we take it as contradictory then the whole edifice of this theory of Hydrogens collapses. Instead we assume that it is indeed valid and that the apparent anomalies are explained by the difference between on atoms as conceived by Objective Science and atoms as conceived by modern science.

From the point of view of modern science's atomic structures, the atoms of hydrogen, fluorine, chlorine, bromine, iodine, astatine and "ununseptium" each have a single electron missing from their outer orbit, and thus there is a very definite structural similarity. The elemental halogens are toxic to most life forms, particularly bacteria, as are some of the compounds they form. We use compounds involving the middle halogens (chlorine, bromine and iodine) as disinfectants. Fluorine is one of the most reactive elements. It can react with otherwise inert materials such as glass, and it will even form compounds with the heavier noble gases.

In *The Tales*, Gurdjieff describes the final two halogens, astatine and ununseptium as the "principal necessary factors" for our existence. This seems absurd. While four of the first five elements in that octave (hydrogen, fluorine, chlorine and iodine) play some role in the biochemistry of man, it is almost certain that neither astatine nor "ununseptium" do. Indeed, as all the halogens are toxic, it is quite likely that both astatine and ununseptium would be toxic if ingested. Both elements would also be radioactive.

If either element exists on Earth as a compound at all, it is likely to be discovered only in the Earth's core. As such it is hard to imagine how either element could be relevant to man. However, if we take a completely different perspective and consider the Hydrogens that serve as food for man and the octave that they carve out as illustrated in the Food Diagram, we note that the octave of normal food for man run from H768 to H12. If "ununseptium" is H768, it strikes a fundamental note in the Inner Ansapalnian octave and so does astatine (H384) then maybe these two substances are indeed principal necessary factors for man's existence, since they are the fundamental notes of the hydrogen classifications of food (for man) and water.

And while we currently have no theory as to the meaning of the neologism Hydro-oomiak (for astatine), the initial morpheme of this word, "hydro," clearly suggests water. Currently we have no theory as to the meaning of Petrkarmak (for ununseptium).

The Four Elements Revisited

We can now look at the Hydrogens from the classification of Earth, Water, Air and Fire. Hydrogens H3072 and H1536 are clearly Earth (i.e. solid). H768, food for man, is somewhere between liquid and solid, best described as a colloid - we attempt to make it such by the action of chewing. H384 is liquid. H192, is gaseous (Air), while H96 is likely to be gaseous (immersed in the liquid of the blood) at body temperature. In that context such molecules may be ionic (i.e. have an electric charge), but they are not plasma (Fire). (Physicists define plasma by specific atomic/molecular behavior.) With H48, H24 and H12, we must be in the realm of Fire.

Note that if we consider the Ansapalnian Octave of Halogens at normal (room) temperatures, we get a different picture. Ununseptium and Astatine are Earth, Iodine and Bromine are Water, Chlorine, Fluorine and Hydrogen are all Air. Hydrogen can very easily become Fire and perhaps should be classified as such, but would not be classified by physicists as plasma when at room temperature.

It would appear that these states are not easily applied to the Hydrogens since, for example with H192, Iodine is a liquid, and not Air.

The Step Diagram at First Blush

If we refer to figure 2 on page 87, we note the strange appearance of Hydrogen 3. This is odd because there is no such Hydrogen, and, given the way that the Hydrogens are derived, there cannot be an H3. Our assumption is that this label H3 is simply a device introduced by Gurdjieff entirely for his depiction of The Step Diagram. Gurdjieff stepped the Hydrogens down twice and in doing so he eliminated the top level hydrogen. That's fine for the study of man, (the Food Diagram shows H768 to H6) but it is not tenable for the study of Everything Living. For that reason we have made a small adjustment to the Step Diagram (see figure 4 on page 91) eliminating H3 by replacing it with H1 and introducing H0. (Mathematically H0 is really H1/6, but H0 is adequate, in our view, to represent a Hydrogen higher than H1).

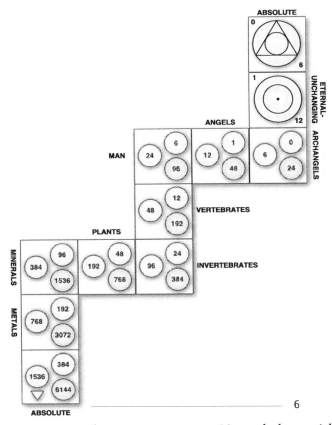

In this diagram, each square is a classification of living things. We are accustomed to think of four of these classifications as alive: plants, invertebrates, vertebrates and man. Most if not all of us know nothing of angels and archangels except by mention in holy books, or by rumor. The concepts of Eternal Unchanging and Absolute as living things are foreign to us except for the very amorphous concept of "one God." Beneath plants in the diagram, we have no concept of life forms in the realm of minerals and metals. If such things are alive, we have no means of separating them out as individualities. We can ask questions such as "Is a stone itself a mineral life form or is it a part of a mineral life form?" But we can only guess at answers. Nevertheless, with this diagram, Gurdjieff challenges us to find a way to see all of these categories as alive.

As regards these categories, Gurdjieff never specifically stated whether each of these categories were to be taken as a collection or as individual exemplars. So, for example, the square depicting Man might refer to an individual Man or Mankind as a whole. For the moment, we will assume that the latter is meant, for the following reason: Gurdjieff suggests that the intelligence of something is determined by what it can be food for. He gives the example that a boiled potato is more intelligent than a raw potato as the former can be food for Man but the latter is indigestible by Man. Man himself may thus be food for the Moon, but may also be food for the Earth (at death his body returns to the Earth) and may also be food for something higher. It would seem then that what an individual man can be food for may vary, but what mankind (including its inner circle) is food for may be constant.

It is worth emphasizing, as Gurdjieff did, that we are not discussing food in its normal sense. First of all, that is what is depicted in the Food Diagram and as far as that is concerned there are not one food but three.

If we look at the Hydrogens in the Step Diagram we see that H768 (first food for Man) is shown as food for Plants. H192 (air or second food) is what Plants are, and H48 (impressions or third food) is what feeds on Plants. The three types of food is clearly not what is implied here.

Curiously, this arrangement of Hydrogens reflects the Law of Three directly, in the following way. Any given Hydrogen cannot combine with the adjacent Hydrogen but only with one above or below the adjacent Hydrogen. Thus H24 can combine with H6 producing H12 or it can combine with H196 producing H48. As Gurdjieff writes,

" ... the higher blends with the lower to actualize the middle."[1]

Once we view the Step Diagram with this idea in mind, we immediately realize that the diagram is constructed entirely on this basis. So if Plants are H192 then that class can only combine with (feed on?) H768. It can be active in respect of H768 and then it will combine with H768, alternatively it can be passive in respect of H48 and thus will combine with (be fed on by?) H48. In respect of the Law of Three these are its only possibilities. And so it is with all of the 9 lower squares.

The two highest squares cannot (on this scale) be food for anything but can feed on H12 and H6 respectively.

The Four Elements Again

When Gurdjieff presented Objective Science's concept of the atom, he insisted that atoms of different densities interpenetrated one another. If we take the diagram of the Atoms (of different densities and the various orders of Laws that apply at each level), it appears that we can assign the Four Elements to the four densest atoms as illustrated in figure 7. So an atom of the Sun is Fire (plasma), an atom of the Planets is Air (gases), an atom of the Earth is Water (liquids) and an atom of the Moon is Earth (solid).

Such an assignment not only appears to be reasonably accurate (yes, we see these elements interpenetrating the lower ones) but it highlights the fact that there are most likely seven elements not four, with the three highest elements being entirely invisible to us, although for all we know, traces of them may have been detected by modern science.

We also note here that these four elements do indeed appear to be under clearly different physical laws. Solids do not flow, liquids do, but exhibit surface tension, which is not a characteristic of gases that thus are capable of diffusion, while plasmas are clearly electrical and have corresponding properties.

If we now overlay the idea of the four elements onto the Step Diagram, we arrive at the diagram in figure 8 on the next page (which also shows the Lateral Octave from the Sun).

Clearly the first three squares in the Step Diagram correspond to Earth. There are over 3000 known minerals, the 9 most common (Quartz, Feldspar, Muscovite, Biotite, Amphibole, Pyroxene, Olivine, Calcite and Dolomite) are estimated to make up 95% of the Earth's crust. Most of these 9 are silicates—combinations of silicon, oxygen and various metals. Minerals are presumed to have formed from chemical reactions that happened long ago as the Earth formed.

It is hard to know how to distinguish metals from minerals in this diagram. The most common metals

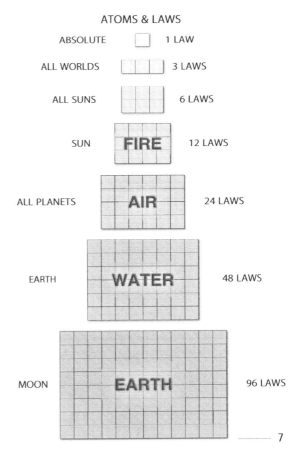

ATOMS & LAWS

ABSOLUTE		1 LAW
ALL WORLDS		3 LAWS
ALL SUNS		6 LAWS
SUN	FIRE	12 LAWS
ALL PLANETS	AIR	24 LAWS
EARTH	WATER	48 LAWS
MOON	EARTH	96 LAWS

7

1 Gurdjieff, *Beelzebub's Tales*, p 751.

are Aluminium (usually as Bauxite) and Iron (usually as Haematite). We note that some minerals (such as sandstone or coal) are produced by biological activity, while other such as granite are produced by volcanic activity. It may be that this is what distinguishes minerals from metals, but we are not confident in this theory.

However if this is so, then we can view minerals as sitting on the dividing line between Earth and Water, with water acting as a means of breaking minerals down, in a direct way through the action of waves or rivers on rocks and in a less obvious way through the action of microbes and plants, often with the assistance of soil. At the heart of Water is plants, who employ water as blood, to transfer minerals through the organism as well as to feed individual cells with water.

On the dividing line between Water and Air we find invertebrates, a class of organisms that are particularly suited to a liquid environment sometimes employing minerals (oysters, snails, crustaceans) as an exoskeleton. These organisms breath air directly and are particularly distinct from plants in that they are capable of motion.

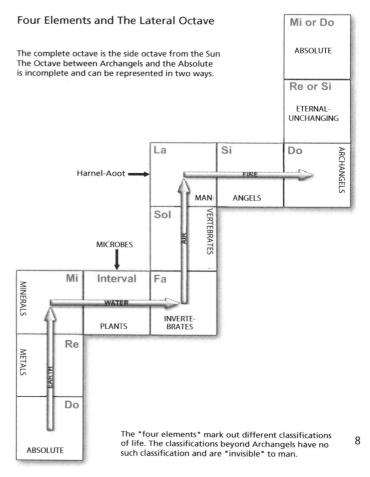

Four Elements and The Lateral Octave

The complete octave is the side octave from the Sun
The Octave between Archangels and the Absolute is incomplete and can be represented in two ways.

The "four elements" mark out different classifications of life. The classifications beyond Archangels have no such classification and are "invisible" to man.

8

The vertebrates utilize air in a sophisticated manner, this is particularly the case with warm blooded animals that maintain a constant body temperature and can move at impressive speed often for a considerable time. The blood of these creatures rapidly circulates air throughout their body. Man, in turn, stands on the diving line between Air and Fire, the Fire enabling him to support a sophisticate nervous system that includes a thinking center and has the potential to digest impressions.

About Angels and Archangels we can only speculate. However we note that the word Angel comes from the Greek Angelos meaning messenger or "one who announces." Within some parts of the Sufi tradition it is suggested that Angels confer knowledge and that all real knowledge comes from this level and is passed to man by revelation. Whether this is true or not, such activity very likely involves magnetic and electronic interactions.

The Lateral Octave From The Sun

The first thing to note about how we have placed the Lateral Octave onto the Step Diagram is that we have assigned Do, Re, Mi to the realm of Earth, but have placed the Mi-Fa Interval in the square labelled Plants. In doing this we have a correspondence with Gurdjieff's statement that Organic life on Earth corresponds to "Fa-Sol-La of the Lateral Octave from the Sun," since we can envisage Fa as including the interval.

In the top two squares we have provided alternatives (Re or Si and Mi or Do) for the notes of the next octave. We have done this because of uncertainty. The Hydrogens appearing in those squares suggest that we do not reach the Absolute (the Hydrogens were stepped down twice) and at Mi we will encounter an Interval which may define "the Absolute for Man." However in case that interpretation is incorrect, we have also indicated that the notes Si and Do may belong there as the true notes of the Sun Absolute (Eternal Unchanging) and the true Absolute.

Microbes

We know very little about the microbial world. There are many, probably millions, of species of microbes of which we are currently unaware. Modern science has focused quite naturally on the microbes that inhabit our bodies. Recently was it estimated that there are 10 times as many microbes that inhabit our bodies as there are cells of our own (the claim was made by Jeffrey Gordon, professor at Washington University). This is quite surprising, given that the evidence also suggests that newly born babies (until they come into contact with bacteria in the birth canal) have none.

However what may be of greater interest to us are what are termed Extremophiles, microbes that seem to thrive in extreme conditions that would be fatal to most life-forms. They exist in the following ranges:

- Temperatures between 266°F (130°C) well above the boiling point of water and 1 °F (-17°C), well below the freezing temperature of water.
- Acidity/alkalinity, from less than pH 0 up to pH 11.5
- Salinity, up to saturation (the point of crystallization in water)
- Pressure: from 1,000-2,000 atm (deepest part of the ocean) down to 0 atm (pressureless space).
- Radiation: up to 5kGy

The extremophiles are found where no other life is found - high in the atmosphere and deep in the earth's crust. They seem to assist life in every layer (every square in the diagram) from Minerals to Man and, quite possibly beyond. In general the existence of extremophiles suggests that life will arise in almost any circumstance and thus, it is entirely feasible that life exists at the microbe level on many planets and moons in our solar system.

Man

Man's position in this octave is at the Harnel-Aoot–the point at which reason becomes possible for a living organism, since this is the point where an intellectual center is possible. In the "realm of Air" man achieves the most that can be achieved by a physical body and stands at the gate of Reason, which is in the "Realm of Fire."

We note also that man's body has its roots in the realm of Earth (Minerals, as are found in bone, hair and teeth) traverses the realm of Water and culminates in the realm of Air. It is made up of all the Hydrogens from H3072 to H12, spanning the huge distance between bone and psychic processes. However the Kesdjan body (Astral, Emotional Body) while it may have its roots in Water appears to be born of Air and destined for Fire, should it crystallize.

Before we look at the bodies of Man further we believe it wise to consider the Earth itself as a cosmos, since the Step Diagram seems to focus on life on this planet (or if it has application beyond that, we can only study it in terms of this planet).

Consider figure 9 (next page) which shows the realms of our planet. Here we have used various names borrowed from Modern Science although our exact definition of these terms is not in every

9

case identical with modern science. Note, first of all, that we show 9 layers corresponding to the lower 9 squares of the Step Diagram, figure 8, page 96.

The lowest of these is the Earth's Core or Barysphere, consisting, it is believed, of heavy metals many of which may be radioactive and may account for the fact that the Earth's temperature increases as you dig down into the crust. We take this to be The Holy Firm, or a Gurdjieff dubs it in *The Tales*, a point of stability.

The Asphenoshere is constituted of deformable (Greek asthenes means weak) rock and stretches 200 kilometres below the Lithosphere. The realm of Metals may in fact go deeper and include the mantle or parts of it. The Earth's crust is known as the Lithosphere and consists of rock, some of which is formed by materials thrown up from below and some of which will be compressed biological residues.

The Lithosphere gives way to the Pedosphere, the layer of soil which covers the surface and in which we include the sediments at the bottom of seas and oceans. This is the material in which trees, plants and all related forms put down their roots and which is sustained by microbial action.

We place the Hydrosphere, the sphere of water, above the Pedosphere, although of course, the two intermingle. The geological record indicates that the first invertebrates that pervaded the planet lived in the sea. Life on the land developed from them.

Although there are vertebrates in the sea and rivers including some mammals, the land is the primary domain of mammals. In figure 9 we have chosen to call this domain the Biosphere, for want of an appropriate word. (Perhaps Zoosphere would be better.) The lower atmosphere is distinctively the domain of Man in its astrological properties. Standing as he does on the bridge between Air and Fire, man is capable of receiving influences from the planets and stars at a higher level than the rest of nature and is capable of contemplating the vastness of the Universe.

The rest of this diagram is speculative. We presume that the Ionosphere is the domain of Angels and the Magnetosphere the domain of Archangels. These are the two outer spheres of our planet, both of them electrical in nature.

The Bodies of Man

Finally, we can discuss what Gurdjieff may mean when he says that a particular classification of life "is" a given Hydrogen. If we consider the Trogoautoegocrat, every life form is a transformation point for various Hydrogens, able to cause the 'food" they consume to evolve and involve. Clearly living things are apparatuses consisting of a range of Hydrogens capable of transforming other Hydrogens

So, to say that a particular living thing "is" a given Hydrogen can only mean that it is typified by a given Hydrogen. Gurdjieff gives us some sense of this in *In Search of the Miraculous*, when he speaks of the Hydrogens which make up the various bodies of Man. Figure 10 combines two diagrams from the book, showing the Hydrogens of the four possible bodies of Man alongside the Ray of Creation. In the text it says:

> He again drew the diagram of the ray of creation and by the side of earth he placed the physical body of man.
>
> "This is ordinary man," he said, "man number one, two, three, and four. He has only the physical body. The physical body dies and nothing is left of it. The physical body is composed of earthly material and at death it returns to earth. It is dust and to dust it returns. It is impossible to talk of any kind of 'immortality' for a man of this sort. But if a man has the second body" (he placed the second body on the diagram parallel to the planets), "this second body is composed of material of the planetary world and it can survive the death of the physical body. It is not immortal in the full sense of the word, because after a certain period of time it also dies. But at any rate it does not die with the physical body.
>
> "If a man has the third body" (he placed the third body on the diagram parallel to the sun), "it is composed of material of the sun and it can exist after the death of the 'astral' body.

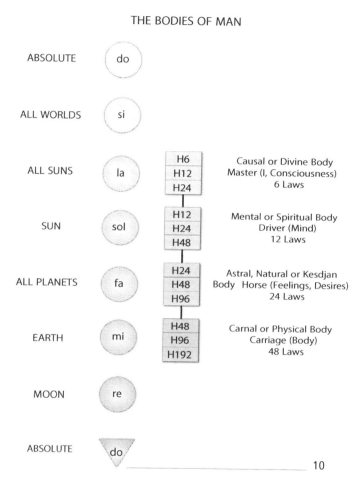

THE BODIES OF MAN

ABSOLUTE	do		
ALL WORLDS	si		
ALL SUNS	la	H6 / H12 / H24	Causal or Divine Body Master (I, Consciousness) 6 Laws
SUN	sol	H12 / H24 / H48	Mental or Spiritual Body Driver (Mind) 12 Laws
ALL PLANETS	fa	H24 / H48 / H96	Astral, Natural or Kesdjan Body Horse (Feelings, Desires) 24 Laws
EARTH	mi	H48 / H96 / H192	Carnal or Physical Body Carriage (Body) 48 Laws
MOON	re		
ABSOLUTE	do		

10

> "The fourth body is composed of material of the starry world, that is, of material that does not belong to the solar system, and therefore, if it has crystallized within the limits of the solar system there is nothing within this system that could destroy it. This means that a man possessing the fourth body is immortal within the limits of the solar system. (Ouspensky, *In Search of the Miraculous*, pp 93-94)

It would appear then, that the carnal body is of Water, which is the level of the Earth. It is built from atoms of Earth (Water) and when destroyed its substances return to the Earth. The Kesdjan body is of Air, the troposphere (lower atmosphere) which is said to be influenced by the planets. It is built from atoms of air, from the breath, and it the vehicle of the emotions. The Mental body is of Fire. It is built by the perfection of reason, from atoms at the level of the Sun.

The Divine Body is beyond the Solar system, built from atoms of the starry world that are subject to just six laws. It takes us beyond the nine lower squares of the Step Diagram. Man numbers 1, 2, 3 and 4 have a carnal body. Man number 5 has a Kesdjan body that, while his physical body persists, pervades the carnal body. Man number 6 has a Mental body which, while the carnal body persists pervades the Kesdjan and carnal bodies. Man number 7 has a divine body that pervades all the three lower bodies.

Later in *In Search of the Miraculous*, Gurdjieff explains the idea of the three levels of Man as worm (carnal body), sheep (Kesdjan body) and Man (Mental body). He then says:

> Man is a complex creature; the level of his being is determined by the level of being of the creatures of which he is composed. The sheep and the worm may play a bigger or a smaller part in man. Thus the worm plays the chief part in man number one; in man number two—the sheep; and in man number three—man. But these definitions are important only in individual cases. In a general sense 'man' is determined by the center of gravity of the middle story.
>
> "The center of gravity of the middle story of man is 'hydrogen' 96. The intelligence of 'hydrogen' 96 determines the average intelligence of 'man,' that is, the physical body of man. The center of gravity of the 'astral body' will be 'hydrogen' 48. The center of gravity of the third body will be 'hydrogen' 24, and the center of gravity of the fourth body will be 'hydrogen' 12.
>
> "If you remember the diagram of the four bodies of man which has been previously given and in which the 'average hydrogens' of the upper story were shown, it will be easier for you to understand what I am now saying."

[G. drew a diagram showing the four bodies, each consisting of three hydrogens. We have represented this in figure 10 on the previous page.]

> "The center of gravity of the upper story is only one 'hydrogen' higher than the center of gravity of the middle story. And the center of gravity of the middle story is one 'hydrogen' higher than the center of gravity of the lower story.
>
> "But, as I have already said, to determine the level of being by the 'table of hydrogens' it is usual to take the middle story. (Ouspenksy, *In Search of the Miraculous*, p 319)

We take this to be Gurdjieff's explanation of the what a being "is" and we can apply it directly to the Step Diagram. Thus in this diagram the square containing Man represents Man with a completed Mental body. There may be only a few such men at any time within Mankind. This is "Man without quotation marks."

So, perhaps, the square of Vertebrates embraces a Man with a perfected Kesdjan body. Again this may include relatively few men. We have no idea whether any other species can perfect a Kesdjan body, but if they can then they also reside here. However the vast majority of humanity and animals really belong in the next lower square, typified by invertebrates. If we look at it this way, then we can view those three squares as an ascent, since the man who develops his possibilities climbs from one to another.

If we look at the Step Diagram in this way, then there are other deductions that we can make from it. However, rather than provide details of this, we leave it as an exercise for those readers who care to pursue it.

Robin Bloor — robin.bloor@gmail.com

··· ∾ ···

QUESTIONS AND ANSWERS

COMMENT: Can you go back to the diagram of the different levels of Man? Is there also an Etheric body?

BLOOR: There may well be. Would anybody like to give an opinion? I don't think *In Search of the Miraculous* mentions the Etheric body as a term.

COMMENT: There is. The Etheric Body is the most physical part of the skin of the Kesdjan Body. The Etheric Body, on the other hand, is the least material part of this body–so it is around you.

COMMENT: Where is this mentioned–in which book is this mentioned?

COMMENT: In Nott–*Teachings of Gurdjieff*, page 174.

COMMENT: *Orage's Commentary on Beelzebub*?

COMMENT: Yes. But, I say it too!

COMMENT: When confronted with these diagrams, the question will come down to how are they practical and in what way do they say something practical about my own work? Because I believe it is quite easy to get side-tracked talking about that Universe being out there, those Suns being out there and something like organic life being around me and the Moon being out there. Whereas I cannot be part of this process, I cannot find practical ways that this process can teach me anything unless I see this process in me–unless I am this process–unless those changes happen. And then the question comes: what kind of cognitive possibilities do I have in terms of these different levels of interactions, of feeding? We definitely cannot have a cognitive relationship with all those Do Re Mi Fa Sols of all the worlds from the Absolute Do to the Absolute Do of the bottom. We live in a certain band of realities and we have the possibilities of a cognitive relationship with those Hydrogens and substances in general and those laws that correspond to this band. The question is, from the minute I realise the Ray of Creation is passing through me and that I have no cognitive relation to the Ray of Creation, unless I study it in me–to what extent does this Ray of Creation pass through anybody else except me? This is something I cannot know, because everything I know about the world is subjective, it passes through my personal perception and the possibility of the primordial laws being laws of perception kind of cocoons me into an individuality of which I can only configure the fact that other people exist and other people have similar ideas and experiences. So there seems to be a constant interrelationship between what is subjective, which is cognitively approachable, and what is objective in the sense of the world we live in outside me, which does not seem to contain the cognitive possibilities of my knowing in any kind of conclusive way other than images–intellectual images. To sum it up, in my understanding, the Ray of Creation is the one passing through me and the primordial laws are the laws of my perception of the world. Would you agree with that?

BLOOR: Kind of. You ask a very big question, because it has a number of aspects. We can first go back to this and say that on this diagram the Ray of Creation doesn't pass through you. This is the one that passes through you–the Side Octave from the Sun. In the sense that you are in that at this note. The Ray of Creation itself is a model for your inner world, so the Ray of Creation that you are interested in is the one that is you. So that is part of it. When we look at it–go back to figure 8–these are feeding points, then this scheme of three octaves is relevant if we start to apply it to us. We feed there; we breathe there; we have perceptions there. This breaking into three octaves here is within us. I would not represent the word 'subjective' in the way that you do, because you are using 'subjective' as though it was diminishing the fact that your inner world is only you. We agree, but once we get into the Work we start to try and create something objective in us and therefore what we actually observe may have been observed, rather than told to us by somebody else, or a theory given to us by somebody else.

COMMENT: Or within us?

BLOOR: I don't know if that answers the question. I don't think it does, but I would say talk to me afterwards because I think it is a long discussion. The other thing I meant to say—the thing that's missing from this is making it relate to *The Tales* and I simply didn't have the time to do that before this conference. I'm intending to do that for the book. One of the things I think is really important is the idea that Djartklom happens as remorse of conscience and that's what makes the Sun shine. The only thing we have got in this that indicates Djartklom is the original genesis where everything breaks into three .... We don't have any model here that's going to help us with that, but we do know this. We have experiences of presence and possibly even second conscious shock and we know we shine like the Sun when that happens.

COMMENT: You mean Aieioiuoa?

BLOOR: It may be that you can pronounce that word and I can't.

COMMENT: I can give you the etymology if you want.

BLOOR: Oh yes.

COMMENT: In the Ouspensky diagrams Hydrogen 96 is on the level of the Moon and, in all esoteric systems, the Moon is a symbol of the etheric body, so if you take the symbols it becomes quite clear. I see also in this scheme—the invertebrates—there is the worm and worm is 'wurm' in German and is the dragon, the kundalini. The middle part there is a sheep and the sheep is the lamb—the transformation of energy in the Astral body and the Man is the essence, which receives the food from the kundalini. So if you take it by symbols and connect it with the laws it becomes, for me, very clear.

BLOOR: That will be in the transcript. That was really useful information that I can work with myself, because I didn't know that.

COMMENT: Quantum physics/quantum mechanics—the world of the super-small. How does that play?

BLOOR: One of the problems with science ... it nearly always turns into a duality. In mathematics we have the functions of a continuous variable and functions of discrete variable. We have variables, we have constants. In language we have verbs, we have nouns; we have consonants, we have vowels. In biology we have it's alive, it's dead; in physics we have is it a wave or is it a particle. We get always this duality, because it is the dualist thinking that does that. So what we have in physics at this time is a duality between Einsteinian physics above the level of quantum mechanics and you have quantum mechanics. There are various things that happen in quantum mechanics and cannot possibly be explained by there being a limit on speed of anything in the Universe. So you have the quantum entanglements where they have measured particles that are 1000 metres apart—they send one in this direction and one in the other direction at exactly the same time, without sufficient time for light to go between them. So we now have a phenomenon of information being passed faster than the speed of light, but the relativistic guys cannot accept that because everything falls apart at their level if they don't have a limit to the speed of light, so you have a division in the world of physics and you discover in the world of quantum physics everything is explained in terms of probabilities. So you have an electron in a shell and it moves to another shell and we know that kind of thing happens in the sense that there is a photon of light that will come out with a given radiation that we presume the model is that it moved from shell to shell, but it does so without passing through the space between. That's how the model works, it has a probability of being in this shell and a probability of being in that shell and no probability of being elsewhere. And that model works for predicting behavior at the quantum mechanical level. I think that what you have ... to resolve those two things ... I think Einsteinian physics is probably wrong, but it doesn't matter in one way, because you are still stuck with two models and the two models work where they work and they don't work where they don't work. It is a set of beliefs–people have a set of beliefs they call science.

COMMENT: I appreciate how you brought Rodney Collin's writing into this, because he has a lot to offer, as you have shown. You refer to his description of the different levels of radiations and in the material that you were referring to there is also the description where man has become god. He offers the explanation of Hitler as an example.

BLOOR: Yes, I remember reading that.

COMMENT: The other thing that might bridge the gap that was presented is this additional information that both Rodney Collin and in particular Maurice Nicoll has added to this–the psychological aspects of the different worlds. World 96 false personality, 48 personality, 24 essence ... and so on. On higher centres ... I think that should have been here.

BLOOR: You are probably right. In the sense that if you want to follow this material up, the first thing you need to do is read the *Theory of Celestial Influence* and you should probably also read the *Theory of Eternal Life* by Rodney Collin. Both of those books have patterns that are very similar to this and explanations that are very interesting. The representation in terms of the whole of the Universe in Maurice Nicoll and also in Orage's presentation in New York has three dimensions of time. The idea of one dimension of time is not ever seen as enough to explain a model of the Universe in total. I could have presented it, but I would be going on for the rest of the week if I tried to do all of that.

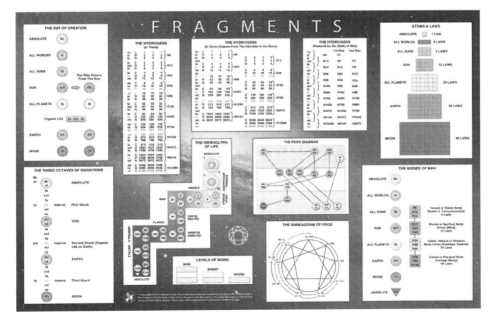

··· ∼ ···

Okhtapanatsakhnian Okhtatralnian Okhterordiapan
Okhti-Noora-Chaka Okhti-Pikan-On Okiartaaitokhsa
Okidanokh Okina Okipkhalevnian Okrualno Oksoseria
Olbogmek Olmantaboor Olooessultratesnokhnian Olooestesnokhnian
Omnipresent Onandjiki Ooamonvanosinian
Ooissapagaoomnian Ookazemotra Oonastralnian
Ooretstaknilkaroolni Oornel Opianine Opium Ori-Noora-Chaka
Ori-Pikan-On Ornakra Orpheist Ors Orthodox
Orthodoxhydooraki Oskiano Oskianotsner Oskianotznel
Oskolnikoo Osmooalnian Otkalooparnian paischakir Paleomothists
palnassoorian Pamir Pandetznokh Pantemeasurability Papaverine
Papaveroon Paramorphine Parijrahatnatioose Partkdolg-duty
Passavus Patetook Pearl-land Pedrini
Perambarrsasidaan Peshtvogner Pestolnootiarly Petrkarmak
phaeton Phormine Photoinzoïn Phykhtonozine Piandjiapan
Piandjoëhary Pianje Pirinjiel Pirmaral Pirotine Pispascana
Pistotorine Planekurab Plef-Perf-Noof Plitazoorali Podkoolad
Podobnisirnian Podotorine Poisonioonoskirian Pokhdalissdjancha
Polorishboorda Polormedekhtic
Polorotheoparl Pooloodjistius Porphiroksine Poundolero
Prana Prnokhpaioch Protocosmos Protopine protoplasts Protoëhary
Prtzathalavr Pseudocodeine pseudophormine Pythoness
Ramadan Rascooarno Rastropoonilo restorial
Resulzarion Revozvradendr Rhaharahr
Riank-Pokhortarz Rimala Rimk
Rirkh Rkhee Roentgen Sakaki Sakookinoltooriko
Sakoor Sakronakari Sakrooalnian Sakroopiaks saliakooriapa
Salkamourskian Salnichizinooarnian
Salounilovian Salzmanino
Sami-Noora-Chakoo Sami-Pikan-On Samlios

∾ Seminars ∾

First Series, *Beelzebub's Tales to His Grandson*, chapter 39. The Holy Planet "Purgatory,"

Second Series, *Meetings with Remarkable Men*, chapter 10. Professor Skridlov

Third Series, *Life Is Real Only Then, When "I Am,"* Prologue

In past years, the Seminars have been focused upon an entire chapter from *Beelzebub's Tales* and from *Meetings with Remarkable Men*. Discussion was open to any aspect of the chapter. As it was felt by many that this approach was too broad, allowing for only a fraction of the material to be explored, it was decided to experiment with a different approach. We chose to read the text of the given chapter together from the beginning with no view to necessarily completing it during the time allowed for the Seminars. Each participant read anywhere from one paragraph to two pages before passing it on to their neighbor who, in turn, continued the reading. Times 'in between' were allotted for anyone to raise their questions, insights, comments, etc..

This year we also added the Third Series, *Life is Real Only Then, When "I Am,"* to the study, beginning with the Prologue. At present, the plan for next year is to pick up where we left off in the respective chapters.

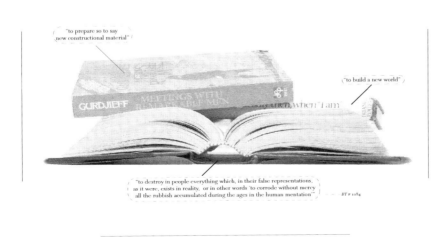

"to prepare so to say new constructional material"

"to build a new world"

"to destroy in people everything which, in their false representations, as it were, exists in reality, or in other words 'to corrode without mercy all the rubbish accumulated during the ages in the human mentation'" — *BT p 1184*

Seminar 1: chapter 39, "Purgatory"

Beelzebub's Tales

COMMENT/MODERATOR: We begin with a prayer:

> Sources of divine
> rejoicings, revolts and sufferings,
> direct your actions upon us.[1]

The plan for the session is to read from the beginning of the chapter. After one or two pages, pause for questions, comments, etc., and then continue.

Reading from "Purgatory:"

CHAPTER XXXIX

The Holy Planet "Purgatory"

AFTER several Dionosks the cosmic ship Karnak left the holy planet, and again began to fall further in the direction of the place of its final destination, and, namely, in the direction of that planet on which Beelzebub had had the place of his arising and whither he was returning to finish his long existence; to finish that long existence of his, which, on account of certain definite circumstances, he had to fulfill on various cosmic concentrations of our Great Universe and always under conditions very unfavorable for him personally, yet which he nevertheless objectively fulfilled quite meritoriously.

And so, when the usual tempo of the falling of the ship Karnak had been re-established, Hassein, the grandson of Beelzebub, again sat down at his feet and turning to him, said:

"Grandfather, oh dear grandfather! Explain to me, please, why, as my uncle Tooilan told me, does our COMMON ALL-EMBRACING UNI-BEING AUTOCRAT ENDLESSNESS appear so often on this holy planet on which we have just been?"

At this question of his grandson, Beelzebub this time became thoughtful a little longer than usual and then, also with greater concentration than was usual for him, slowly said:

"Yes . . . I do not know, my dear boy, with what to begin this time in order to answer this question of yours in such a form as would satisfy me also, since among many other tasks I have set myself in respect of you, as regards your 'Oskiano,' there is also this, that you, at your age, should have an exhaustive knowledge and understanding about this holy planet.

---

1 Gurdjieff, *Beelzebub's Tales*, P 752.

"In any case, you must first of all be told that this same holy planet, which is called Purgatory, is for the whole of our Great Universe, as it were, the heart and place of concentration of all the completing results of the pulsation of everything that functions and exists in the Universe.

"OUR COMMON-FATHER-CREATOR-ENDLESSNESS appears there so often only because this holy planet is the place of the existence of the, in the highest degree, unfortunate 'higher-being-bodies,' who obtained their coating on various planets of the whole of our Great Universe.

"The 'higher-being-bodies' who have already merited to dwell on this holy planet, suffer, maybe, as much as anybody in the whole of our Great Universe.

"In view of this, our ALL-LOVING, ENDLESSLY-MERCIFUL and ABSOLUTELY-JUST CREATOR-ENDLESSNESS, having no other possibility of helping these unfortunate 'higher-being-bodies' with anything, often appears there so that by these appearances of HIS HE may soothe them, if only a little, in their terrible inevitable state of inexpressible anguish.

"This planet began to actualize that aim for which it now exists, much later than that period of the flow of time when the completing process of the 'creation' of the now existing 'World' was finished.

"In the beginning all these 'higher-being-bodies' who at the present time have the place of their existence on this holy planet, went direct on to our Most Most Holy Sun Absolute, but later when that all-universal calamity, which we call the 'Choot-God-litanical period' occurred in our Great Universe, then after this terrifying common-cosmic calamity, similar 'higher-being-bodies' who now dwell on this holy planet, cease to have the possibility of blending directly with our Most Most Holy Sun Absolute.

"Only after this 'Choot-God-litanical period' did the necessity appear for such a kind of general-universal functioning which this holy planet 'Purgatory' actualizes at the present time.

"It was just from this time that the whole surface of this holy planet was correspondingly organized and adapted in such a way that these 'higher-being-bodies' might have the place of their already unavoidable existence on it."

Having said this, Beelzebub became a little thoughtful and with a slight smile continued to tell the following:

"This holy planet is not only the center of the concentrations of the results of the functioning of all that exists, but it is also now the best, richest, and most beautiful of all the planets of our Universe.

"When we were there, you probably noticed that we always saw and sensed that from there all the space of our Great Universe or, as your favorites would say, all the 'skies' reflected, as it were, the radiance which recalls the radiance of the famous and incomparable 'Almacornian turquoise.' Its atmosphere is always pure like the 'phenomenal-Sakrooalnian-crystal.'

"Everywhere there, every individual with all his presence senses 'everything external,' 'Iskoloonizinernly,' or as your favorites would say, 'blissfully-delightfully.'

"On that holy planet, as the informed say, of springs alone, both mineral and fresh which for purity and naturalness are unequalled on any other planet of our Universe, there are about ten thousand.

"There, from the whole of our Universe are gathered the most beautiful and best songbirds, of which as the informed also say, there are about twelve thousand species.[2]

COMMENT/MODERATOR: Relative to the previous talk concerning suffering, joy and bliss (Lee van Laer's talk), it is interesting that (or how) he uses "bliss" here. In the chapter "Justice," he describes the 'higher-being-bodies' as "blissful." Anyone wondered about that?

Continuing reading from "Purgatory:"

"And as for the surplanetary formations, such as 'flowers,' 'fruits,' 'berries,' and all others of the same kind, words are inadequate. It can be said that there are collected and acclimatized there almost the whole 'flora,' 'fauna,' and 'foscalia' from all the planets of our Great Universe.

"Everywhere on that holy planet, in corresponding gorges, are convenient caves of all kinds of 'interior form'–made partly by Nature Herself and partly artificial-ly–with striking views from their entrances, and in these caves there is everything that can be required for a blissful and tranquil existence, with the complete absence of any essence-anxiety whatever in any part of the presence of any cosmic independent Individual, such as 'higher-being-bodies' can also become.

"It is just in these caves that those 'higher-being-bodies' exist by their own choice, who, owing to their merits, come to this holy planet from the whole of our Great Universe for their further existence.

"Besides all I have mentioned, there are also there the very best, in regard to con-venience as well as to speed, what are called 'Egolionopties,' or, as they are still some-times called, 'Omnipresent-platforms.'

"These Egolionopties freely move in all directions in the atmosphere of the holy planet, at any desired speed, even at that speed in which the second degree suns of our Universe fall.

"The system of this kind of 'Egolionopty' was, it seems, invented specially for this holy planet by the famous angel, now already Archangel Herkission.

Having uttered these last words, Beelzebub suddenly became silent and again deeply thoughtful, and Hassein and Ahoon looked at him with surprise and inter-rogation.

After a fairly long time had passed, Beelzebub, shaking his head in a special man-ner, again turned to Hassein and said:

"I am just now thinking that it would be very reasonable on my part, if to this question of yours–'why our ENDLESSNESS so often rejoices this holy planet with HIS appearance'–I would answer in such a way, so that I could, apropos, explain to you also what I have already several times promised you to explain.

"That is to say, about the fundamental cosmic laws by which our present World is maintained and on the basis of which it exists; and this moreover should be done, because if both of these questions are taken together, only then will you have all-round material for a complete representation and exhaustive understanding about

2 Gurdjieff, *Beelzebub's Tales*, PP 744-46.

this holy planet Purgatory, and at the same time learn something more about the three-brained beings who have interested you and who arise on the planet Earth.

"I wish to give you also now as many clear and detailed explanations as possible concerning this holy planet, as, sooner or later, you will have to know about this, because every responsible three-brained being of our Universe, irrespective of the nature of the causes and place of his arising and also of the form of his exterior coating, will ultimately have to learn about everything concerning this holy planet.

"And he must know all this in order to strive to exist in that direction which corresponds just to the aim and sense of existence, which striving is the objective lot of every three-brained being, in whom, whatever the causes might be, the germ arises for the coating of a 'higher-being-body.'

"And so . . . my boy, first of all I must once more and in greater detail repeat that our ENDLESSNESS was forced to create the whole World which now exists at the present time.

"In the beginning, when nothing yet existed and when the whole of our Universe was empty endless space with the presence of only the prime-source cosmic substance 'Etherokrilno,' our present Most Great and Most Most Holy Sun Absolute existed alone in all this empty space, and it was on this then sole cosmic concentration that our UNI-BEING CREATOR with his cherubim and seraphim had the place of HIS most glorious Being.

"It was just during this same period of the flow of time that there came to our CREATOR ALL-MAINTAINER the forced need to create our present existing 'Megalocosmos,' i.e., our World.

"From the third most sacred canticle of our cherubim and seraphim, we were worthy of learning that our CREATOR OMNIPOTENT once ascertained that this same Sun Absolute, on which HE dwelt with HIS cherubim and seraphim was, although most imperceptibly yet nevertheless gradually, diminishing in volume.

"As the fact ascertained by HIM appeared to HIM very serious, HE then decided immediately to review all the laws which maintained the existence of that, then still sole, cosmic concentration.

"During this review our OMNIPOTENT CREATOR for the first time made it clear that the cause of this gradual diminishing of the volume of the Sun Absolute was merely the Heropass, that is, the flow of Time itself.

"Thereupon our ENDLESSNESS became thoughtful, for in HIS Divine deliberations HE became clearly aware that if this Heropass should so continue to diminish the volume of the Sun Absolute, then sooner or later, it would ultimately bring about the complete destruction of this sole place of HIS Being.

"And so, my boy, in view of this, our ENDLESSNESS was then just compelled to take certain corresponding measures, so that from this Heropass the destruction of our Most Most Holy Sun Absolute could not eventually occur.

"Further, again from the sacred canticle of our cherubim and seraphim, but this time the fifth sacred canticle, we were worthy of learning that after this Divine ascertainment of HIS, our ENDLESSNESS devoted HIMSELF entirely to finding a possibility of averting such an inevitable end, which had to occur according to the lawful commands of the merciless Heropass, and that after HIS long Divine deliberations, HE decided to create our present existing 'Megalocosmos.'

"In order that you may more clearly understand how our ENDLESSNESS decided to attain immunity from the maleficent action of the merciless Heropass and of course how HE ultimately actualized it all, you must first of all know that before this, the Most Most Holy Sun Absolute was maintained and existed on the basis of the system called 'Autoegocrat,' i.e., on that principle according to which the inner forces which maintained the existence of this cosmic concentration had an independent functioning, not depending on any forces proceeding from outside, and which were based also on those two fundamental cosmic sacred laws by which at the present time also, the whole of our present Megalocosmos is maintained and on the basis of which it exists, and, namely, on the basis of those two fundamental primordial sacred cosmic laws, called the sacred Heptaparaparshinokh and the sacred Triamazikamno.[3]

COMMENT: A significant word is "diminishing" because of Heropass and Almighty decides to change the basic law from Autoegocrat to Trogoautoegocrat. In my mind, this is a very potent image and it is crucial to the presentation of what Gurdjieff is doing with this system, of his thoughts. It is essential because it is a point that connects these ideas with science, official science.

I believe Autoegocrat and the diminishment of the Autoegocratic Universe is quite simply the results of entropy, of the systems of the Universe diminishing because of the second law of thermodynamics which describes inevitable death of all systems. By the change of Autoegocrat to Trogoautoegocrat, there is an element that is being introduced here of Trogo. "Trogo" means eating, eating means "life, living organisms" in the sense we know living organisms–and the difference is consciousness–the difference from Autoegocrat to Trogoautoegocrat. Trogoautoegocrat involves consciousness; it involves living beings.

So what it states here is that living beings provide for a force that counterbalances entropy and counterbalances entropic death. I think this is a representation of a structure where consciousness can fit in the scientific system used by ordinary science.

COMMENT: I don't think it is appropriate to introduce science into this at all. If Gurdjieff had wanted to introduce the idea of entropy, you would find the word "entropy" in this book. I don't think it is there at all. I don't think it is helpful to try to marry one system to another. We could try to marry it to Christianity or marry it to Buddhism or any particular set of beliefs and science is just another set of beliefs.

COMMENT: I agree that "entropy" is a word but the idea Gurdjieff used was that the forces were weakened or diminished. In the revised version it says "space" or "volume" is diminished, before he said "forces." The idea is really about decaying.

My thinking is the following. The chapter "Purgatory" doesn't aim to teach us how the worlds were created, the purpose is to encourage us to work on ourselves for having a higher-being-bodies. The theory of creating the words just served this purpose. How? It is a fact that we do not exist on Sun Absolute. This is obvious. So if God exists on Sun Absolute and we human beings are not there and we are supposed to work on ourselves to have higher bodies in order to arrive at Sun Absolute, the practical question is: how is it possible? If we are existing now in Sun Absolute, we should know it and feel it but we are definitely separated and the question is how to cross the barrier.

In accordance to known theologies and ideas since 700 years of gradual development from body to soul to higher soul, this is not new; it is many centuries known.

3 Gurdjieff, *Beelzebub's Tales*, PP 746-50.

Every octave with the Stopinders is a kind of a ladder. You can imagine that we are split into half; we have a higher soul and a lower soul but our higher soul is a part of the lower soul of the level above us. It means we are connected and we have a possibility to climb one step, Kesdjan Body, whatever. When we are at that level, again, our higher parts are the lower parts of the higher level. Ouspensky uses SOL and DO are resonating.

I believe the only idea in this cosmological explanation is not so much to tell us how the Cosmos was created. I don't think Gurdjieff knows how the Cosmos was created; it was long ago but I do think it gives us a very solid rational, semi-scientific explanation how it is possible to spiritually develop.

Gurdjieff was aware the people in the beginning of the century started looking and thinking scientifically, so he puts here the basis even intelligent people like us can accept the idea that it is possible to progress to a higher level. So it was a practical idea behind this theory.

Reading from "Purgatory:"

"About both of these fundamental cosmic primordial sacred laws, I have already once told you a little; now however I shall try to explain to you about them in rather more detail.

"The first of these fundamental primordial cosmic sacred laws, namely, the law of Heptaparaparshinokh, present-day objective cosmic science, by the way, formulates in the following words:

"'The-line-of-the-flow-of-forces-constantly-deflecting-according-to-law-and-uniting-again-at-its-ends.'

"This sacred primordial cosmic law has seven deflections or, as it is still otherwise said, seven 'centers of gravity' and the distance between each two of these deflections or 'centers of gravity' is called a 'Stopinder-of-the-sacred-Heptaparaparshinokh.'

"This law, passing through everything newly arising and everything existing, always makes its completing processes with its seven Stopinders.

"And in regard to the second primordial fundamental cosmic law, and, namely, the Sacred-Triamazikamno, common-cosmic objective science also formulates with the words:

"'A new arising from the previously arisen through the "Harnel-miaznel," the process of which is actualized thus: the higher blends with the lower in order to actualize the middle and thus becomes either higher for the preceding lower, or lower for the succeeding higher; and as I already told you, this Sacred-Triamazikamno consists of three independent forces, which are called:

the first, 'Surp-Otheos';
the second, 'Surp-Skiros';
the third, 'Surp-Athanotos';

which three holy forces of the sacred Triamazikamno the said science calls as follows:
the first, the 'Affirming-force' or the 'Pushing-force' or simply the 'Force-plus';
the second, the 'Denying-force' or the 'Resisting-force' or simply the 'Force-minus';
and the third, the 'Reconciling-force' or the 'Equilibrating-force' or the 'Neutralizing-force.'"

At this place of my explanations concerning chiefly the fundamental laws of 'World-creation' and 'World-maintenance,' it is interesting to notice by the way, that the three-brained beings of this planet which has taken your fancy, already began, at that period when the consequences of the properties of the organ Kundabuffer were not yet crystallized in their common presences, to be aware of these three holy forces of the Sacred-Triamazikamno and then named them:

the first, 'God-the-Father';
the second, 'God-the-Son';
and the third, 'God-the-Holy-Ghost';

and in various cases expressed the hidden meaning of them and also their longing to have a beneficent effect from them for their own individuality, by the following prayers:

'Sources of Divine
Rejoicings, revolts and sufferings,
Direct your actions upon us.'

. . .

or   'Holy-Affirming,
Holy-Denying,
Holy-Reconciling,
Transubstantiate in me
For my Being.'

. . .

or   'Holy God,
Holy Firm,
Holy Immortal,
Have mercy on us.'

"Now, my boy, listen further very attentively.

"And so, in the beginning as I have already told you, our Most Most Holy Sun Absolute was maintained by the help of these two primordial sacred laws; but then these primordial laws functioned independently, without the help of any forces whatsoever coming from outside, and this system was still called only the 'Autoegocrat.'

"And so, our ALL-MAINTAINING decided to change the principle of the system of the functionings of both of these fundamental sacred laws, and, namely, HE decided to make their independent functioning dependent on forces coming from outside.

"And so, in consequence of the fact that for this new system of functioning of the forces which until then maintained the existence of the Most Most Holy Sun Absolute, there were required outside of the Sun Absolute corresponding sources in which such forces could arise and from which they could flow into the presence of the Most Most Holy Sun Absolute, our ALMIGHTY ENDLESSNESS was just then compelled to create our now existing Megalocosmos with all the cosmoses of different scales and relatively independent cosmic formations present in it, and from then on the system which maintained the existence of the Sun Absolute began to be called Trogoautoegocrat.

"OUR COMMON FATHER OMNI-BEING ENDLESSNESS, having decided to change the principle of the maintenance of the existence of this then still unique cosmic concentration and sole place of HIS most glorious Being, first of all altered the process itself of the functioning of these two primordial fundamental sacred laws, and HE actualized the greater change in the law of the sacred Heptaparaparshinokh.

"These changes in the functioning of the sacred Heptaparaparshinokh consisted in this, that in three of its Stopinders he altered the, what are called 'subjective actions' which had been until then in the Stopinders, in this respect, that in one he lengthened the law conformable successiveness; shortened it in another; and in a third, disharmonized it.

"And, namely, with the purpose of providing the 'requisite inherency' for receiving, for its functioning, the automatic affluence of all forces which were near he lengthened the Stopinder between its third and fourth deflections.

"This same Stopinder of the sacred Heptaparaparshinokh is just that one, which is still called the 'mechano-coinciding-Mdnel-In.'

"And the Stopinder which he shortened, is between its last deflection and the beginning of a new cycle of its completing process; by this same shortening, for the purpose of facilitating the commencement of a new cycle of its completing process, HE predetermined the functioning of the given Stopinder to be dependent only upon the affluence of forces, obtained from outside through that Stopinder from the results of the action of that cosmic concentration itself in which the completing process of this primordial fundamental sacred law flows.

"And this Stopinder of the sacred Heptaparaparshinokh is just that one, which is still called the 'Intentionally-actualized-Mdnel-In.'⁴

COMMENT/MODERATOR: Is it crystal clear about what is meant by "... the 'requisite inherency' for receiving, for its functioning, the automatic affluence of all forces which were near...?" What is meant by "requisite inherency?" How do we understand these words? Bottom of page 753.

COMMENT: It is certainly not crystal clear so please correct me when I am wrong but is he not talking here of the "mechano-coinciding-Mdnel-In?" He is talking about the automatic affluences of all forces which were near, so a shock coming from outside being able to reach us. So he has provided us with the required inherency for receiving such a mechano-coinciding-Mdnel-In or shock from outside. That is what I hear.

COMMENT: It is not crystal clear to me either but I want to say something about an issue: why this Conference exists. It was precisely the discussion of this point between Bert Sharp, Sy Ginsberg, Nick Tereschenko and Russell Smith that brought them all together because it was exactly this point that Russell Smith was trying to clarify by showing a hand intervening on an octave which was stretching in an elastic piece of something like elastic paper or something and pushing one side and having the elastic band kind of being distorted. It was exactly this point that started the whole discussion.

So maybe if we solve it, we don't have any reason to have any other Conferences in the future! [laughter]

COMMENT: In the 1931 edition, it puts it slightly differently so for the purposes of a slightly new light on it. Again, he is talking about the difference between Autoegocrat and Trogoautoegocrat:

4 Gurdjieff, *Beelzebub's Tales*, PP 750-54.

From the 1931 manuscript of the chapter "Purgatory:"

> "... Autoegocrat ... was formed only of two laws, namely the law of 'Triamonia' and the law of 'Eftologodiksis'. To these two laws OUR CREATOR added a third force, called 'Fagologiria', by means of which the "Autoegokrat' became the 'Trogoautoegokrat', that is, a force depending on other forces exterior to itself. Or, as is might be said, after the addition of the Fagologiria, the Laws of Triamonia and Eftologodiksis could function only by feeding on the substances and forces coming from without.[5]

So this is the adjustment he had to make so that something coming in at that point caused the further evolution of whatever it is, everything.

COMMENT: Of course it is not crystal clear but I have been thinking many, many years about this because, like many others, I like to understand what we read. I also believe that whatever Gurdjieff writes has a sense. I also believe in my ability to understand. So what I have come up with comes from many years.

Regarding the two Stopinders, one is called "mechano," one is called "intentional." They are corresponding to the going down of the Worlds, decay. The Worlds automatically become less and less; you can call it entropy, you can call it whatever you want.

The other force, which Ouspensky called the organic life which transfer back the energy by taking the level of Earth and spiritualize it, send it back to the Moon or no matter what, that is the intentional Stopinder.

So, I understand these two things in the following way. Creation of the Worlds is automatic. Shortening the Stopinder means that planets, suns can now be created with a span of time, shorter that Sun Absolute Itself. In Sun Absolute, everything takes millions of years but now with the shortening of the new cycle, Worlds may be created and they are created mechanically. Suns create planets, planets create moons, etc., you don't need intentional consciousness or the effort of human beings for the creation of these Worlds.

In order to feed back the system, which is the purpose of Trogoautoegocrat, you need intentional intelligence, human beings that will have, in themselves, the ability to intentionally spiritualize matter. That is the second Stopinder. These two Stopinders created the third Stopinder, the disharmony.

There is a very simple symbol of this, which is a human being, to explain the idea. When I was born and I am growing, this is mechanical Stopinder; I came from my parents, very quickly, very smoothly. If I want or not want, I will die and decay. That is very good, the remains of my body will serve other forms of life, etc.. That is the first Stopinder that things go one after the other. I was born.

Now in me there is the ability and craving to come back to God and the love for God. This creates disharmony between my ego, natural tendency to enjoy and to exploit physically enjoyment and my spiritual craving to be more than a man. Here comes the third Stopinder, that is the disharmony.

You can use the symbol of two triangles; the one going down and the one going up, the seal of David, Ouspensky spoke about it. But this reminds me of what we spoke about concerning suffering and bliss because it is exactly this. By putting us in a state, we have to intentionally suffer in order to come back to God. This is suffering; living here is suffering. But by arriving at God at the end, this is bliss. So–no suffering, no bliss.

---

5 Gurdjieff, *Beelzebub's Tales*, 1931 manuscript, chapter "The Holy Planet Purgatory," P 2.

Here we have a system that corresponds to what I tried to explain before–that these Stopinders are difficult words to explain; they actually mean two forces–going down force, going up force. The going up force has to do with human beings and with coating of Higher Beings and suffering and the going down is mechanical, automatic.

The end picture is the following: instead of have a stagnated Universe without the movement, there is no movement, energy goes down, becomes less and less, arrives to us, where we are. By our inner Godly forces, we strive; we are becoming Godly; we come back to God. So it is like water coming back to the sea.

My end remark is the following: this is very sad. It means that our spiritual actions maintain the realm of God; that what we are doing is important to God. At the same time, God gave us life so there is a dependence from the point of view of God. Maybe it is frustrating to be dependent upon creatures like us because, if we are accepting of what Gurdjieff is saying, he tells what we are doing as human beings to evolve spiritually is essential to existence of the Sun Absolute. So it puts us in a very important place and it puts us in a place where we, if we love God, we have to try to be higher.

COMMENT: Well, I think your analysis is as good as it can get. The only thing I would like to add is nothing you omitted–just to say how this analysis is in step with the idea of the Work being about metabolizing negative emotions into positive emotions. It is making suffering becoming bliss.

COMMENT/MODERATOR: Please let us stick with the text, let us try.

COMMENT: I hope I am not going to deviate. I think that what has been said is quite informative. What interests me the most is that in the second Stopinder, the implication is that one assumes responsibility in one's work for how impressions are taken in. That is the way I understand it. One becomes responsible in this action and we can perhaps agree that is where intentional suffering is indicated, that we become responsible for the way that the impressions we take in act in ourselves and it is quite interesting that the third disharmonization divides the world into inner and outer circumstances which interact in a complex way.

To bring that back around to Autoegocrat versus Trogoautoegocrat. The word "Autoegocrat" basically means existing alone in a sense and is a singular authority but Trogoautoegocrat, when this was introduced, was a Universe of relationships.

The point I was making this morning about intentional suffering is that he is very specific in saying that it takes place in relationship. So the sacrifice that was made in the change of the Universal Laws was actually, if you want to be conceptual about it, a surrender of authority on the part of HIS ENDLESSNESS so that other beings would participate, through choice, through responsibility, in an exchange. Trogoautoegocrat implies an exchange and responsibility for my impressions of others as well as myself.

For me, the heart of these rather complicated ideas lies that dynamic.

COMMENT: Regarding "... the purpose of providing the 'requisite inherency' for receiving, for its functioning, the automatic affluence of all forces which were near...." The 'mechano-coinciding-Mdnel-In' is almost certainly the breathing and the automatic affluence of all forces is almost certainly the breath. That is the MI-FA interval. These things are just corresponding so the purpose of lengthening the Stopinder would imply that it would give it the requisite inherency to make you want to breathe.

COMMENT: I'd like to go back to the words. It is a very short sentence. What are the active words? For me, " 'requisite inherency for receiving' " and the "automatic affluence of all forces which were near."

If we look outside the windows here, we can see waterways flowing all around. When these waterways are wide there is the opportunity for more current to flow. By creating a "'requisite inherency for receiving'," the term in electrical engineering is "lowering the impedance."

A funnel has a wide mouth and a narrow bottom. A big part of that is a low impedance; it opens things up to the outside. When we have a lower impedance between Stopinders three and four, more can flow in from outside.

Prior to that, the Autoegocrat has all the Stopinders equally dispersed and everything is equally difficult and equally easy for things to flow but there is an inherent resistance to all of that. We are lowering the resistance when the Stopinder is lengthened between three and four. We are lowering the impedance to flow.

Then he says "all forces which were near," making it easier for things that are in the immediate vicinity, what is coming in the door to get in from the outside. Prior to that it is equally easy to get in and equally not easy to get in Autoegocrat.

I think the metaphor of impedance is exactly what he is talking about.

COMMENT/MODERATOR: I get the impression that we think the Law of Seven is only happening to us but he is talking about a cosmic perspective. Yes, this book is absolutely about myself but it seems intentional that he is giving this great cosmic perspective. So what is the first Stopinder in the creation of the Suns and the planets? If we think the 'Intentionally-actualized-Mdnel-In' has only to do with a three-brained being, that doesn't compute when he is speaking about completion of Suns and planets and the active elements. It seems that cosmic element helps bring more impartiality.

COMMENT: Yesterday, when we read the text of the 1931 edition, I was struck by the use of the word "Eftologodiksis" (changed to "Heptaparaparshinokh" in the 1950 edition). In Greek, the etymology is "Eft" is "Hepta." It is the same—it means "seven." "Logo" is a very complicated word but is also is "reason" or "explanation." "Diksis" is to demonstrate—for you to show. So what it means is that if you want to demonstrate, you have seven reasons for everything. This is what the word says: demonstration is by sevenfold reasoning.

We should seek all the explanations—cosmic, planetary, in ourselves, breathing and probably all food, because "trogo" means "eating" and what substitutes this in the older text is "Fagologiria." "Fago" is the same as "trogo;" it is a different word but it has exactly the same meaning with no deviation; it is just used in different circumstances. Two different words used in different circumstances, always meaning the same thing: "Fago" and "trogo." And "logo" again is the reason so Fagologiria means the reason that there is eating.

Eating is very important in this business.

COMMENT: A very small point and that is, if you remember, the Creation of mobile beings was an afterthought, as we will meet later on. In other words, the initial Creation, which is described here, doesn't depend on human beings.

COMMENT: I believe whatever works for men, works for the Cosmos because the man is in the creation of God. I used man as breathing just as an example, not as the only thing. We are human beings; there are other beings that do the same work, not only us of course.

··· ∾ ···

Seminar 2: chapter 39, "Purgatory"

Beelzebub's Tales

FACILITATOR: I will continue to read from where we left off and pass the book until we come to a point where somebody wishes to raise a question.

Continuing Reading from "Purgatory:" – P 754

"This same Stopinder of the sacred Heptaparaparshinokh is just that one, which is still called the 'mechano-coinciding-Mdnel-In.'

"And the Stopinder which HE shortened is between its last deflection and the beginning of a new cycle of its completing process; by this same shortening, for the purpose of facilitating the commencement of a new cycle of its completing process, HE predetermined the functioning of the given Stopinder to be dependent only upon the affluence of forces, obtained from outside through that Stopinder from the results of the action of that cosmic concentration itself in which the completing process of this primordial fundamental sacred law flows.

"And this Stopinder of the sacred Heptaparaparshinokh is just that one, which is still called the 'intentionally-actualized-Mdnel-In.'

"As regards the third Stopinder, then changed in its 'subjective action' and which is fifth in the general successiveness and is called 'Harnel-Aoot,' its disharmony flowed by itself from the change of the two aforementioned Stopinders.

"This disharmony in its subjective functioning, flowing from its asymmetry so to say in relation to the whole entire completing process of the sacred Heptaparaparshinokh, consists in the following:

"If the completing process of this sacred law flows in conditions, where during its process there are many 'extraneously-caused-vibrations,' then all its functioning gives only external results.

"But if this same process proceeds in absolute quiet without any external 'extraneously-caused-vibrations' whatsoever, then all the results of the action of its functioning remain within that concentration in which it completes its process, and for the outside, these results only become evident on direct and immediate contact with it.

"And if however during its functioning there are neither of these two sharply opposite conditions, then the results of the action of its process usually divide themselves into the external and the internal.

"Thus, from that time, the process of actualization began to proceed in the greatest as well as in the smallest cosmic concentrations with these Stopinders of this primordial sacred law of Heptaparaparshinokh changed in this way in their subjective actions.

"I repeat, my boy: Try very hard to understand everything that will relate to both these fundamental cosmic sacred laws, since knowledge of these sacred laws, particularly knowledge relating to the particularities of the sacred Heptaparaparshinokh, will help you in the future to understand very easily and very well all the second-grade and third-grade laws of World-creation and World-existence. Likewise, an all-round awareness of everything concerning these sacred laws also conduces, in general, to this, that three-brained beings irrespective of the form of their exterior coating, by becoming capable in the presence of all cosmic factors not depending on them and arising round about them—both the personally favorable as well as the unfavorable—of pondering on the sense of existence, acquire data for the elucidation and reconciliation in themselves of that, what is called, 'individual collision' which often arises, in general, in three-brained beings from the contradiction between the concrete results flowing from the processes of all the cosmic laws and the results presupposed and even quite surely expected by their what is called 'sane-logic'; and thus, correctly evaluating the essential significance of their own presence, they become capable of becoming aware of the genuine corresponding place for themselves in these common-cosmic actualizations.

COMMENT: On page 754 he speaks of what can complete the process in regards to the disharmony in the Harnel-Aoot. And I think I should read that small section which I am referring to:

> "... but if this same process proceeds in absolute quiet, without any external extraneously caused vibration whatsoever, then all the results of the action of the functioning remain within that concentration in which it completes its process and for the outside these results only become evident on direct and immediate contact with it.

So he is pointing to this absolute quiet. Now this quiet, for me, is that place in myself where I can go now and then—momentarily blank. The cultivation of this ability seems to me not only to be dependent on repeating, but it refers to when I go blank and sort of an inner listening, where I can hear and I can feel the urgency of participating and it is when I am anchored in what I call this silent point that I can go on and on and experience a cultivation of a gradually more and more reliable force that can counterbalance these disturbances and they vary from enthusiasm and to worry or other associative reactions that come up during the completion of the task. What I am referring to is, for example, when I am restoring a painting and there is the possibility to use the disturbances that come up in me, then these disturbances can be counterbalanced by going to this silent point. There is a lot of force in it.

Then he is referring to another aspect, where he says: if the completing process of this sacred law flows in conditions where, during its process, there are many extraneously caused vibrations, then all its functions gives only external results. And to me the external results that he points to when a process is completed and there are extraneously caused vibration is results which is right in form, but wrong in content. And in reference to what he writes on pages 750/51, he speaks of triads–using an opportunity through becoming quiet and cultivating the ability to become quiet is definitely the triad of regeneration.

The other example he gives–to me this is where–then all the functions gives only external results–refers to the triad of corruption. And then he goes on to the third one and maybe I should just read it: and if however during its function, there are neither of these two sharply opposite conditions, then the result of the action and its process usually divide themselves into external and internal–which also to me represent the triad or regeneration but on a completely different level, where the ability is of a more permanent character. I hope it makes sense to someone, it does to me.

Continuing reading from "Purgatory:"

"In short, the transmutation in themselves of an all-round understanding of the functioning of both these fundamental sacred laws conduces to this, that in the common presences of three-brained beings, data are crystallized for engendering that Divine property which it is indispensable for every normal three-brained being to have and which exists under the name of 'Semooniranoos'; of this your favorites have also an approximate representation, and they call it 'impartiality.'

"And so, my dear boy, our COMMON FATHER CREATOR ALMIGHTY, having then in the beginning changed the functioning of both these primordial sacred laws, directed the action of their forces from within the Most Holy Sun Absolute into the space of the Universe, whereupon there was obtained the what is called 'Emanation-of-the-Sun-Absolute' and now called, 'Theomertmalogos' or 'Word-God.'

"For the clarity of certain of my future explanations it must here be remarked that, in the process of the creation of the now existing World, the Divine 'Will Power' of our ENDLESSNESS participated only at the beginning.

"The subsequent creation went on automatically, of its own accord, entirely without the participation of His Own Divine Will Power, thanks only to these two changed fundamental primordial cosmic laws.

"And the process itself of creation proceeded then in the following successiveness:

"Thanks to the new particularity of the fifth Stopinder of the sacred Heptaparaparshinokh, these emanations issuing from the Sun Absolute began to act at certain definite points of the space of the Universe upon the prime-source cosmic substance Etherokrilno from which, owing to the totality of the former and the new particularities of the sacred primordial laws, certain definite concentrations began to be concentrated.

"Further, thanks to these factors and also to their own laws of Heptaparaparshinokh and Triamazikamno which had already begun to arise in these definite concentrations with their action upon each other, everything which had to be gradually began to be crystallized in these concentrations, and as a result of all this, those large concentrations were obtained which exist also until now and which we now call 'Second-order-Suns.'

"When these newly arisen Suns had been completely actualized and their own functionings of both the fundamental laws had been finally established in them, then in them also, similarly to the Most Most Holy Sun Absolute, their own results began to be transformed and to be radiated, which, together with the emanations issuing from the Most Most Holy Sun Absolute into the space of the Universe, became the factors for the actualization of the common-cosmic fundamental process of the sacred law of Triamazikamno, and that is to say:

"The Most Most Holy Theomertmalogos began to manifest itself in the quality of the third holy force of the sacred Triamazikamno; the results of any one of the newly arisen Second-order-Suns began to serve as the first holy force; and the results of all the other newly arisen Second-order-Suns in relation to this mentioned one newly arisen Sun, as the second holy force of this sacred law.

"Thanks to the process of the common-cosmic sacred Triamazikamno thus established in the space of the Universe, crystallizations of different what is called 'density' gradually began to be formed around each of the Second-order-Suns out of that same prime-source Etherokrilno, and grouping themselves around these newly arisen Suns, new concentrations began to take form, as a result of which more new Suns were obtained, but this time 'Third-order-Suns.'

"These third-order concentrations are just those cosmic concentrations which at the present time are called planets.

"At this very place in the process of the first outer cycle of the fundamental sacred Heptaparaparshinokh, namely, after the formation of the Third-order-Suns or planets, just here, owing to the changed fifth deflection of the sacred Heptaparaparshinokh, which as I have already said is now called Harnel-Aoot, the initially given momentum for the fundamental completing process, having lost half the force of its vivifyingness, began in its further functioning to have only half of the manifestation of its action outside itself, and the other half for itself, i.e., for its very own functioning, the consequences of which were that on these last big results, i.e., on these said Third-order-Suns or planets, there began to arise what are called, 'similarities-to-the-already-arisen.'

"And as after this, surrounding conditions of actualizations were everywhere established corresponding to the manifestation of the second particularity of the fifth Stopinder of the fundamental sacred Heptaparaparshinokh, therefore from then on the actualization of the fundamental outer cycle of the sacred Heptaparaparshinokh ceased, and all the action of its functioning entered forever into the results already manifested by it, and in them there began to proceed its inherent permanent processes of transformation, called 'evolution' and 'involution.'

"And then, thanks this time to a second-grade cosmic law which is called 'Litsvrtsi,' or the 'aggregation of the homogeneous,' there began to be grouped on the planets themselves, from the mentioned 'relatively independent' new formations named 'similarities-to-the-already-arisen,' yet other also 'relatively independent' formations.

"Thanks just to these processes of 'evolution' and 'involution' inherent in the sacred Heptaparaparshinokh, there also began to be crystallized and decrystallized in the presences of all the greatest and smallest cosmic concentrations, all kinds of definite cosmic substances with their own inherent subjective properties, and which objective science calls 'active elements.'

"And all the results of the 'evolution' and 'involution' of these active elements, actualizing the Trogoautoegocratic principle of existence of everything existing in the Universe by means of reciprocal feeding and maintaining each other's existence, produce the said common-cosmic process 'Iraniranumange,' or, as I have already said, what objective science calls 'common-cosmic-exchange-of-substances.'

"And so, my boy, thanks to this new system of the reciprocal feeding of everything existing in the Universe, in which our Most Most Holy Sun Absolute Itself participated, there was established in it that equilibrium which at the present time no longer gives the merciless Heropass any possibility of bringing about anything unforeseen whatsoever to our Most Great and Most Most Holy Sun Absolute; and thus, the motive for the Divine anxiety of our ALMIGHTY UNI-BEING ENDLESSNESS concerning the wholeness of HIS eternal place of dwelling, disappeared forever.

COMMENT: The question has been raised whether one can find the enneagram in the Tales. It has been given several answers. One of them was a presentation of the second order laws like Litsvrtsi and Iraniranumange that are mentioned in this chapter. There was a presentation, in Prague I think it was. And this chapter, at least a part of this chapter, can be seen as a description of the enneagram. And the point of that presentation was that these are laws–Litsvrtsi and all that–are exactly a representation of the 123, 231, 312 interchanges that you were mentioning before.

COMMENT: Is the second particularity of the tree of the fifth Stopinder the functioning when there are neither these two sharply opposite conditions then the results of the actions of these processes usually divide themselves into the internal and external? Would we agree that this is the second particularity or peculiarity?

COMMENT: Yes

COMMENT: Okay, then how does that result to evolution and involution? How do we get evolution and involution out of the fifth Stopinder?

COMMENT: I would like to remind what Ouspensky wrote about this. Ouspensky wrote that the organic creatures on the planet serve the cosmic purposes by processing food, etc, but, he says, that if the individual chooses, he can utilise part of this energy for inner development and getting a higher body. It means he said that the general rule is that everybody cannot do it, but few people choose– they go under the radar–and they can utilise this energy for themselves. I think this is the same idea and it is also what you have said. When you act mechanically, responding to external circumstances: you are hungry, you go to work, you eat food, you buy food, that is all external influences cause you mechanical things, then nothing grows inside you, but when you are in quietness, inner peace, impartial to what is going on, not mechanically respond to stimuli, then you accumulate energy and force and this builds yourself and it can be either one of these extremes, that is you can be a monk that only works on himself and very quickly maybe become a saint, the other extreme is a normal person who only reacts to their conditions, but there are intermediate stages, let's say some times we are meditating–we are trying to do some inner work or quiet–so then we are preserving spiritual material that builds our higher bodies. I think this is relating to that, but I'm not sure.

COMMENT: I would like to share a new image that appeared to me when this passage was read. Before I saw just the evolution of solar system and the planets, but now there appear to me the image of the master and his disciples. So the second order Suns are exemplified by the masters and the third order suns are exemplified by his disciples and these involutionary and evolutionary processes are appearing in the disciples because of the presence of the master. And together of course they work to prevent the diminishing of the Holy Sun Absolute, which is God, Father, Christ and his disciples.

COMMENT: I just wanted to add something to what A said. This silent—what I call the silent point—is the second of the three possibilities. And I think it is when we try to work without being noticed, it is that kind of work that can enable our work to become equally balanced between the inner and the outer world. I remember this: someone is doing something good as long as fiancés father is looking. So there is an order in the three ways of doing things and the third way when the outer and the inner is working, that quality of the triad of regeneration manifesting is a consequence of working invisibly. Then again at the end of that passage he says that it can be recognized through some kind of immediate confrontation, which means somebody on the same level might be able to recognise it.

COMMENT: The word "evolution" comes from a Latin word that related to the rolling and unrolling of a text. So I think that my own associative perception of the word is that somehow evolution is an upward movement which biologists of course would tell you isn't correct and that involution is a downward movement and yet I think that when we ask about the connection between the internal and the external and the question of involution and evolution that it is actually in a sense a reference to breathing. There is a breathing process that takes place, in which in the inhalation and the exhalation or the rolling and unrolling, there is an exchange which once again brings me back to the question of the relationships that are formed in this action, because it's always about the formation of new relationships that weren't there before.

COMMENT: The thing that strikes me here is this question of what is a Stopinder. And let's look at what he says sits between those two points and it's Harnel-miatznel. Which he describes as: the higher blends with the lower in order to actualize the middle and thus becomes either higher for the preceding lower, or lower for the succeeding higher. So what does this mean in terms of evolution and involution? In evolution, then you have an active higher and therefore there is a corresponding passive lower which actualizes the middle. So the process goes in that direction–that sits between those two points. Therefore, in order to be involutionary, which is ascending, then we start with the lower –the lower opens to receive the higher and actualizes the middle which is higher than the lower, and therefore it is ascending. So it's exactly the same thing and it raises a question for me–we think of being active, of working, as something that starts with a doing and in fact what is said here is that in order to be ascending, we have to start with a receiving, so that the lower can receive the higher in order to actualize the middle. I don't know. Same triad, different directions.

FACILITATOR: Just a minor point. I'm kind of agreeing with you in saying that the ascending octaves take the passive position and the descending octave … the Do is created in the descending octave; the Do is passive in the ascending octave. Would you like to continue to read?

Continuing reading from "Purgatory:"

"Here it is necessary to tell you that when this most wide Divine actualization was finished, our triumphant cherubim and seraphim then gave, for the first time, to all the newly arisen actualizations those names which exist even until today. Every 'relatively independent concentration' in general they then defined by the word 'cosmos,' and to distinguish the different orders of arising of these 'cosmoses,' they added to this definition 'cosmos' a separate corresponding name.

"And, namely, they named the Most Most Holy Prime-Source Sun Absolute itself—'Protocosmos.'

"Each newly arisen 'Second-order-Sun' with all its consequent definite results they called 'Defterocosmos.'

"'Third-order-Suns,' i.e., those we now call 'planets,' they called 'Tritocosmos.'

"The smallest 'relatively independent formation' on the planets, which arose thanks to the new inherency of the fifth Stopinder of the sacred Heptaparaparshinokh and which is the very smallest similarity to the Whole, was called 'Microcosmos,' and, finally, those formations of the 'Microcosmos' and which also became concentrated on the planets, this time thanks to the second-order cosmic law called 'mutual attraction of the similar,' were named 'Tetartocosmoses.'

"And all those cosmoses, which together compose our present World, began to be called the 'Megalocosmos.'

"And then also our cherubim gave names, also existing until now, to the emanations and radiations issuing from all these cosmoses of different scales, by means of which the process of the most great cosmic Trogoautoegocrat proceeds.

(1) The emanation of the Most Most Holy Sun Absolute Itself they called, as I have already told you, 'Theomertmalogos' or 'Word-God.'

(2) The radiation of each separate Second-order-Sun, 'Mentekithzoin.'

(3) The radiation of each planet separately they called Dynamoumzoin.'

(4) That given off from the Microcosmoses they called 'Photoinzoin.'

(5) The radiations issuing from the 'Tetartocosmoses' they called 'Hanbledzoin.'

(6) The radiations of all the planets together of any solar system they called 'Astroluolucizoin.'

(7) The common radiations of all the 'Newly-arisen-second-order-Suns taken together they called 'Polorotheoparl.'

"And all the results issuing from all the cosmic sources, great and small, taken together, were also then named by them the 'common-cosmic Ansanbaluiazar.'

"It is interesting to remark that concerning this 'common-cosmic Ansanbaluiazar,' present-day objective science has also the formula: 'Everything issuing from everything and again entering into everything.'

"Independent names were then given also to all the, as they are called, 'temporarily independent crystallizations' arising in each of the innumerable cosmoses by the evolutionary and involutionary processes of these fundamental sacred laws.

"I shall not enumerate the names of the large number of these independent 'centers of gravity' which become crystallized in all separate cosmoses, but shall indicate only the names of those definite 'center-of-gravity active elements' which become crystallized in each separate cosmos, and which have a direct relation with my following elucidations and, namely, those which are crystallized in the presences of Tetartocosmoses and have such a 'temporarily independent center of gravity.'

"In Tetartocosmoses the following names were given to these independent arisings:

(1) Protoëhary
(2) Defteroëhary
(3) Tritoëhary
(4) Tetartoëhary
(5) Piandjoëhary
(6) Exioëhary
(7) Resulzarion

COMMENT: Do I understand correctly that after all these cosmoses were created and they began to emanate and radiate, that was the purpose for which HIS ENDLESSNESS changed the laws and that gave HIS ENDLESSNESS what the Holy Sun Absolute needed to exist forever?

COMMENT: I think it says that nothing unforeseen would occur, rather than it would never diminish. So it doesn't say it worked, it just said it ... but not because ...

COMMENT: The reason he changed the laws ... produced the result that he needed.

COMMENT: Yes

COMMENT: As I understand it these are seven gradients of radiations corresponding to known systems of spheres in the Kabbalah for example and many others, starting from Will, the highest, then Wisdom – I don't know Greek, but maybe someone will tell me whether Mentek has something to do with thinking or Wisdom. Menteki? No? Anyway, I think that maybe this means the word of God, the Will, Wisdom, Action–Dynamo, Photo–like photosynthesis–what happens on Earth. Then there is Hanbledzoin, which is later explained, the kind of psychic energy that we human beings can produce. So we have here seven types of energies and they are interrelating, that is, that we can observe any being, any cosmos, according to its place. It absorbs some energies, radiates some other energies and these energies are connected according to what was explained before: the higher with the lower they create the middle one, so for example the very high radiation–again I take man as an example–the very godly radiation is also in us as part of our soul, for example and it interacts with our mentation, which is Hanbledzoin, so the result could be some higher coating, my Kesdjan Body, or maybe even a higher body. So this explains the interchange between various stages, or different degree of refinement of energies, that can blend together, feed one another, interact and create possibilities of going up, going down, have middle situation, etc., etc.. I strongly believe this is resembling the Kaballistic sefirot, like wisdom, action, until Earth.

COMMENT: I don't have much to say about that really. The only thing is to remind that Hanbledzoin is blood and ...

COMMENT: No, no.

COMMENT: Hanbledzoin is the blood of the Kesdjan body.

COMMENT: And these cosmoses have consciousness, they know they exist. It was in that sense that it was mentioned before that the creation of a new order which involved consciousness, cosmoses, trogoautoegocrat, one organism eating another, is the maintenance of consciousness that counterbalances entropy. This is the image I have about the general order of things which comes down to what A said in terms of one world feeding the other in a vertical sense–emanations from the higher blending with emanations of the lower to create middle entities and create a vertical movement.

COMMENT: It seems to me that one interpretation of these is based on the words that are there. Photoinzoin is electromagnetism, Hanbledzoin is animal magnetism, Dynamoumzoin is motion, the laws of motion in mass based bodies, Astroluocizoin, astral influences from stars and so on. I don't know how to explain every one of these, but obviously the top one, Theomertmalogos is everything that comes from the mouth of God, so it's the fundamental radiation of creation.

COMMENT: It seems a little strange: he starts out with Theomertmalogos, emanation. Everything else is a radiation, but he goes to a separate second order Sun and then a planet and then microcosmos, then tetartocosmoses, then six he goes back to all the planets together and then all the radiations of the second order suns. I find that a little strange and I wonder why it is in that order.

COMMENT: It's like a Stopinder.

COMMENT: I just want to thank you because Gurdjieff made a very big difference between emanations and radiations in one of the texts, so thank you for clarifying.

Continuing reading from "Purgatory:"

> "And now, my boy, after everything that I have elucidated to you we can return to the question why and how 'higher-being-bodies' or, as your favorites name them, souls, began to arise in our Universe, and why our UNI-BEING COMMON FATHER turned HIS Divine attention particularly to just these cosmic arisings.

"The point is that when the 'common-cosmic-harmonious-equilibrium' had become regularized and established in all those cosmoses of different scales, then in each of these Tetartocosmoses, i.e., in each separate 'relatively-independent-formation-of-the-aggregation-of-microcosmoses' which had its arising on the surface of the planets—the surrounding conditions on the surface of which accidentally began to correspond to certain data present in these cosmoses, owing to which they could exist for a certain period of time without what is called 'Seccruano,' i.e., without constant 'individual tension'—the possibility appeared of independent automatic moving from one place to another on the surface of the given planets.

"And thereupon, when our COMMON FATHER ENDLESSNESS ascertained this automatic moving of theirs, there then arose for the first time in HIM the Divine Idea of making use of it as a help for HIMSELF in the administration of the enlarging World.

"From that time on HE began to actualize everything further for these cosmoses in such a direction that the inevitable what is called, 'Okrualno'— i.e., the periodic repetition in them of the completing process of the sacred Heptaparaparshinokh—might be accomplished in such a way that, under conditions of a certain kind of change in the functioning of the common presences of some of these Tetartocosmoses, there might be transformed and crystallized, besides the crystallizations which had to be transformed for the purpose of the new common-cosmic exchange of substances, also those active elements from which new independent formations might be coated in them themselves with the inherent possibility of acquiring 'individual Reason.'

"That this idea first arose just then in our ENDLESSNESS, we can also see from the words of that sacred canticle with which at the present time, at all divine solemnities, our cherubim and seraphim extol the marvelous works of our CREATOR.

"Before continuing to relate further how this was actualized, it is necessary to tell you that the functioning of the mentioned common-cosmic Iraniranumange is harmonized in such a way that all the results obtained from transformations in different cosmoses localize themselves together according to what is called 'qualitativeness of vibrations,' and these localizations penetrate everywhere throughout the Universe and take a corresponding part in planetary as well as in surplanetary formations, and generally have as the temporary place of their free concentration the what are called atmospheres, with which all the planets of our Megalocosmos are surrounded and through which connection is established for the common-cosmic Iraniranumange.

COMMENT: My question is: do we have a clear image of the difference between tetartocosmoses and human beings?

COMMENT: Don't tetartocosmoses have independent, automatic motion? Those beings that have independent, automatic motion.

COMMENT: I think that further on it will be said that beings, so human beings as well, they have two natures, whereas tetartocosmoses they are like animals – they're not developing a psyche, but human beings have a body and a psyche, so they are two natured.

COMMENT: It's explained in the next page that when these tetera creatures have the ability to have a second body they are called beings that are two natured. So a being is development of the tetartocosmoses. It is a refinement.

Continuing reading from "Purgatory:"

"And so, the further results of this Divine attention in respect of the mentioned Tetartocosmoses consisted in this, that during their serving as apparatuses for the most great cosmic Trogoautoegocrat, the possibility was obtained in them that from among the cosmic substances transformed through them, both for the needs of the Most Most Great common-cosmic Sacred Trogoautoegocrat, as well as for the supply of substances expended by them for the process of their own existence, and composed exclusively of cosmic crystallizations which are derived from the transformations of that planet itself on which the given Tetartocosmoses arose, such results began to be obtained in their common presences under the mentioned conditions as proceed from cosmic sources of a higher order and, consequently, composed of what are called vibrations of 'greater vivifyingness.'

"Now from such cosmic results, exactly similar forms began to be coated in their common presences, at first from the cosmic substances Mentekithzoin, i.e., from the substances transformed by the sun and by other planets of that solar system within the limits of which the given Tetartocosmoses had the place of their arising, and which cosmic substances reach every planet through the radiations of the said cosmic concentrations.

"In this way, the common presences of certain Tetartocosmoses began beforehand to be composed of two different independent formations arisen from two entirely different cosmic sources, and these began to have a joint existence, as if one were placed within the other.

"And so, my boy, when similar coatings of previously coated Tetartocosmoses were completed and began to function correspondingly, then from that time on they ceased calling them Tetartocosmoses and began to call them 'beings,' which then meant 'two-natured,' and these same second coatings alone began to be called 'bodies-Kesdjan.'

"Now when in this new part of these 'two-natured-formations' everything corresponding was acquired, and when all that functioning which it is proper to such cosmic arisings to have was finally established, then these same new formations in their turn on exactly the same basis as in the first case and also under the conditions of a certain kind of change of functioning, began to absorb and assimilate into themselves such cosmic substances as had their arising immediately from the Most Most Holy Theomertmalogos, and similarities of a third kind began to be coated in them which are the 'higher sacred-parts' of beings and which we now call 'higher being-bodies.'

··· ∿ ···

Seminar 3: Chapter 39, "Purgatory"

Beelzebub's Tales

Darlene Franz introduced participatory music: I invite all of you to sing. This is the Prayer we will sing together. It is very simple. It is a mantric, repetitive prayer. I will sing it once with the harmonium. You may listen as many times as you feel is necessary until you are ready to join in. If you feel you hear a different part, a harmonizing part, to what the main melody is, please feel free to sing that, to add that to what we are all doing together. The harmonies are improvisatory. I invite you if you wish, as you sing, to divide your attention between listening to the sound of your own voice and cultivating an awareness of the specific sensations of singing in the body, the vibrations of the vocal chords, of the chest cavity, anywhere you are aware of vibration in the body. The words are:

> Holy God
> Holy Firm
> Holy Immortal
> Have Mercy on us[1]

We will sing as long as seems good; we will go on maybe 20–30 times or so. Just relax and sing.

MODERATOR: I'd like to introduce one small addition, that is, if you want to make a comment, try to make the distinction between whether your comment is descriptive of the words that Gurdjieff wrote or whether it is an example. In other words, when you make a comment, preface by saying whether this is your understanding of the words or whether it is an example.

Reading from Chapter XXXIX The Holy Planet "Purgatory:"

    (1) The emanation of the Most Holy Sun Absolute Itself they called, as I have already told you, 'Theomertmalogos' or 'Word-God.'
    (2) The radiation of each separate Second-order-Sun, 'Mentekithzoin.'
    (3) The radiation of each planet separately they called 'Dynamoumzoin.'
    (4) That given off from the Microcosmoses they called 'Photoinzoin.'
    (5) The radiations issuing from the 'Tetartocosmoses' they called 'Hanbledzoin.'
    (6) The radiations of all the planets together of any solar system they called 'Astroluolucizoin.'
    (7) The common radiations of all the 'Newly-arisen-second-order-Suns taken together they called 'Polorotheoparl.'
    "And all the results issuing from all the cosmic sources, great and small, taken together, were also then named by them the 'common-cosmic Ansanbaluiazar.'
    "It is interesting to remark that concerning this 'common-cosmic Ansanbaluiazar,' present-day objective science has also the formula: 'Everything issuing from everything and again entering into everything.'

---

1 Gurdjieff, *Beelzebub's Tales*, p 752.

"Independent names were then given also to all the, as they are called, 'temporarily independent crystallizations' arising in each of the innumerable cosmoses by the evolutionary and involutionary processes of these fundamental sacred laws.

"I shall not enumerate the names of the large number of these independent 'centers of gravity' which become crystallized in all separate cosmoses, but shall indicate only the names of those definite 'center-of-gravity active elements' which become crystallized in each separate cosmos, and which have a direct relation with my following elucidations and, namely, those which are crystallized in the presences of Tetartocosmoses and have such a 'temporarily independent center of gravity.'

"In Tetartocosmoses the following names were given to these independent arisings:

> (1) Protoëhary
> (2) Defteroëhary
> (3) Tritoëhary
> (4) Tetartoëhary
> (5) Piandjoëhary
> (6) Exioëhary
> (7) Resulzarion.

"And now, my boy, after everything that I have elucidated to you we can return to the question why and how 'higher-being-bodies' or, as your favorites name them, souls, began to arise in our Universe, and why our UNI-BEING COMMON FATHER turned HIS Divine attention particularly to just these cosmic arisings.

"The point is that when the 'common-cosmic-harmonious-equilibrium' had become regularized and established in all those cosmoses of different scales, then in each of these Tetartocosmoses, i.e., in each separate relatively-independent-formation-of-the-aggregation-of-microcosmoses' which had its arising on the surface of the planets–the surrounding conditions on the surface of which accidentally began to correspond to certain data present in these cosmoses, owing to which they could exist for a certain period of time without what is called 'Seccruano,' i.e., without constant 'individual tension'– the possibility appeared of independent automatic moving from one place to another on the surface of the given planets.

"And thereupon, when our COMMON FATHER ENDLESSNESS ascertained this automatic moving of theirs, there then arose for the first time in HIM the Divine Idea of making use of it as a help for HIMSELF in the administration of the enlarging World.

"From that time on HE began to actualize everything further for these cosmoses in such a direction that the inevitable what is called, 'Okrualno'–i.e., the periodic repetition in them of the completing process of the sacred Heptaparaparshinokh–might be accomplished in such a way that, under conditions of a certain kind of change in the functioning of the common presences of some of these Tetartocosmoses, there might be transformed and crystallized, besides the crystallizations which had to be transformed for the purpose of the new common-cosmic exchange of substances, also those active elements from which new independent formations might be coated in them themselves with the inherent possibility of acquiring 'individual Reason.'

"That this idea first arose just then in our ENDLESSNESS, we can also see from the words of that sacred canticle with which at the present time, at all divine solemnities, our cherubim and seraphim extol the marvelous works of our CREATOR.[2]

2 Gurdjieff, *Beelzebub's Tales*, PP 760-63.

COMMENT: Does anyone have any idea what this "Seccruano" is? Yes, it says "constant individual tension" but what does that mean?

COMMENT: I have an idea. It is written that this human being had the ability to move so, if we understand it not to move like animals on the surface of the planet but the ability to move means the possibility to develop, then we can understand this word as the opposite of being able to develop. So I understand it to be the ability of the human being to develop as opposed to have a tension and be the same all the time.

COMMENT: I think we are going from plants to things that can move from location to location so I think the constant individual tension the individual rigidity of plant because this goes from plants to one-brained to two- to three-brained in this section.

COMMENT: Do you think plants are tense? He uses the word "tension."

COMMENT: I would have thought so. They have a rigidity.

COMMENT: He uses "tension" doesn't he; I don't think he uses that word for nothing.

COMMENT: Right.

COMMENT: I would like to offer an explanation for this point. Protoëhary, Defteroëhary, Tritoëhary, etc., are substances that are found in the body as sequential results of phases of digestion. Protoëhary means "first grace," Defteroëhary means "second grace," Tritoëhary, "third grace."

So there is an enhancement of the importance of these phases of digestion and of food as it is transubstantiated in the body. So what is happening here I believe is also the fact that these creatures that move about, there is a correspondence of what is happening inside them with what is going on outside. That means when they are hungry, they can find food. Things that are happening outside, the existence of things that they could possibly consume as food corresponds to the needs that happen inside. When they are hungry, when they are in tension, they go about to satisfy their hunger but at some point they have more time than needed to find their food. And it is at this time that the idea of development could enter the general picture.

COMMENT: But not just food, sex and protection as well.

COMMENT: Possibly. I have just connected it with the words "Protoëhary," "Defteroëhary," etc., which are in direct reference to food.

COMMENT: I also hear plants in this Seccruano. There is this tension in stillness against gravity so there is a pressure of a plant that interacts with gravity that is constant individual tension.

COMMENT: On a slightly different point, and this comes up a number of times in *The Tales*, are the words "them themselves" together: "... also those active elements from which new independent formations might be coated in them themselves with the inherent possibility of acquiring 'individual Reason.'"

I think there is something indicated there because it doesn't just say "coated in them." "Them themselves" gives the impression there is something active going on there is some required effort.

COMMENT: For those whose mother tongue is not English, may I ask for all to speak a little slower?

Continuing to read from Chapter XXXIX The Holy Planet "Purgatory:"

"Before continuing to relate further how this was actualized, it is necessary to tell you that the functioning of the mentioned common-cosmic Iraniranumange is harmonized in such a way that all the results obtained from transformations in different cosmoses localize themselves together according to what is called 'qualitativeness of vibrations,' and these localizations penetrate everywhere throughout the Universe and take a corresponding part in planetary as well as in surplanetary formations, and generally have as the temporary place of their free concentration the what are called atmospheres, with which all the planets of our Megalocosmos are surrounded and through which connection is established for the common-cosmic Iraniranumange.

"And so, the further results of this Divine attention in respect of the mentioned Tetarto-cosmoses consisted in this, that during their serving as apparatuses for the most great cosmic Trogoautoegocrat, the possibility was obtained in them that from among the cosmic sub-stances transformed through them, both for the needs of the Most Most Great common-cosmic Sacred Trogoautoegocrat, as well as for the supply of substances, expended by them for the process of their own existence, and composed exclusively of cosmic crystallizations which are derived from the transformations of that planet itself on which the given Tetar-tocosmoses arose, such results began to be obtained in their common presences under the mentioned conditions as proceed from cosmic sources of a higher order and, consequently, composed of what are called vibrations of 'greater vivifyingness.'

"Now from such cosmic results, exactly similar forms began to be coated in their common presences, at first from the cosmic substances Mentekithzoin, i.e., from the substances transformed by the sun and by other planets of that solar system within the limits of which the given Tetartocosmoses had the place of their arising, and which cosmic substances reach every planet through the radiations of the said cosmic concentrations.

"In this way, the common presences of certain Tetartocosmoses began beforehand to be composed of two different independent formations arisen from two entirely different cosmic sources, and these began to have a joint existence, as if one were placed within the other.

"And so, my boy, when similar coatings of previously coated Tetartocosmoses were completed and began to function correspondingly, then from that time on they ceased called them Tetartocosmoses and began to call them 'beings,' which then meant 'two-natured,' and these same second coatings alone began to be called 'bodies-Kesdjan.'

"Now when in this new part of these 'two-natured-formations' everything correspond-ing was acquired, and when all that functioning which it is proper to such cosmic arisings to have was finally established, then these same new formations in their turn on exactly the same basis as in the first case and also under the conditions of a certain kind of change of functioning, began to absorb and assimilate into themselves such cosmic substances as had their arising immediately from the Most Most Holy Theomertmalogos, and similarities of a third kind began to be coated in them which are the 'higher sacred-parts' of beings and which we now call 'higher being-bodies.'

"Further, when their 'higher being-bodies' were finally coated and all the corresponding functions had been acquired in them, and chiefly when it became possible for the data for engendering the sacred function, named 'objective Reason,' to become crystallized in them, which data can become crystallized exclusively only in the presences of those cosmic arisings, and when what is called 'Rascooarno' occurred to these 'Tetartocosmoses' or 'beings,' i.e., the separation of these diverse-natured 'three-in-one' formations from each other, only then did this 'higher-being-part' receive the possibility of uniting itself with the Cause-of-Causes of everything now existing, i.e., with our Most Most Holy Sun Absolute, and began to fulfill the purpose on which our ALL-EMBRACING ENDLESSNESS had placed HIS hope.

"Now it is necessary to explain to you in more detail in what successiveness this first sacred Rascooarno then occurred to these first Tetartocosmoses and how it occurs also now, to the as they are called 'three-brained beings.'

"At first on the planet itself the 'second-being body,' i.e., the body-Kesdjan, together with the 'third-being-body' separate themselves from the 'fundamental-planetary-body' and, leaving this planetary body on the planet, rise both together to that sphere where those cosmic substances–from the localizations of which the body-Kesdjan of a being arises–have their place of concentration.

"And only there, at the end of a certain time, does the principal and final sacred Rascooarno occur to this two-natured arising, after which such a 'higher being-part' indeed becomes an independent individual with its own individual Reason. Previously–i.e., before the Choot-God-Litanical period this sacred cosmic actualization, was, only after this second process of the sacred Rascooarno, either thought worthy of uniting with the presence of our Most Most Holy Sun Absolute or went into other cosmic concentrations where such independent holy Individuals were needed.

"And if at the moment of the approach of the final process of the sacred Rascooarno these cosmic arisings had not yet attained to the required gradation of Reason of the sacred scale of Reason, then this higher being-part had to exist in the said sphere until it had perfected its Reason to the required degree.

"It is impossible not to take notice here of that objective terror which occurs to the already risen higher-being-parts, who, owing to all results in new cosmic processes unforeseen from Above, have not yet perfected themselves up to the necessary gradations of Reason.

"The point is, that according to various second-grade cosmic laws, the 'being-body-Kesdjan' cannot exist long in this sphere, and at the end of a certain time this second being-part must decompose, irrespective of whether the higher being-part existing within it had by that time attained the requisite degree of Reason; and in view of the fact that as long as this higher being-part does not perfect its Reason to the requisite degree, it must always be dependent upon some Kesdjanian arising or other, therefore immediately after the second sacred Rascooarno every such still unperfected higher being-body gets into a state called 'Techgekdnel' or 'searching-for-some-other-similar-two-natured-arising-corresponding-to-itself' so that when the higher part of this other two-natured arising perfects itself to the required degree of Reason and the final process of the sacred Rascooarno occurs to it, and the speedy disintegration of its Kesdjan body is not yet clearly sensed, this higher being-body might instantly enter this other body Kesdjan and continue to exist in it for its further perfection, which perfection must sooner or later be inevitably accomplished by every arisen higher being-body.[3]

3 Gurdjieff, *Beelzebub's Tales*, PP 763-66..

COMMENT: I would like to ask about something that was read previously. Does anybody know if there is a relationship between the Choot-God-Litanical period and the time the Laws were changed by HIS ENDLESSNESS?

COMMENT: I think it is self-explanatory because the Laws were changed in order to effect the Creation and the Choot-God-Litanical period occurred after the Creation.

COMMENT: Is it immediately after? Is it the introduction to the Choot-God-Litanical period? When the Creation occurred, is that the introduction of the Choot-God-Litanical period?

COMMENT: No, the Choot-God-Litanical period occurred after the discovery that mobile beings could assist in the administration of the enlarging Universe. The first higher being-bodies went straight the Sun Absolute and there they began to radiate in miniature but the quality of their Theomertmalogos was not the same as that emanating from the Prime Source. Therefore, it caused a contamination of Theomertmalogos, which was then incorporated into the new higher being-bodies. This is part of the "Gurdjieffian Cosmic Cock-up Theory," first mentioned in *The Tales*, with the collision of the comet Kondoor, breaking the Earth into three fragments and the perceived need to introduce the organ Kundabuffer.

Continuing to read from Chapter XXXIX The Holy Planet "Purgatory:"

"And that is why, in that sphere to where the higher being-part goes after the first sacred Rascooarno, that process proceeds called 'Okipkhalevnian-exchange-of-the-external-part-of-the-soul' or 'exchange-of-the-former-being-body-Kesdjan.'

"Here, you might as well be told that your favorites also have, as it were, a similar representation about the 'Okipkhalevnian exchange' and they have even invented a very clever name for it, namely, 'metempsychosis' or 'reincarnation'; and that branch of their famous science which in recent centuries has been created around this question also gradually became, and at the present already is, one of those minor maleficent factors, the totality of which is gradually making their Reason, already strange enough without this, always more and more, as our dear Mullah Nassr Eddin would say: 'Shooroomooroomnian.'

"According to the fantastic branch of this theory of their 'science,' now called spiritualism, they suppose among other things that each of them already has a higher being-part or, as they call it, a soul, and that a transmigration must be occurring the whole time to this soul, i.e., something of the kind of this same 'Okipkhalevnian exchange' of which I have just spoken.

"Of course, if these unfortunates would only take into consideration that according to the second-grade cosmic law called 'Tenikdoa' or 'law of gravity,' this same being part–if in rare cases it does happen that it arises in them–instantly rises after the first Rascooarno of the being, or, as they express it, after the death of the being, from the surface of their planet; and if they understood that the explanations and proofs, given by this branch of their 'science,' of all sorts of phenomena which proceed as it were among them there thanks to those fantastic souls of theirs, were only the fruits of their idle fancy–then they would already realize that everything else proved by this science of theirs is also nothing else but Mullah Nassr Eddin's 'twaddle.'

"Now as regards the first two lower being-bodies, namely, the planetary body and the body-Kesdjan, then, after the first sacred Rascooarno of a being, his planetary body, being formed of Microcosmoses or of crystallizations transformed on that planet itself, gradually decomposes and disintegrates there on that same planet, according to a certain second-grade cosmic law called 'Again-Tarnotoltoor,' into its own primordial substances from which it obtained its arising.

"As regards the second-being-body, namely, the body-Kesdjan, this body, being formed of radiations of other concentrations of Tritocosmoses and of the Sun itself of the given solar system, and having entered after the second process of the sacred Rascooarno into the sphere just mentioned, also begins gradually to decompose, and the crystallizations of which it is composed go in various ways into the sphere of its own primordial arisings.

"But the higher being-body itself, being formed of crystallizations received directly from the sacred Theomertmalogos into the solar system within the limits of which the being arises and where his existence proceeds, can never decompose; and this 'higher part' must exist in the given solar system as long as it does not perfect itself to the required Reason, to just that Reason, which makes similar cosmic formations what are called 'Irankipaekh' i.e., such formations of the mentioned Most Most Sacred substances as can exist and be independent of Kesdjanian arisings and at the same time not be subject to what are called 'painful' influences from any external cosmic factors whatsoever.

"And so, my boy, as I have already told you, after these cosmic arisings had perfected their Reason to the necessary gradation of the sacred scale of Reason, they were in the beginning taken on to the Sun Absolute for the fulfillment of roles predestined for them by our CREATOR ENDLESSNESS.

"It is necessary to tell you that concerning the determination of the degree of individuality, our cherubim and seraphim also then at the very beginning established that still now existing sacred 'Determinator-of-Reason' which is applied for the determination of the gradations of Reason or, more exactly, the 'totality-of-self-awareness' of all separate large and small cosmic concentrations, and by which not only are the gradations of their Reason measured, but there is also determined their, as it is called, 'degree-of-justification-of-the-sense-and-aim-of-their-existence,' and also the further role of each separate Individual in relation to everything existing in our great Megalocosmos.[4]

COMMENT: For some reason, when this was being read, it hits me that this immediate feeling of urgency, not stealing from thinking but coming from the experience of being somewhere. It hits me that this experience of urgency is actually one of the manifestations of the Kesdjan Body—the experience of urgency without linking to meaning stemming from thinking. I just wanted to share that.

COMMENT: Thank you.

COMMENT: It is very important to note that the 'Determinator-of-Reason' is a 'totality-of-self-awareness'. And that is not only thinking. The 'totality-of-self-awareness' is also feeling and sensing, so it is three things. And I completely agree about what was said about the Kesdjan Body; this whole very dense material in this part of the chapter "Purgatory" gives us a feeling of urgency and hopefully also a feeling that you are absolutely nothing.

COMMENT: I would like to thank U. when she was reading the passage: 'degree-of-justification-of-the-sense-and-aim-of-their-existence.' The way she read it was an example of the use of syntax and

4 Gurdjieff, *Beelzebub's Tales*, pp 767-69.

punctuation to emphasize certain things. It makes you stop and take in what he is actually saying. She changed the way she read it so it emphasized the important points. Thank you.

Continuing to read from Chapter XXXIX The Holy Planet "Purgatory:"

"This sacred determinator of 'pure Reason' is nothing else than a kind of measure, i.e., a line divided into equal parts; one end of this line is marked as the total absence of any Reason, i.e., absolute 'firm-calm,' and at the other end there is indicated absolute Reason, i.e., the Reason of our incomparable CREATOR ENDLESSNESS.

"In this place I think it might as well be explained to you further about the various kinds of sources, present in the common presences of all three-brained beings for the manifestation of being-Reason.

"In every three-brained being in general, irrespective of the place of his arising and the form of his exterior coating, there can be crystallized data for three independent kinds of being-mentation, the totality of the engendered results of which expresses the gradation of his Reason.

"Data for these three kinds of being-Reason are crystallized in the presence of each three-brained being depending upon how much–by means of the 'being-Partkdolg-duty'–the corresponding higher-being-parts are coated and perfected in them, which should without fail compose their common presences as a whole.

"The first highest kind of being-Reason is the 'pure' or objective Reason which is proper only to the presence of a higher being-body or to the common presences of the bodies themselves of those three-brained beings in whom this higher part has already arisen and perfected itself, and then only when it is the, what is called, 'center-of-gravity-initiator-of-the-individual-functioning' of the whole presence of the being.

It was requested the previous paragraph be re-read (which it was).

"The second being-Reason, which is named 'Okiartaaitokhsa,' can be in the presences of those three-brained beings, in whom their second-being-body-Kesdjan' is already completely coated and functions independently. "As regards the third kind of being-Reason, this is nothing else but only the action of the automatic functioning which proceeds in the common presences of all beings in general and also in the presences of all surplanetary definite formations, thanks to repeated shocks coming from outside, which evoke habitual reactions from the data crystallized in them corresponding to previous accidentally perceived impressions.[5]

COMMENT: It is very interesting to read these the other way around–to start reading with the third being-reason and then the second and then the first. It gives a very interesting impression. Also it is very related to the chapter "Form and Sequence" where he talks about the Reason-of-knowing and the Reason-of-understanding,[6] an expression of your individuality.

"Now, my boy, in my opinion, before going on to a more detailed explanation of how their higher-parts were then coated and perfected in the common presences of the first Tetartocosmoses, as well as in the common presences of those who were afterwards named 'beings,' it is necessary to give you more information about the fact that we, beings arisen

5 Gurdjieff, *Beelzebub's Tales*, PP 769-70.
6 Ibid., PP 1166-70.

on the planet Karatas, and also the beings arisen on your planet called Earth, are already no longer such 'Polormedekhtic' beings as were the first beings who were transformed directly from the Tetartocosmoses, i.e., to say, beings called Polormedekhtic or, as it is still now said, 'Monoenithits' but are beings called 'Keschapmartnian,' i.e., nearly half-beings, owing to which the completing process of the sacred Heptaparaparshinokh does not proceed at the present time through us or through your favorites, the three-brained beings of the planet Earth, exactly as it proceeded in them. And we are such Keschapmartnian beings because the last fundamental Stopinder of the sacred Heptaparaparshinokh, which at the present time almost all the beings of the Megalocosmos call the sacred 'Ashagiprotoëry,' is not in the centers of those planets upon which we arise–as it occurs in general in the majority of the planets of our great Megalocosmos–but is in the centers of their satellites, which for our planet Karatas is the little planet of our solar system which we call 'Prnokhpaioch,' and for the planet Earth, its former fragments now called the Moon and Anulios.

"Thanks to this, the completing process of the Sacred Heptaparaparshinokh for the continuation of the species, for instance, proceeds not through one being, as it proceeded with the Tetartocosmoses, but through two beings of different sexes, called by us 'Actavus' and 'Passavus,' and on the planet Earth, 'man' and 'woman.'

"I might say here, that there even exists in our Great Megalocosmos a planet on which this sacred law Heptaparaparshinokh carries out its completing process for the continuation of the species of the three-brained beings, through three independent individuals. You might as well be acquainted somewhat in detail with this uncommon planet.[7]

COMMENT: What is the origin or meaning of Anulios?

COMMENT: I believe "Anulios" is an anagram of "soi luna" which means "our moon."

"This planet is called Modiktheo and belongs to the system of the 'Protocosmos.'

"Beings arising on this planet are three-brained, like all other three-brained beings arising on all the planets of our Great Megalocosmos, and in their exterior appearance are almost similar to us, and at the same time are–and are also so considered by all others–the most ideal and perfect of all the innumerable various-formed exterior coatings of three-brained beings in all our Great Universe; and all our now existing angels, archangels, and most of the Sacred Individuals nearest to our COMMON FATHER ENDLESSNESS arise just upon this marvelous planet.

"The transformation through them of the cosmic substances required for the common-cosmic Trogoautoegocratic process, according to the sacred law of Heptaparaparshinokh, proceeds on these same principles on which it proceeds through our common presences and also through the presences of your favorites, the three-brained beings breeding on the planet Earth. For the continuation of their species alone does this sacred law effect its completing process through three kinds of beings, wherefore such three-brained beings are called 'Triakrkomnian'; separately, however, just as among us beings of different sexes are called Actavus and Passavus or are called on your planet man and woman, so there on the planet Modiktheo they call the beings of the different sexes 'Martna,' 'Spirna,' and 'Okina,' and although externally they are all alike, yet in their inner construction they are very different from each other.

7 Gurdjieff, *Beelzebub's Tales*, PP 770-71.

"The process of the continuation of their species proceeds among them in the following manner:

"All three beings of different sexes simultaneously receive the 'sacred Elmooarno,' or as your favorites say 'conception,' through a special action, and for a certain period they exist with this sacred Elmooarno or 'conception' apart from one another, entirely independently, but each of them exists with very definite intentional perceptions and conscious manifestations.

"And later, when the time approaches for the manifestation of the results of these conceptions, or when, as your favorites say, the time of birth approaches, there becomes evident in all these three uncommon beings, as it is called, an 'Aklonoatistitchian' longing for each other, or as your favorites would say, there appears in them a 'physico-organic-attraction.' And the nearer the time of this being-manifestation or birth approaches, the more they press close to each other and ultimately almost grow on to each other; and thereupon at one and the same time, they actualize in a certain way these conceptions of theirs.

"And so, during their actualization of their conceptions, all these three conceptions merge one with another, and in this way there appears in our Megalocosmos a new three-brained being of such an uncommon construction.

"And the three-centered beings of this kind are ideal in our Megalocosmos, because at their very arising they already have all the being-bodies.

"And they have all three being-bodies because the producers of such a being, namely, Martna, Spirna, and Okina, each separately conceives the arising of one of the three-being bodies, and owing to their special corresponding being-existences they aid the Sacred Heptaparaparshinokh to form the given being-body in themselves to perfection and afterwards, at the moment of appearance, merge it with the other bodies into one.

"Note, by the way, my boy, that the beings arising on that incomparable and marvelous planet have no need, like the three-brained beings arising on other ordinary planets of our Megalocosmos, to coat their higher-being-bodies with the help of those factors which our CREATOR designed as means of perfecting–namely, those factors which we now call 'conscious labors' and 'intentional suffering.'

"Now, my boy, to continue the further, more detailed elucidation concerning the process of the transformation of cosmic substances through beings in general, we shall take as an elucidatory example the common presences of your favorites.

"Although the process of the transformation of substances for the continuation of the species by means of us or by means of the common presences of your favorites does not proceed exactly as it proceeded in the first Tetartocosmoses who were transformed into beings, nevertheless we shall take them as an example, since the process itself of the transformation of cosmic substances for the needs of the Most Great common-cosmic Trogoautoegocrat proceeds through their common presences exactly as it proceeded through the first Tetartocosmoses; at the same time you will acquire information concerning several other small details of the strange particularities of their psyche, and also gain information relating to how they in general understand, and how they regard, their being-duty in the sense of serving the common-cosmic process of Iraniranumange, destroying for the beatification of their own belly every kind of law-conformable foreseeing actualization for the welfare of the whole Megalocosmos.

"As for those particularities of the transformation of cosmic substances, thanks to which the continuation of the species of different beings at the present time proceeds differently, for the present I will say only this, that the cause depends on the place of concentration of the sacred Ashagiprotoëry, i.e., on the place of concentration of those cosmic substances, which are the results of the last Stopinder in the common-cosmic Ansanbaluiazar.

"Now, my boy, I shall begin by repeating: all your favorites, even the contemporary, are–like us and like all the other three-centered beings of our Megalocosmos–such apparatuses for the Great cosmic Trogoautoegocrat just as the Tetartocosmoses were, from whom arose the first ancestors of the now existing beings as well as the beings now existing everywhere. And through each of them the cosmic substances arising in all seven Stopinders of the Sacred Heptaparaparshinokh could be transformed, and all of them, again even the contemporary, besides serving as apparatuses for the Most Great cosmic Trogoautoegocrat, could have all possibilities for absorbing from those cosmic substances which are transformed through them what is corresponding for the coating and for the perfecting in them of both higher-being-bodies; because each three-brained being arisen on this planet of yours represents in himself also, in all respects, just as every three-brained being in all our Universe, an exact similarity of the whole Megalocosmos.

"The difference between each of them and our common great Megalocosmos is only in scale.[8]

8 Gurdjieff, *Beelzebub's Tales*, pp 771-75.

··· ∿ ···

Seminar: chapter 10, "Professor Skridlov"

Meetings with Remarkable Men

FACILITATOR: So, we'll start. I think we agreed only to make comments and raise questions between the readers.

FACILITATOR: We started this chapter at the last conference, and were shown a map of the travels so we got a few pages into the chapter. It seems to be a chapter of chance meetings. Gurdjieff and Skridlov have met by chance and decided to go to Bukhara together to answer questions regarding psychological and archeological knowledge. Then a series of chance meetings with a Greek tailor and, through him, a Turkoman nomad, lead them to discover that the people of Kafiristan, although hostile to outsiders, love very much men of God. They see that this can be their way in to this region and decide to prepare by disguising themselves as Persian holy men. They even practice Persian chants and we will try now to invoke Skridlov and Gurdjieff by playing the piece to Professor Skridlov.

PARTICIPANT plays "Professor Skridlov" on oboe.

FACILITATOR: Top of page 230. The previous conversation was about the people of Kafiristan's love of the men of God.

> "After this thought had been expressed by a nomad whom we had met by chance, and who had spoken perhaps thanks only to Russian vodka, all our deliberations, that night and the next day, were based on the idea that we might get into this country, not as ordinary mortals, but by assuming the appearance of persons who are shown special respect there and who have the possibility of going freely everywhere without arousing suspicion.
>
> The following evening, still in the midst of our deliberations, we were sitting in one of the Tekinian chaikanas of New Merv, where two parties of Turkoman libertines were indulging in kaif with batchi, that is with boy dancers, whose chief occupation— authorized by local laws, and also encouraged by the laws of the great Empire of Russia which then had a protectorate over this country—is the same as that carried on in Europe, also legally, by women with yellow tickets; and here in this atmosphere, we categorically decided that Professor Skridlov should disguise himself as a venerable Persian dervish and I should pass for a direct descendant of Mohammed, that is to say, for a Seïd.
>
> To prepare ourselves for this masquerade, a long time was necessary, as well as a quiet, isolated spot. And that is why we decided to settle down in the ruins of Old Merv, which met these requirements and where, moreover, we could at times, for a rest, make some excavations. Our preparation consisted in learning a great many sacred Persian chants and instructive sayings of former times, as well as in letting our hair grow long enough for us to look like the people for whom we intended to pass; make-up in this case was quite out of the question. After we had lived in this way for

about a year and were finally satisfied both with our appearance and our knowledge of religious verses and psalms, one day, very early in the morning, we left the ruins of Old Merv, which had come to be like home for us, and going on foot as far as the station of Baïram Ali on the Central Asiatic Railway, we took a train to Chardzhou, and from there set off by boat up the river Amu Darya.

It was on the banks of this river Amu Darya, in ancient times called the Oxus and deified by certain peoples of Central Asia, that the germ of contemporary culture first appeared on earth. And during my journey up this river with Professor Skridlov an incident occurred—extraordinary for Europeans but very characteristic of the local patriarchal morality, as yet unaffected by contemporary civilization—the victim of which was an exceedingly good old Sart. The memory of this incident has often evoked in me the feeling of remorse of conscience, since it was because of us that this good old man lost his money, perhaps forever. I therefore wish to describe this part of our journey to that country, then inaccessible to Europeans, in as much detail as possible and to describe it more or less in the style of a literary school which I happened to study in my youth and which arose and nourished, so it seems, just here on the shores of this great river—a style called the 'creation of images without words'.

The Amu Darya, which higher up in its course is called the river Pyandzh, has its main sources in the Hindu Kush mountains and flows at the present time into the Aral Sea, though formerly, according to certain historical data, it emptied into the Caspian Sea.

At the period to which the present story relates, this river washed the boundaries of many countries—the former Russia, the Khivan khanate, the Bukharian khanate, Afghanistan, Kafiristan, British India and so on. It was formerly navigated by rafts of a special kind, but, when the region was conquered by Russia, a river fleet of flat-bottomed steamboats was launched which, besides fulfilling certain military needs, provided passenger and cargo service between the Aral Sea and the upper reaches of the river.

And so I begin, also of course for the purpose of resting, to wiseacre a little in the style of the aforementioned ancient literary school."[1]

COMMENT: I never read it in this way. Is anybody acquainted with the ancient literary school that creates images without words. Is that reliefs?

FACILITATOR: I hear something that reminds me of a paper at the Canterbury Conference about autostereograms. I gave this a lot of thought, what does this mean, the creation of images without words? How can any image be created without words (through literature), because even if you start speaking in a different style, it's still words. It seems to me, as is the case in *The Tales*, that there are images that arise between the words. Autostereograms are these images that perhaps you have seen, my children were fascinated by them when they were younger, it just looks like a mass of dots all over a paper. You can't really make anything out if you look directly at it, but if you relax your vision, take a wider vision, something appears that isn't really there.

I haven't investigated all real literary schools or styles in relation to this chapter, but to me it is sufficient that there is a change of tone and that we are being alerted to that there might be something beyond the words. This whole book has been quite difficult to me because of its realism. I've got stuck

1 Gurdjieff, *Meetings*, PP 230-31..

again and again in the mind-set that this is real stories about real people and that this is what really happened to Gurdjieff, whereas with *Beelzebub's Tales,* because its space ships and crazy words, it's kind of ok. I'm listening with a different part of myself, so perhaps these are some of the images that are being created without words.

COMMENT: Just to add to what the facilitator says. I think the reason why he uses the word 'ancient' here is that there are other texts that are written in the same way. Although we don't necessary read them or see them in the same way, there are people who might consider the Bible to be written the same way, for example. On the surface you have historical accounts of Adam and Eve and Moses and Aaron and so on, but there is also a meaning beyond the words, or without the words, that means standing outside of the words.

COMMENT: I'd just like to go to the beginning of what we read. They're going to Kafiristan, and 'kafir' means unbeliever, but it's strange that these unbelievers have respect and love for believers! It's Arabic. And he mentions a number of times Old Merv, Old Bukhara, Old Samarkand, and then New Merv, New Samarkand, New Bukhara. When the Russians started to build the railway system for military purposes, they didn't want to aggravate the local population so they built the stations just a little outside of these big cities. If you take this as a metaphor, it's the distortion of traditional values and the introduction of corruption and prostitution, because soldiers have to live somewhere, and if you have 20,000 soldiers you need women, so this brings all kind of backward movement as old Bukhara is ancient, and relates to what is good, patriarchality and so on.

COMMENT: There's something I want to say about these places. It's about an ongoing investigation and study being carried out in our groups. It's been going on for a few years now. Kafiristan and the whole valley of Amu Darya is inhabited by a tribe called Kalas. I don't know if you know of it? They claim they're Greek and this is collaborated by the text, as they're approached by people who speak to them in Greek, repeatedly. The region has been inhabited in two waves, one was supposedly with Iskandar, Alexander. He passed through Amu Darya and Oxus down from Afghanistan, through the areas below. The other wave was just after Justinian, which was about 520 AD when Justinian, the emperor of Byzantium, forbade all the practices of the old religion. Consequently, the platonic schools left Athens and other cities and went to Persia, where they were given the right to establish themselves and the right to practice their own religion. They still do this, so they're 'kafir' to the locals who are Muslims. For some reason they have respected them.

Right now they're in the middle of Taliban country. It's a spot within Taliban country, and there are records dated about 1000 AD of Turks, Seltzuck and Ottoman Turks, passing through this region and reporting the existence of ancient Greek philosophical schools. These are the direct descendants of the old Platonic schools, which influenced Sufi thinking in Bukhara. These areas are connected with the Silk Road.

COMMENT: Just to mention the yellow tickets. Yellow tickets were issued for prostitutes in Russia under the government, and I just want to mention Vivitskaya, she was sold in the white slave trade, so there is a connection back to Vivitskaya.

FACILITATOR: One more thing I'd like to say is that this next passage, which is quite different in tone, shows very clearly what Gurdjieff was capable of in terms of literature. *Beelzebub's Tales to His Grandson* was not written "badly" because he was a bad writer. I think here is an indirect proof that it was a conscious choice. So let's hear this style.

"Amu Darya . . . clear early morning. The mountain peaks are gilded by the rays of the still hidden sun. Gradually the nocturnal silence and the monotonous murmur of the river give place to the cries of awakened birds and animals, to the voices of people, and to the clatter of the steamboat's wheels.

On both banks the fires which had burned out during the night are being re-kindled, spirals begin to rise from the funnel of the boat's kitchen, mingling with the suffocating smoke of damp saksaul spreading everywhere.

Overnight the banks have noticeably changed in appearance, although the boat has not moved. It is the ninth day since it left Chardzhou for Kerki.

Although on the first two days the boat moved forward very slowly, it was not held up, but on the third day it ran aground and stopped for a whole day and night, until the Amu Darya, by the force of its current, washed away the sandbank and made it possible to move on. Thirty-six hours later the same thing occurred, and now it is already the third day that the steamer has been stationary, unable to move further.

The passengers and crew are patiently waiting until this wayward river takes pity and lets them proceed. Here this is quite usual. The river Amu Darya runs through sands for almost its entire course. Having a very strong current and an irregular volume of water, it is always either washing away its unstable banks or depositing sand on them; and its bed is thus constantly changing, with sandbanks forming where before there were whirlpool depths. Boats going upstream go very slowly, particularly at certain seasons of the year, but downstream they fly like mad, almost without the engine.

One can never determine beforehand, even approximately, the time it will take to travel from one point to another. Knowing this, people who travel upstream provide themselves for any emergency with enough food for several months. The time of year in which this journey of ours up the Amu Darya takes place is the least favorable, owing to the low water. Winter is approaching, the rainy season is over, and, in the mountains where the river chiefly takes its source, the thawing of snow has ceased. Travel is also not particularly agreeable because just at this season the cargo and passenger traffic on these boats is at its height. The cotton has been picked everywhere; the fruit and vegetables of the fertile oases have been gathered and dried; the caracul sheep have been sorted; and the inhabitants of the regions through which the Amu Darya flows are all travelling on it. Some are returning to their villages; others are taking their cheeses to market to exchange them for articles needed for the short winter; still others are going on pilgrimages or to their relatives.

That is why, when we came on board, the boat was so crammed with passengers. Among them are Bukharians, Khivans, Tekkis, Persians, Afghans and representatives of many other Asiatic peoples.

In this picturesque and motley crowd, merchants predominate; some are transporting goods, others going upstream for supplies of cheese.

Here is a Persian, a merchant of dried fruits; here an Armenian going to buy Kirghiz rugs on the spot, and a Polish agent, a cotton-buyer for the firm of Posnansky; here is a Russian Jew, a buyer of caracul skins, and a Lithuanian commercial traveller with samples of picture frames in papiers-Maché and all kinds of ornaments of gilt-metal set with artificial coloured stones.

Many officials and officers of the frontier guard, and fusiliers and sappers of the Transcaspian Regiment are returning from leaves or from their posts. Here is a soldier's wife with a nursing baby, going to her husband who has stayed for an extra term of service and has sent for her. Here is a travelling Catholic priest on his official rounds, going to confess Catholic soldiers.

There are also ladies on board. Here is the wife of a colonel, with her lanky daughter, returning home from Tashkent where she has taken her son, a cadet, to see him off to Orenburg to study in the cadet corps. Here is the wife of a cavalry captain of the frontier guard who has been to Merv to order some dresses at the dressmakers there; and here is a military doctor's wife escorted by his orderly, travelling from Ashkhabad to visit her husband, who is serving in solitude because his mother-in-law cannot live without 'society', which is lacking where he is stationed."[2]

FACILITATOR: We'll just take a pause there. See if there are any questions or comments. It's a very sensory, lively description. Smells, sounds, sight, touch, movement, exchange, life, vibrancy. It shows what a writer this is.

COMMENT: I would like to say something about the numbers relating to the travel. First, they travelled for three days. So its do, re mi, and then they hit a sandbank, so it's a gap. And then, he doesn't say a day and a half, he says thirty six hours, so this connects three and six, end and middle, which is do, re, mi, fa, sol. The middle is Harnel-Aoot, so there has to be another sandbank there.

COMMENT: I just noticed that the material they were supplying themselves with doesn't include fresh food. All the things they collect were forms of nourishment that could last for some time. What could that mean? That there was no fresh food except for the food that would be a supply for a long time?

COMMENT: As far as I know, on the market there were the traded goods, rice and things, but everybody had a vegetable garden near their house, so the fresh food you had nearby or maybe you would make an exchange with your neighbor, but not on the market.

COMMENT: He also says that when you go up the stream it's very difficult, but when you go down the stream you fly like mad! This again is Harnel-Aoot, and its either evolution or involution. I like playing with words, and Amu Darya can be pronounced as AMU (I'm you) and DARYA (ja) darju in Russian is sort of 'I give to you.' I'm getting out of my egoism and opening towards you, the other, my neighbor. So it's opening up from me, going outside, reaching others, so this could be connected with Harnel-Aoot as well.

"Here is a stout woman with an enormous coiffure undoubtedly of artificial hair, with many rings on her fingers and two enormous brooches on her chest; she is accompanied by two very good-looking girls who call her 'aunt', but you can see by everything that they are not at all her nieces.

Here are also many Russian former and future somebodies, going God knows where and God knows why. Also a troupe of travelling musicians with their violins and double-basses. From the very first day out of Chardzhou, all these people, as it were, sorted themselves out; the so-called intelligentsia, the bourgeoisie and the peasants formed separate groups, where, making acquaintances among themselves,

2 Gurdjieff, *Meetings*, PP 231-33.

they soon began to feel as though among old friends. The members of each of these groups began to regard and to act towards the passengers belonging to the other groups either haughtily and disdainfully or timidly and ingratiatingly, but at the same time they did not hinder one another from arranging things each according to his own wishes and habits, and little by little they became so accustomed to their surroundings that it was as though none of them had ever lived in any other way."[3]

COMMENT: This whole section where he makes us look at this list of people that he is referring to reminds me of a passage in the chapter France in *Beelzebub's Tales*, where he's also pointing to a list of people. You may know this section, its very emotional I think: "There in front of me, that stout gentleman with an enormous growth on his neck, sitting with two young street girls dress him in the costume of a 'Zairian'—would he not look exactly like that type I once saw sitting in a 'kaltaan' in the city of Koorkalai?" and the list goes on. I'm not sure what to make of it, but I definitely feel there is a signpost for relating these two.

FACILITATOR: I hear here the formation of groups of I's in the language of Ouspensky, like-minded parts of myself clumping together with other like-minded parts of myself, forming distinct groups, and then the emergence of buffers between these distinct groups. They don't hinder one another but look down a little on one another or look up ingratiatingly on one another. But I've become so used to it that I don't notice it, and it feels like "none of them had ever lived in any other way."

COMMENT: I think he's collecting all these different parts of us in one place. He says they cannot go anywhere. They're waiting for higher forces to appear, to have pity on them. He's in a state where he's collecting all that is good and bad and ugly and waiting. Making room for something to appear.

> "Neither the delays in the steamer's progress nor its crowdedness disturbed anyone; on the contrary, they all accommodated themselves so well that the whole journey was like a series of picnics. As soon as it became clear that this time the steamer was thoroughly grounded, almost all the passengers gradually went ashore. By the end of the day there appeared on both banks clusters of tents, made from whatever came to hand. Smoke arose from many fires, and, after an evening gaily spent with music and song, most of the passengers stayed on shore overnight.
>
> In the morning the life of the passengers resumes its rhythm of the day before. Some build fires and make coffee, others boil water for green tea, still others go in search of saksaul poles, get ready to go fishing, go out to the steamer and back in small boats, call back and forth between the steamer and shore or from one bank to the other; and all is done calmly and unhurriedly, as everyone knows that, as soon as it is possible to move on, the big bell of the steamer will ring an hour before departure and there will be plenty of time to return on board."
>
> In that part of the boat where we had settled ourselves an old Sart made his place beside us. It was evident that he was a rich man because among his things were many bags of money.
>
> I do not know how it is now, but at that time, in Bukhara and the neighboring countries, there were no coins of high value.
>
> In Bukhara, for instance, the only coin worth anything was called a tianga—an irregularly cut piece of silver equivalent to approximately half a French franc. Any sum

3 Gurdjieff, *Meetings*, P 234.

larger than fifty francs had therefore to be carried in special bags, which was very inconvenient, especially for travellers.

If one had thousands in this coinage and had to travel with this money, it was necessary to have literally a score of camels or horses to carry it from place to place. On very rare occasions the following method was used: the quantity of tiangi one wished to transport was given to some Bukharian Jew who gave in exchange a note to some acquaintance of his, also a Jew, who lived at the place to which one was going, and there the latter, deducting something for his trouble, returned the same amount of tiangi.

And so, on arriving at the town of Kerki, which was as far as the boat went, we left our steamer, changed to a hired kobzir 1 and continued further.

When we were already quite a long way from Kerki and were making a stop at Termez, where Professor Skridlov had gone ashore with some Sart workmen to get provisions in a near-by village, our kobzir was approached by another one carrying five Sarts, who without saying a word began to unload from their kobzir on to ours, twenty-five large sacks filled with tiangi.

At first I did not understand what it was all about; only after the unloading was finished did I gather from the oldest Sart that they had been passengers on our steamer, and that when we had disembarked these sacks of tiangi were found in the place which we had occupied. Certain that we had forgotten them and having learned where we were going, they decided to make haste to catch up with us and give us back the tiangi we had obviously forgotten in the confusion. And he added: 'I decided to catch up with you without fail because the same thing happened to me once in my life and so I understand very well how disagreeable it is to arrive in a strange place without the necessary tiangi. And as for me, it makes no difference if I arrive in my village a week later; I shall regard it as if our steamer had run aground an extra time.'

I did not know how to reply or what to say to this queer fellow; it was just too unexpected for me and all I could do was pretend that I understood very little Sart and wait for the return of the professor. Meanwhile I offered him and his companions some vodka.

When I saw Skridlov returning, I quickly went ashore to meet him as if to help him carry the provisions, and told him all about it. We decided not to refuse the money, but to find out the address of this still unspoiled man, in order to send him a pesh kesh in gratitude for his trouble, and then to hand over the tiangi to the nearest Russian frontier post, giving the name of the boat and the date of its last trip and explaining in as much detail as possible all the facts which could serve to identify our fellow-traveller, the Sart, who had forgotten these sacks of money on the boat. And so we did.

Soon after this incident, which, in my opinion, could never have occurred among contemporary Europeans, we arrived at the famous town associated with the name of Alexander of Macedonia, which is now nothing more than an ordinary Afghan fort. Here we went ashore and, assuming the roles thought out beforehand, continued our journey on foot.

Passing from one valley to another and coming in contact with many different tribes, we finally came to the central settlement of the Afridis, in a region considered to be the heart of Kafiristan.

On the way, we did everything required of a dervish and a Seïd, that is to say, I sang religious verses in Persian, and the professor, after a fashion, beat out corresponding rhythms on the tambourine, in which he then collected alms.[4]

FACILITATOR: Are there any comments or observations? There's a lot here about money, money lending for example. The Bukharian Jew gives a note in exchange for money to be received at a later date. I think the English word is usury. Gurdjieff is dealing with this aspect of money, and then of course he speaks of the honesty of the unspoilt patriarchal Sart. Usury is where you charge money for lending money. We call it interest now. This was a big moral, ethical issue in the middle ages and it's only become acceptable practice relatively recently in the west. This seems to be a section about the right relationship with money. It describes the practice of a sort of banking, where notes replace tiangi.

COMMENT: Sorry for speaking too much, but I just love this passage, it's so picturesque. It was just said that some kind of exchange is going on. I think it's connected with Amu Darya, because once you go more upstream, the Amu Darya becomes the Pyandzh river, so piandjoëhary, and this is exactly where the Harnel-Aoot is. If it's just one indication, you can say that maybe it's a coincidence, but I have found many details that build up the story. Another detail is the place Termez. Termez means place of transformation. We have a kobzir, it's a raft, and if you remember in the Karpenko chapter, he is making a raft with the bourdouks, but here the emphasis is on bourdok. This was when they had to kill the goats and inflate them. In Skridlov, the emphasis is not on air, or inflating something, the emphasis is on the vehicle, the vessel, that's going to take them up the river, where the sun is hiding just behind the mountains!

COMMENT: If we try to envisage a picture, one possibility is that the river is the access, it is where things flow, and at one end of it there are two bodies of water, Amu Darya and the Caspian Sea. At the moment, the river is flowing to Amu Darya, and before it used to flow to the Caspian Sea. There are places in *Beelzebub's Tales*, I don't know where exactly, where water and blood are linked to each other, water is the blood of something, and blood is the water of something, so if you could imagine the water being blood flowing, flowing to two possible areas where there's a lot of blood, could this be an anatomical picture that is coming out? That the river represents our central axis, where air and blood flow and end up at one end, which is our brain which has two hemispheres? Usually, one side is more active, and maybe that's where the blood is flowing. When the boat stops and people go to either side, could this be an image of an exchange? An exchange of air, an exchange of blood, what is going on in the lungs? This might be farfetched, but is he picturing a kind of breathing or exchange of air through blood?

COMMENT: Something minor perhaps. Skridlov comes in and out. The substance of what we've been reading brings up for me emotional questions and conscientious questions, and he's waiting for Skridlov, to confer with the professor.

COMMENT: What I wanted to talk about is the situation with the five Sarts bringing the money. This is perhaps a question of temptation. They had the choice to keep the money for themselves, but they decide to bring the money, to arrange everything so that this energy or this money goes back to the person who is the owner. They do not tell these five sarts, I guess the five has a certain meaning, what they are going to do, that they are not the owners, they just do what is needed without making the five sarts feel bad. They just do what is needed. Mr. Gurdjieff mentions that this would not be possible nowadays in the western world.

4 Gurdjieff, *Meetings*, PP 234-36.

COMMENT: Well thank you for that, because I'm taking some significance from the number five. We have five senses. And we have this money. And we put them to sleep with the vodka.

COMMENT: This evoked in me the golden rule, because Pogossian says never do unto other one... so this is temptation, this is the moment of temptation, and again this takes us back to Harnel-Aoot, this is the moment of substance.

COMMENT: All these talks about money and the significance of money, that they had to carry the money in big bags that had to be carried by camels, reminds me of the well-known biblical parable that it is as difficult for a rich man to pass into heaven as it is for a camel to pass through the eye of a needle. The Eye of the Needle is a gate in Jerusalem, and usually you had to remove any bags because it was so small that you could just push through. At the same time, this is assigned to the Harnel-Aoot position. They have to become poor again, and they have to resist the temptation of keeping all this money so that they cannot pass through this Harnel-Aoot.

COMMENT: With regards to money, it seems to me to represent energy and what puzzles me is there was something about the difficulty of carrying the bags for a traveller, and what does say to us about the energy that we have right here and now? Can we find it resonant? Is there some energy that we have that we find difficult to carry? What is that difficulty? Is it straying away on cloud nine, inner talking?

COMMENT: I would like to talk about sharing the energy that is there, you have to share the energy. Talking about exchange was a good example, you give your energy to everybody and so you don't keep this bag of luggage yourself. When you share it, everybody can travel and we don't need these bags.

I would like to say something about the playing of roles by Skridlov and Gurdjieff. They have been rehearsing for a year, they are very conscious of their roles every second. What he describes here about these people, is that most people are not even aware that they are playing a role, whether it's the role of mother or whatever kind of role you have, the aunt, the niece. And this is prostitution. When you show yourself unconsciously. You think you are who you are and that everybody can see it. All the roles we have in life, we should be aware of them and we should know when we show anybody else the different roles we have. Gurdjieff is showing what work means, to be conscious of the roles you play is work.

I shall not describe the rest of our trip and the many extraordinary adventures connected with it, but will go on to the account of our accidental meeting with a certain man, not far from the aforementioned settlement—a meeting, the result of which gave quite another direction to our inner world, and thereby changed all our expectations, intentions and the plan itself of our future movements.

We left the settlement of the Afridis with the intention of proceeding towards Chitral. In the market of the next fairly large place I was accosted by an old man in native dress, who said to me softly in pure Greek: 'Please do not be alarmed. I quite accidentally learned that you are a Greek. I do not want to know who you are or why you are here, but it would be very pleasant for me to talk with you and see how a fellow countryman breathes, for it is fifty years since I saw a man who was born in the land where I myself was born.'

By his voice and the expression of his eyes, this old man made such an impression on me that I was immediately filled with a perfect trust in him, as in my own father, and I answered him, also in Greek: 'To talk here now is, I think, very awkward. We, at least I, may run great danger, so we must think where we can talk freely without fear of undesirable consequences; perhaps one of us can think of some way or find some suitable place, and meanwhile I can only say that I myself will be unspeakably glad of this opportunity, for I am utterly weary of having to deal for so many months with people of alien blood.'

Without replying, he went on his way, and the professor and I went about our business. The next day another man, this time in the habit of a certain monastic order well known in Central Asia, placed in my hand, instead of alms, a note.

I read this note when we arrived at the askhana where we had lunch. It was written in Greek and I learned from its contents that the old man of the day before was also one of the, as they were called, 'self-freed' monks of this order, and that we would be allowed to come to their monastery since, regardless of nationality, all men were respected there, who strove towards the One God, Creator of all nations and races without distinction.[5]

COMMENT: I think we're coming towards the end of this session. So, this is another chance meeting. There are many chance meetings of help coming from outside if we are open and available to it. And this World Brotherhood of Self-freed Monks—it's going to be very interesting to continue with it. Let's round off with any comments on what we've read so far, and then we can look forward to the next conference! It gets better and better and better. He even tells us how to build a soul, even though he says he's going to do it elsewhere, and then he does it in here. But I'm intrigued by Father Giovanni and this Greek connection that you pointed out with Kafiristan. Father Giovanni is an Italian Greek, his father was Italian and his mother Greek. And Giovanni is also John.

FACILITATOR: First I was associating this with the passage in Purgatory where they are separating outer and inner effect, so that it's dangerous now to talk Greek because this would give only outer results, bad results, so they have to separate themselves to give an inner result.

This father Giovanni is connected with the myth of Prester John who founded a branch of Asian Christianity. It's a legend of the Middle Ages and it's also in the Grail stories. They're going to look for certain Prester John and in some legend he's situated in India and founded a Christian Indian branch, so it's Asiatic Christianity. In another legend he lives somewhere in Ethiopia and teaches there. This is fairly close to the ancient trade routes to India, so this is how the Christian impulse came into central Asian mythology and his name is connected with this.

It seems to me that this is a good place to stop so we'll finish the session here, now.

5 Gurdjieff, *Meetings*, PP 236-37.

Seminar: *Life is Real Only Then, When "I Am"*

"Prologue"

I am. . .? But what has become of that full-sensing of the whole of myself, formerly always in me in just such cases of self-questioning during the process of self-remembering. . . .

Is it possible that this inner ability was achieved by me thanks to all kinds of self-denial and frequent self-goading only in order that now, when its influence for my Being is more necessary even than air, it should vanish without trace?

No! This cannot be! . . .

Something here is not right!

If this is true, then everything in the sphere of reason is illogical.

But in me is not yet atrophied the possibility of actualizing conscious labor and intentional suffering! . . .

According to all past events I must still be. I wish! . . . and will be!!

Moreover, my Being is necessary not only for my personal egoism but also for the common welfare of all humanity.

My Being is indeed necessary to all people; even more necessary to them than their felicity and their happiness of today.

I wish still to be ... I still am!

By the incomprehensible laws of the association of human thoughts, now, before beginning to write this book which will be my third—that is, my instructive—series of writings, and in general my last book, through which I wish to share with the other creatures of our Common Father similar to myself almost all the previously unknown mysteries of the inner world of man which I have accidentally learned, there has reoccurred to me the above-quoted self-reasoning which proceeded in me during an almost delirious state exactly seven years ago today, and even, it seems to me, at this very hour.

This fantastic soliloquy proceeded in me the 6th of November, 1927, early in the morning in one of the Montmartre night cafes in Paris when, tired already to exhaustion from my "black" thoughts, I had decided to go home and there once more to try whether I might perhaps succeed in sleeping at least a little.

Although my health was, then too, in general bad—yet on this morning I felt particularly miserable.

My miserable state on that morning was also further aggravated by the fact that during the last two or three weeks I had slept not more than one or two hours in twenty-four, and this last night I had not been able to sleep at all.

The fundamental cause of such sleeplessness and general disorder, in those days already excessive, of nearly all the important functions of my organism, was the uninterrupted flowing in my consciousness of "heavy" thoughts about the apparently insoluble situation which had then unexpectedly arisen for me.

In order to be able to explain, at least approximately, what this insoluble situation for me was, I must first say the following:

For more than three years up till then I had been writing, almost day and night, with constant self-driving, the books I had resolved to publish.

I say with constant self-driving because, due to the consequences of an automobile accident which happened to me just before beginning to write these books, I had been very ill and weak, and therefore, of course, had not had the possibility tor any active action.

Yet I had not spared myself, and had worked very hard in such a state, chiefly thanks to the factors that formed in my consciousness, from the very beginning, the following *idée fixe* notion:

Since I had not, when in full strength and health, succeeded in introducing in practice into the life of people the beneficial truths elucidated for them by me, then I must at least, at any cost, succeed in doing this in theory, before my death.

While writing out in outline during the first year the different fragments intended for publication, I had decided to write three series of books.

I had decided with the contents of the first series of books to achieve the destruction, in the consciousness and feelings of people, of deep-rooted convictions which in my opinion are false and quite contradictory to reality.

With the contents of the second series of books to prove that there exist other ways of perceiving reality, and to indicate their direction.

With the contents of the third series of books to share the possibilities which I had discovered of touching reality and, if so desired, even merging with it.

With such intentions I began from the second year to write out this material in definite books, in a form now for general understanding.

And just before the events I am now describing, I had finished writing all the books of the first series and was already working on the books of the second series.

As I had the intention of publishing the first series of my writings the following year, I therefore decided, parallel with working on the books of the second series, to hold frequent public readings of the first series.

I decided to do this in order, before finally sending them to press, to review them once more but this time in accordance with the impressions with which different fragments were received by people of different typicalities and different degrees of mental development.

And in view of this aim, I began from then on to invite to my city apartment different persons of my acquaintance of corresponding individuality to hear the chapter proposed for correction, which was read aloud by somebody in their presence.

At that time I had my principal place of residence for my whole family as well as for myself at Fontainebleau, but because of my frequent visits to Paris I was obliged also to have an apartment there.

During these common readings, in the presence of listeners of many different typicalities, while simultaneously observing the audience and listening to my writing, now ready for publication, I for the first time very definitely established and clearly, without any doubt, understood the following:

The form of the exposition of my thoughts in these writings could be understood exclusively by those readers who, in one way or another, were already acquainted with the peculiar form of my mentation.

But every other reader for whom, strictly speaking, I had goaded myself almost day and night during this time, would understand nearly nothing.

During this common reading, by the way, I enlightened myself for the first time with regard to the particular form in which it would be necessary to write in order that it might be accessible to the understanding of everyone.

So, when I had clarified all this to myself, there just then appeared before me, in all its splendor and full majesty, the question of my health.

Above everything else, there then flowed in my consciousness the following thoughts:

If all this, which was written during three or four years of almost unceasing day and night work, were to be rewritten from the beginning in another form more accessible to the understanding of every reader, at least the same length of time would be required. . . . But time is needed for the exposition of the second and third series; and time will be also necessary for introducing into practical life the essence of these writings of mine. . . . But where can so much time be obtained? . . .

If my time depended solely upon me I could, of course, rewrite all this anew. Moreover, from the very beginning of this new writing, I would acquire the certainty of a peaceful end, for now, knowing how to write, I could fully expect that at least after my death the principal aims of my life would certainly be realized.

But, due to all kinds of accumulated consequences of my past life, it so happens that just now my time depends not upon me but exclusively upon the "self-willed" Archangel Gabriel. And indeed there remains to me but one or two or perhaps, at the most, three years more of life.

Concerning this, that is, that I have soon to die, any one of hundreds of physician-specialists knowing me can now confirm.

Besides this, I myself in my past life had not in vain been known as a good, above the average, diagnostician.

Not for nothing had I during my life held many conversations with thousands of candidates for a speedy departure from this world.

It would, strictly speaking, even be unnatural if it were not so. . . . For the processes of the involution of my health during my past life had proceeded many times more rapidly and intensively than the processes of its evolution.

In fact, all the functions of my organism which previously had been, as my friends said, "steel-cast," had gradually degenerated, so that at the present moment due to constant overworking not one of them was, even relatively, functioning properly.

This is not at all to be wondered at . . . . Even without considering the many other events unusual in human experience which had taken place in the accidentally peculiar pattern of my past life, it would be enough to recall that strange and inexplicable destiny pursuing me, which consisted in my having been wounded three times in quite different circumstances, each time almost mortally and each time by a stray bullet.

If the full significance of only these three incidents were comprehended, which inevitably implanted ineffaceable results in my body, one could understand that they in themselves were sufficient to have caused my final end long ago.

The first of these three incomprehensible fateful events happened in 1896, on the island of Crete, one year before the Greco-Turkish War.

From here, while still unconscious, I was brought, I don't know why, by some unknown Greeks to Jerusalem.

Soon, with consciousness returned, although with my health not yet quite restored, I in the company of other just such as myself–"seekers of pearls in manure" set out from Jerusalem for Russia not by water, as normal people ordinarily do, but by land, on foot.

From such wandering, continuing about four months nearly always through places almost impassable, with my health still in precarious condition, there must, of course, have been implanted in my organism for the rest of my life some "chronically manifesting" factors of evil influence upon my health.

In addition to everything else, during this foolish trip, there visited me and found delight in my body, for quite a long stay, some specific "delicacies" of local character, among which, by the way, were the honored and famous "Kurdistan tzinga" [scurvy], the not less famous "Armenian dysentery" and, of course, that common and omnipresent favorite of many names: *la grippe*, or influenza.

After this, willy-nilly, I had to live some months, without absenting myself, at home in Transcaucasia, and then again began, animated of course as always by the idée fixe of my inner world, various trips through all kinds of bush and jungle.

And this time in my unfortunate physical body I again played host, during their long visits, to many other specific delicacies of local character.

Among such new guests were the honored "Ashkhabadian bedinka," "Bokharian malaria," "Tibetan hydropsy," "Beluchistan dysentery" and many others who also left their calling cards permanently whenever they called.

In the following years my organism, although it had already acquired immunity from all such local delicacies, nevertheless could not, of course, due to its increasing tenseness, eradicate the consequences of these old delicacies.

COMMENT: First of all, what does he mean by "stray bullet?" Secondly, why is he attaching the names of towns or whole countries to diseases? Does anyone have an opinion on this? I can add something Paul Beekman Taylor told me. He went for steam baths with Gurdjieff. Gurdjieff never had any indication of bullet holes anywhere on his body.

COMMENT: I think stray bullets mean no more than the mishaps, physically, of life. It's not real bullets.

COMMENT: I would say so too but the question for me would be, in the chapter "Religion," the leader of the seven Tibetan saints was also hit by a stray bullet. That also doesn't make sense. I just don't have any idea; I don't think it can be that simple, that it is just law of accident. Is it really?

COMMENT: If I think back to *Meetings with Remarkable Men*, there is the chapter about the spider and there are quite a few places that the change of the course of their travels is abrupt. Something comes in from outside, like the spider, and then there is an abrupt change and they end up going to Egypt or place like that. Probably, I would be looking for something coming in from the outside, some kind of MI–FA interval and changing his course. In this case, I haven't mapped it all out for myself but that is what I would be looking for in this story of the stray bullets.

COMMENT: I think that is good. If you were injured by a bullet in Crete and then were taken to Jerusalem for treatment seems like a long journey. It is a deflection.

COMMENT: I have read a lot of things about near-death experiences and people changing their lives totally after that so this may be this kind of shock for changing totally his whole system of vision. He calls this the bullet that nearly killed him.

COMMENT: This is interesting relative to how he ends *The Tales* with the new organ and begins this Series with a lot of near death experiences. I don't ordinarily think when I am reading things like this in the Third Series of his stated purpose of it:
With the contents of the third series of books to share the possibilities which I had discovered of touching reality and, if so desired, even merging with it.
Each book has a context. This quite a context!

COMMENT: And this is what the Work is about: how to die.

COMMENT: This is a thought I have had for a long time about this issue here about the first bullet in Crete. Cretans are very … "nationalistic" is not the word, perhaps "localistic" is the word. 1896 was the year of a revolution in Crete. It was the Cretan revolution that ended up with a Greek–Turkish war. The revolution was against the Turks then Greece got involved in the war because of that revolution and Greece lost very bad to the Turks; it was a disaster.

Now, the effect of this paragraph is that Gurdjieff is thought very highly of in Crete. It has been proposed that they build a statue to him because he fought for that cause, which was a lost cause, which means he is so much more respected that he went there to fight in 1896.

So, I don't know. Do you make who you are? Do you craft it with your memoirs?

COMMENT: It just entered my mind that when he speaks about this stray bullet it is spoken from some experience. Maybe this car accident was one stray bullet.

COMMENT: When he talks about his predicament of reading his work in front of the people and they are not understanding anything. This brought the picture of the chapter of "Hadji-Asvatz-Troov" where the sheik asked Hadji, as a specialist in stringed instrument, to make a mechanical device so that any dervish could play it.

> """Hadji, you, as a specialist in stringed instruments, try–perhaps you can manage to make a stringed musical instrument on which any dervish, without being a specialist, can produce the sounds of the necessary melody merely by a mechanical action, such as, for example, turning, striking, pressing, and so on.""[1]

Later on, he invents this small Greek hand organ. This reminded me of the chapter "Arousing of Thought" where he mentions "pianola" which is another hand organ.

I was wondering; when he re-wrote *The Tales*, are *The Tales* this new stringed instrument that we have to turn, because when you turn the pages, you are turning them mechanically and he said he is going to put some notions into us and the notions are going to work mechanically.

COMMENT: I read this as a symbol of what we read about yesterday: the 'mechano-coinciding-Mdnel-In.' This is life. I feel we have this, all of us. We meet something in our life that can put us on a different course if we take it in a special way.

COMMENT: After the car crash, that was when he decided to start writing the books. He may have understood that this is the time to start writing books.

COMMENT: I don't remember which book I read the following story: a woman came to Gurdjieff in Paris and she asked him to teach her the secret of life. He took her to a cabaret and said to watch very carefully what is happening. He introduced himself to a whore there and he took a cherry and he asked her what did she think it was. The said it was a cherry. He said, no, you are wrong, this is not a cherry, this is a very special fruit that I brought from another planet because, if you see me, I am not a regular man. I am a man who came from another planet. If you don't believe me, taste it. So she tasted it. Gurdjieff then asked her what she thought of this wonderful fruit. And she said, it is a cherry. And then he told the woman, you see, that is the secret of life.

What it tells me in relation to what we are discussing is we have to maintain our simple and sane mind. Many times Gurdjieff makes jokes about people and tells them fantastic things, like to eat to ice cream with mustard when he was in the Prieuré; he told some woman, you should mustard on your ice cream; it is better and she does it. He did it just to mock how people can give up simple and straightforward thinking.

1 Gurdjieff, *Beelzebub's Tales*, p 881.

So I would say that is the character. He was a Caucasian, not in the sense of white skin. He liked to make jokes especially about European people who were very naïve. He had many, many stories how he succeeded to squeeze money from people with birds he painted and with the writing machines. It was part of his character, a rascal to make fools of people which he said in order to step on the toes to show them how naïve they are; how they lost their ability to think straight forward.

Therefore, with many, many things, we have take with a little pepper; he is a person who wants to shock you, wants to test your ability to see through simple things. That is why I think he thought it was necessary to make impressions, like pretending he is this and this and these accidents, I don't know why, I think it didn't happen.

[continued reading from *Life is Real Only Then, When "I Am"*]

> Under such conditions of tension years passed; then, for this unfortunate physical body of mine, came another year of destiny, 1902, when I was punctured by a second stray bullet.

> This occurred in the majestic mountains of Tibet one year before the Anglo-Tibetan War.

> On this second occasion, my unfortunate physical body was able to elude destiny because near me there were five good physicians—three of European education and two specialists of Tibetan medicine, all five very sincerely devoted to me.

> After three or four months of unconscious life, for me there flowed still another year of constant physical tenseness and unusual psychic contrivance—and then came my third fateful year.

> This was at the end of 1904 in the Transcaucasian region in the neighborhood of the Chiatura Tunnel.

> Speaking about this third stray bullet, I cannot here deny myself the opportunity, for the pleasure of some and for the displeasure of others of my acquaintances of the present time, of now saying openly about this third bullet that it was plunked into me, of course unconsciously, by some "charmer" from among those two groups of people, who, fallen on one side under the influence of the revolutionary psychosis and on the other under the sway of imperious superiors, accidental upstarts, together laid then, also of course unconsciously, the basic foundation stones of the groundwork of the, at least today, indeed "great Russia."

> There then proceeded firing between the so-called Russian army, chiefly Cossacks, and the so-called Gourians.

> In view of the fact that certain events in my life, beginning with this third nearly fatal wound and up to the present time, have among themselves, as I have recently noticed, a very strange, and at the same time very definite, connection in terms of one physical law, I will therefore describe some of these events with as much detail as possible.

> It is necessary before going further to mention here also that on the evening of November 6, 1927, when, after a good sleep, I began to think of the situation that had

arisen for me, then into my consciousness flashed one idea, among others, which then appeared to me entirely absurd; but now, after having constated unexpectedly and having elucidated during the last seven years various facts previously unknown to me, I have become convinced without any doubt that it must be true.

And so, at the time of this third bullet, near me there was only one man, and at that a very weak one. As I learned later, he, surmising that the situation and surrounding circumstances were such that very undesirable consequences might arise for me, quickly somewhere found a donkey and, placing me, completely unconscious, on it, in haste drove it far into the mountains.

There he put me in some cave, and himself went to look for help.

He found some kind of a "barber-physician" and necessary bandages and returned with them late in the evening.

They did not find anyone in the cave and were astounded, because neither could I have left by myself nor could anyone else have come there, and as far as wild animals were concerned, they knew well that in this region, aside from deer and goat and sheep, there were no animals.

They noticed traces of blood, but it was impossible to follow them because the night had already fallen.

COMMENT: This is a pretty far out idea but is it possible that these stray bullets that Gurdjieff is describing something metaphorically happening to peoples associated with those wars, those events. Those of you who know the course of history better than me, know that these things start with one bullet here or there. Is it possible that that event in Crete and the next one and the next one are actually skirmishes involving countries?

COMMENT: I don't think so. Even if it is, I don't think it is important. I think he must be talking about us, something about you, in fact or me. He doesn't want to give us history lessons, we are not interested in history, we are interested in survival, as it were.

Here is another crazy thought. What happens when you are hit with a bullet? You bleed. Blood comes out of you. And we have different kinds of blood, planetary and other kinds of blood. The blood is connected to the word "bless." It could be a blessing to be hit by a bullet, perhaps. So all of things may not be what they look like; they may not be as bad as they sound. To be hit by bullets, if it is a blessing, it might be a good thing.

COMMENT: What I wonder about is all these data–years, months and days. Whenever I count them together I mostly come to a three or six or nine. I don't think it is accidental. We also have a five with the five physicians and maybe this is again a moment of temptation because of the five physicians, three are of European education and two are from Tibetan medicine. Maybe also it is to show that things go down or go up. I have the impression of what is going on is a big turmoil around him or ourselves this word "unconscious" is mentioned very often with the war and now he is unconscious going into this cave. It may be a new way because now he goes into this unconsciousness in a cave, which is a strong symbol. So maybe there is a new step; maybe it is more about our inner travel.

COMMENT: However one interprets the bullet, when he is hit, he goes on and on and on. That is a very clear message. In the beginning if you take this car accident as a bullet, that is when he started. He doesn't stop. That is advice to us even if we are hit with a bullet, we must go on and on and on.

[continued reading from *Life is Real Only Then, When "I Am"*]

Only the next morning, when it began to dawn, after spending the whole night in anxiety and fruitless search in the forest did they find me between some rocks, still alive and apparently sound asleep.

The barber immediately found some roots, and with these he made a temporary tourniquet, and after giving instructions to my weak friend what to do, he at once set out somewhere.

Late in the evening he returned accompanied by two of his friends, called "Khevsurs," with a two-wheeled cart to which were harnessed two mules.

That evening they drove me still higher into the mountains and again placed me in a cave, but this time a large one, adjacent to another immense cave in which, as later appeared, sat and reclined, perhaps contemplating human life of past and future ages, several score Khevsurian dead, "mummified" by the rarefied air of that high place.

In this cave where they placed me, for two weeks, in the presence of the aforementioned weak man, the barber and one young Khevsur, there proceeded in me the struggle between life and death.

After that my health began to improve at such a pace that in one week more my consciousness had entirely returned, and I could already move about with the help of someone and a stick, and a couple of times even visit the "secret meeting" of my "immortal neighbors."

At this time it was ascertained that below, in the process of civil war, the upper hand, as it is said, had been taken by the Russian army and that already everywhere the Cossacks were poking about and arresting every "suspicious" inhabitant who was not a native.

As I was not a native, and knew also the process of the mentation of people fallen under a "revolutionary psychosis," I decided to flee from these parts as soon as possible.

Taking into consideration the surrounding conditions of the Transcaucasian region as a whole, and my personal prospects for the future, I decided to go into the Transcaspian region.

Subjected to incredible physical sufferings, I set out in the company of the above-mentioned weak man.

I experienced unbelievable sufferings chiefly because I had everywhere on the way to preserve an unsuspicious exterior.

An exterior not arousing suspicion was necessary so as not to become a victim either of this "political psychosis" or of the so-called "national psychosis."

The fact of the matter is that, in places where the railroad passed, there had only recently been completed a so-called "realization of a higher gradation" of the "national psychosis," in this instance between the Armenians and Tartars, and some peculiarities of this human scourge still continued to flow by momentum.

My misfortune in this case consisted in the fact that, having a "universal appearance," I represented to the Armenians a pure-blooded Tartar and to the Tartars a pure-blooded Armenian.

To make a long story short, I, by hook or by crook, in the company of this weak friend of mine, and with the help of a "mouth harmonica," arrived in the Transcaspian region.

This mouth harmonica, which I discovered in the pocket of my coat, rendered us a great service.

COMMENT: When he speaks about the civil war, he specifies it is not just a war, it is a civil war. How do you see that? It is not any war, it is a civil war.

COMMENT: I think what you might be pointing to is possibly a war within an individual, between two parts of an individual.

COMMENT: Yes. He is pointing to a war inside us.

COMMENT: It is quite obvious that there are so many questions that arise by reading this text, questions that cannot have an easy answer and may never have an answer, really.

On the other hand, the truth is I am intrigued by all this commotion, all this moving from Crete to Jerusalem to these places. What was said about this being only internal, the paradigms used here, yes, they could be and I am sure they are. I am sure they have internal dimension.

At the same time, there is the question. Why did Gurdjieff go to these places and not any other places? He was a boy of very little means and a vast world in front of him to look into and the conditions were very difficult; there was no tourism at that point he could hide amongst.

So how do you make the decisions where to go? I think an element of chance would have to be there and possibly bullets are obstacles that were really insurmountable–objective obstacles that had to be avoided because of the circumstances–he had to move on; he had to be moved on.

So I am left with a curiosity of actually looking into the geography of these particular occurrences so it is a task I am undertaking myself to look into that because I am intrigued by all this conversation that seems not to have any ready answers.

COMMENT: There is one really mysterious thing he keeps referring to and it is the weak man. He did travel through these areas and I believe he was shot (as James Moore refers to) but he does refer to this weak man and he is always referred as this "weak" man.

Is anyone clear why he is weak? He calls him a weak man but what has he done that is weak? We will read on and he disappears; that is his role to be called a weak man. Can anyone see why he is weak?

COMMENT: I wasn't going to try and answer that but also to point out that pretty much everyone else has a name has some other classification in terms of where they come from or some other attribute but to be a weak man is a bit unusual in terms of his style so, yes, I noticed that as well.

COMMENT: In *Meetings with Remarkable Men*, there are several places where he mentions the weak man but it also mentioned with a strong spirit. So this is the situation where the mechanics have to stop to do their job and something else has to take over.

COMMENT: It is interesting that this man, although he is weak, is not in inverted commas so it could be a kind of a nascent real I that is still developing.

COMMENT: To go back to what was spoken of earlier, these three engagements he is talking about–it is not the first time he has mentioned these. The Anglo-Tibetan war is there in *The Tales*; the Crete rebellion is there in *The Tales* in the first chapter; the Russian Revolution is all over *The Tales*. So these are referring to other things and this happening again and again. He mentioned these diseases, there are seven diseases and he's pointing out the places where they occurred. I am sure those diseases are not associated with national things. We also have something else that seems to be an absurdity–that Gurdjieff couldn't pass himself off as an Armenian ("to the Armenians a pure-blooded Tartar"). Well I would have thought not. I would have thought being able to speak Armenian and having been able to do so from very young, he probably would be able to pass himself off as an Armenian. So this is kind of odd. These are questions, no answers.

COMMENT: To follow on with these absurdities, because I wonder if something could be mapped out. These three stray bullets are like three shocks coming in from the outside that change the course that he was going in. The other place where he speaks in detail about these three shocks is in the digestion of physical food in the chapter "Purgatory" in *The Tales*.

He says these same laws of digestion hold true for the digestion of Air and the digestion of Impressions. This would be an interesting to explore. Is this another digestive octave? We have three distinct shocks. What was pointed out about the second shock (the second bullet) there is the number five and there is something involving and evolving.

It seems this is all given in *The Tales*, and here this book, *Life is Real Only Then, When "I Am"* is the esoteric part of the series.

COMMENT: I was looking at that. When there is the question of the weak man, the first thought that came to my mind (I like these first thoughts because they are crazy) – it is the operational laws of the changed Stopinders. He shortened the last Stopinder so made it weaker for the commencement of the new cycle and the weak man carries him into the caves. I have to look into this more deeply but this is the first picture that came.

COMMENT: The three Theological regions of the Fourth Way: Judaism, Tibetan and then the Christian or you can say Muslim. So we have the Armenian representing the Christian, the enemies may be the Muslims, Tibet and Jerusalem. A few times Gurdjieff said he studied the Kabala and he was in Monastery of the Essenes. We know that he was in Tibet; we know, of course, he was in Kars in the school of Christianity so maybe he refers to four influences that built his system. He wants to say that he got the influences accidently but it was very, very impressive–it did something to him; it changed him, maybe he says it wounded him but it could be this–just an idea.

COMMENT: This is the Third Series and he has every right to believe that the reader has been through the other material. So the other material has prepared the reader in a variety of ways to interpret this now in a way that has some skill. If the reader has gotten through *Meetings* and figured out it is not just literal, for sure, we get to point now where it is not just literal.
The two tunes that are coming up in the reading are real pieces of music, you can find them on youtube easily.

[continued reading from *Life is Real Only Then, When "I Am"*]

On this original instrument I then played, I confess, not badly —although I played only two tunes: "The Peaks of Manchuria" and "Valse Ozhidanie."

Arriving in the Transcaspian region we decided for the time being to establish ourselves in the city of Ashkhabad.

We rented two good rooms in a private house with a charming garden, and I could finally rest.

Yet, on the first morning when my only near person there went to a pharmacy to get for me the necessary medicaments, he did not return for a long time.

Hours passed, but still he did not come … he did not come.

I began to be anxious, chiefly because I knew that he was here for the first time and did not yet know anybody.

Night is falling and I have no more patience. … I am going to look for him.

But where? First of all I go to the pharmacy. There they know nothing.. . .

Suddenly, listening to my questions, the druggist's boy says that he saw this same young man, who was there in the morning, arrested by the police in the street not far from there, and taken away somewhere.

What is to be done? Where to go? I know no one here, and besides I am hardly able to move because during the last few days I have become completely exhausted.

When I leave the pharmacy, it is almost completely dark in the street.

By chance an unoccupied carriage passes. I ask to be taken to the center of the city, somewhere near the bazaar where after the stores close there is still life.

I decide to go to such a place in the hope of meeting, perhaps in one of the cafes or *chaikhanas*, someone of my acquaintance.

I am barely moving through narrow streets, and come across only small *ashkhanas*, where only the Tekinians sit.
I am weakening more and more, and in my thoughts already flashes a suspicion that I may lose consciousness.

I sit down on the terrace in front of the first *chaikhana* I pass, and ask for some green tea.

While drinking tea, I come to—thank God!—and look around on the space dimly lit by the street lantern.

I see a tall man with a long beard, in European clothing, pass by the *chaikhana*.

His face seems familiar. I stare at him while he, already coming near, also looking at me very intently, passes on.

Proceeding further, he turns around several times and looks again at me.

I take a risk and call after him in Armenian:

"Either I know you, or you know me!"

He stops, and looking at me, suddenly exclaims, "Ah! Black Devil!"and walks back.

It was enough for me to hear his voice, and already I knew who he was.

He was no other than my distant relative, the former police court interpreter.

I already knew that several years before he had been exiled to some place in the Transcaspian region, but to where I did not know.

And I also knew that the reason for his exile was that he had stolen the affections of the paramour of the chief of police.

Can you imagine my inner exultation at such a meeting?

COMMENT: Two comments: First, the previous page and a half at least he switched back to the picture language and now he has left it. Second, the "Can you imagine my inner exultation at such a meeting?" reminds me of finding the map [in *Meetings with Remarkable Men*].

[continued reading from *Life is Real Only Then, When "I Am"*]

I will not describe how and about what we talked, while sitting on that terrace of the small *chaikhana* and continuing to drink green tea.

I will only say that on the following morning this distant relative of mine, the former police official, came to me accompanied by his friend, a police lieutenant.

From them I learned, first, that nothing serious threatened my companion.

He was arrested only because he was here for the first time and nobody here had ever seen him before.

And as there were now many dangerous revolutionaries everywhere, he was arrested only in order to establish his identity.

This, they say, is not a complicated thing. They will write to the place where his passport was issued and order an inquiry into his political reliability; but if he must, in the meanwhile, disport himself with fleas and lice, what of it? To experience this is a very good thing as a preliminary education for the future life.

And secondly, added my distant relative, lowering his voice, your name appears on the list of sources disturbing for the peace of visitors to "Montmartre," places of frivolous amusement.

On this account, and also because of some other considerations, I, still in a very sick condition, decided to leave this place also as quickly as possible. For I could do nothing to help my friend.

Now entirely alone, and moreover with very limited funds, I set out in the direction of Central Asia.

After overcoming with unimaginable difficulties every kind of great and small obstacle, I came to the city of Yangihissar in the former Chinese Turkestan, where, from old friends of mine, I supplied myself with money and then found myself in that same place where I had lived several years before, while recovering my health when it had been shattered because of stray bullet number two.

This place is located on the southwestern edge of the Gobi desert and represents to my mind the most fertile of all the parts of the surface of our earth.

And concerning the air of this place and its salutary influence on everyone inhaling it, I will say that it is truly purgatorial.

If in reality there exist paradise and hell, and if from them arises any radiation, then the air in the space between these two sources would surely have to be similar to this.

For on one side is a soil which almost literally pours from itself, as from a cornucopia, all kinds of earthly flora, fauna and phoscalia, and right next to this fertile soil is an area of many thousands of square kilometers representing literally hell, where not only nothing crops up but anything originating elsewhere that happens to get in its midst, is destroyed in a very short time, leaving no trace.

COMMENT: To continue with the notion that the three bullets represent the three shocks coming in from outside. Of chief interest in the chapter "Purgatory" is the practical knowledge of how Food, Air and Impressions are digested, going back to the chapter "Arch-absurd," having one's own law of Three.

Maybe this octave represented by the three bullets, perhaps this indication of the air being purgatorial might be significant.

COMMENT: How to understand such details as a "weak" man. The so-called weak man saved him through difficult and arduous effort.

COMMENT: He himself was weak, he was saying he was weak, so there are two weak men, not just one.

COMMENT: Can Ocke explain something that was in his paper about the third state of consciousness? To balance first the three parts within ourselves and three conscious shocks and three states.

COMMENT, Ocke: To Madam de Salzmann it is pretty accurate because she constantly says in her papers that one should center oneself in the abdomen to allow the spine area and the plexus area and the head to take their natural space. We are normally identified with one part of a center or one center and if we do that, then we can enter another state. In my book, I have written a whole chapter on exploring the third state of consciousness because it is an exploration because you don't know what it is in the beginning; you really have learn, like a baby, to enter that state. I personally think Madam de Salzmann's book, Reality of Being is pointing very much at how she worked with Gurdjieff and with other people to establish that. It is also in my book.

[continued reading from *Life is Real Only Then, When "I Am"*]

> Namely, here on this small singular piece of the hard surface of our Earth the air of which, that is, our second food, originates and is transformed between the forces of paradise and hell, in me there had proceeded at the end of my first visit there, then also in an almost delirious condition, just that same self reasoning concerning which, in my consciousness, on the evening of November 6th, as I have mentioned above, there flashed an idea which appeared to me then entirely absurd.
>
> The first time, my friends brought me here in an unconscious condition, soon after I had been wounded by the second stray bullet.
>
> At the beginning, near me were many friends among whom were also the five mentioned physicians.
>
> And when, after the return of consciousness, I began to improve, all of them gradually went away, and I remained there with only one Tibetan and one very young Kara-Kirghiz.
>
> Living there, far from people of all sorts, attended by these two sympathetic people who treated me almost maternally, and all the time nourished by the above-mentioned "cleansing air," I, within six weeks, recovered so that I already wished and was able at any moment to leave this salutary place.
>
> Everything was already gathered and packed and we awaited the coming of the young Kara-Kirghiz' father, with his three camels, in order to proceed on the journey.
>
> As I had information that in one of the valleys of the mountain, then called "the peak of Alexander III," there were at that time several Russian officers, topographers of the Turkestan Topographical Administration, among whom was one of my very good friends, I intended first to go to them, and from there to join some large caravan and travel first to Andijan, then to the Transcaucasian region to see my relatives.

COMMENT: As was pointed out, it seems to be connected with the different digestions of Food and Air and Impressions. And looking at the bullets, I think it is a point that these bullets changed the original intention. Within the original intention before you start to give yourself the first conscious shock, there is only the Air and the Food. With that in mind, these bullets are very important. Formatorily, we might look at it as some disturbing factors that takes us away from the right route. In fact, they are the necessary bullets in order to start something.

I was trying to see this in terms of the triad of Regeneration. To give yourself the first conscious shock would be starting the triad of Regeneration: form, matter and the neutralizing factor, life. Form is the active force, matter is the consequences of the bullets that try to hold you back from the original direction that you had before you were hit by the bullet. So the form has to work on that matter–matter is the second force in that triad, to give up instead of starting to write the book would be a completely different triad.

So I think it is an important point as looking at it as the three octaves. The bullets are absolutely necessary; we have to be in life; we have to take bullets. If there are no bullets, then the consequences of the Kundabuffer go on and on.

··· ∽ ···

Samliosian Samoniks Samonoltooriko Samookorooazar
Samos sandoor Sarnuonino Saroonoorishan Sarpitimnian
Sart satkaine Scheherazade Seccruano
Sekronoolanzaknian Selchan Selneh-eh-Avaz Selnoano
Selos Selzelnualno Semooniranoos Semzekionally
Senkoo-ori Sensimiriniko Seraph Serooazar
Setrenotzinarco Sevohtartra Sevrodox
Shachermacher-accounting
Shachermacher-workshop-booths shashlik Shat-Chai-Mernis
Sherakhoorian Shila-PlavShmana Shooroomooroomnian
Shooshoonian Shuenists Shvidi-Noora-Chakoo
Shvidi-Pikan-On Sianoorinam Siapora Sidor Sikharenenian Sikitians
Sikt ner chorn Silkoornano
Silnooyegordpana Similnisirnian
Simkalash Sincratorza Sinkrpoosarams
Sinndraga Sinokooloopianian Sinonoums Sinooa
Sirioonorifarab Sirkliniamen
Sitrik Skernalitsionniks Skinikoonartzino Skoohiatchiny
Snipsnapsnorum Sobrionolian Soldjinoha Solianka
Solioonensius Solni Soloohnorahoona
Soniasikra Sonitanis Sooanso-Toorabizo Sooniat
Sooptaninalnian Soorptakalknian Soort Spetsitooalitivian
Spipsychoonalian Spirna Stopinder Stumpsinschmausen
Surp-Athanatos Surp-Otheos Surp-Skiros
Svolibroonolnian Tadjiks
tainolair Tak-tschan-nan Talaialtnikoom Talkoprafarab
Tambak Tandoor Tanguori Taranooranura Tastartoonarian
Tatakh Tazaloorinono Tchaftantouri Techgekdnel Teleoghinoora
Teleokrimalnichnian tempo-Davlaksherian
Tenikdoa Terasakhaboora Terbelnian
Ternoonald Teskooano Tetartocosmos Tetartoëhary Tetetos

Singing a Whole World: Chant Circle as Microcosmos

. . . Darlene Franz . . .

I want to begin with the chant we sang earlier, which is a prayer, an invocation. The words, which we all know, are from the Purgatory Chapter we've been studying this week. All sing:

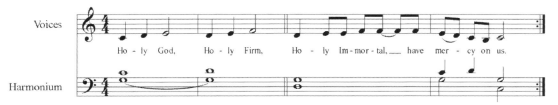

I'd like to read from *The Tales*:

> "Here you should know that your contemporary favorites very often use a notion taken by them from somewhere, I do not know whether instinctively, emotionally, or automatically, and expressed by them in the following words: 'We are the images of God.' These unfortunates do not even suspect that, of everything known to most of them concerning cosmic truths, this expression of theirs is the only true one of them all. And indeed, each of them is the image of God, not of that 'God' which they have in their bobtailed picturings, but of the real God, by which word we some-times still call our common Megalocosmos. Each of them to the smallest detail is exactly similar, but of course in miniature, to the whole of our Megalocosmos, and in each of them there are all of those separate functionings, which in our common Megalocosmos actualize cosmic harmonious Iraniranumange or 'exchange of sub-stances,' maintaining the existence of everything existing in the Megalocosmos as one whole."[1]

And later he goes on to summarize his comments:

> "At any rate, my little Hassein, each of your favorites separately, is, in his whole presence, exactly similar in every respect to our Megalocosmos."[2]

So, the question that arises for me, and I'm sure for many of us, is: what does it take to make our-selves in the image of the Megalocosmos, rather than, as Mr. Gurdjieff laments, to make God in the image of our more constricted selves? According to him, at very least, whole presence is required. And I have no doubt that most of, if not all of us here, have pursued and cultivated practices from the Fourth Way, and from other traditions, other paths, with this aim in mind–of becoming a true image of the whole Megalocosmos.

It's my belief that participatory music making, engaged with intention, also has this possibility, and I'm here to facilitate some experiments in that direction, as I've done with numerous groups of

---

1 Gurdjieff, *Beelzebub's Tales*, p 775.
2 Ibid., p 777.

contemplative Christian seekers. Many of those folks have adopted the false belief–often through acceptance of others' negative judgments on them–that they can't sing. And I find this is common in the population in general. People say, 'Oh, I can't sing.' So right there is a beginning point to work with voice.

I want to reference a couple of comments from earlier presentations. Anthony Blake, this morning, said that we're engaged in making the world intelligible. And this to me, is what we are attempting in a small way, through this singing practice. He also said that we never know the laws apart from our instantiations of them. So how could these laws be instantiated here, now, in the present moment, in our practice of singing together? That's my question, and that's what our experiment is about.

I also want to reference what Robin Bloor said (I believe this was from Rodney Collin): What kind of God is it that we believe in? What God are we making that shows us who we are? And how do we participate in this making?

And finally, from Paul Taylor, and I have this via Tony Blake, since I've not had the privilege of meeting Mr. Taylor. Mr. Gurdjieff said to Paul Taylor at one point, that "all truth disappears in words of telling. Truth must be conveyed, not spoken. Music and dance convey truth that words cannot. You are here to learn this."

So I've been performing this experiment in various contexts, for about seven years now. One of my reasons for wishing to present it here, with all of you, is that I've been doing this for about seven years with Christian Contemplative groups. And I have a sense that something new is required, and what better place to come look for that than with people who are deeply embedded in this practice, these practices that we share.

And so, this work originates in a different context, so I'm a little bit in fear and trembling about placing it here before you all, where perhaps it's not in its native territory, but let's finish our experiment, since we don't know what's going to happen.

I did want to read one other passage from Maurice Nicoll that to me also has tremendous bearing on our work here together, and on this work in particular. In the other context where I've presented this work, there is, as I said, a lot of negativity. Whether it's expressed or not, it's there in the background as "I can't sing. This is terrible. I have a terrible voice. No one wants to hear me," all of these kinds of things.

Our challenge is to transform this type of messaging that we have absorbed in our psychological beings, and sometimes very deeply.

This is from Dr. Nicoll's *Commentaries*, quite early in the first volume. I'm sure many of you have read this:

> "Now I wish to speak to you about how you work on yourselves, and in what spirit you take the work . . . to work in a negative way is useless. It is only through some kind of delight, some kind of joy or pleasure or some genuine affection or desire that a person can work and bring about any change of being in himself. Fear, for example, will not act in this way. A man may have some kind of knowledge of truth, but unless he values it, unless he feels some delight in it, it cannot affect him. It cannot act on him, for a man unites with truth only through his love, as it were, and in this way, his being is changed. But if he is negative, then his love life – that is, his emotional side – is in a wrong state, and it will be same if he is in a state of fear and feels compelled to do something against his will. To do a thing willingly, from a delight in doing it, will effect a change in you. . . This work, if you will listen to it and hear it in your hearts,

is the most beautiful thing you can possibly hear . . . it is about liberation . . . it is as beautiful as if, locked for years in prison, you see a stranger entering who offers you a key."[3]

And so, this is just by way of reminding us that this endeavor of music-making is, or can be, playful and joyful. My intention is to encourage you to experiment, to give yourself permission to try things, and as much as you're able, to enter into this musical undertaking in a spirit of joy and delight, and exploration.

So, let's begin with some chanting with the intention of cultivating a collected state–a balance of all three centers–or, as Beelzebub says:

"I find it necessary to repeat that the 'active mentation' in a being and the useful results of such active mentation are in reality actualized exclusively only with the equal-degree functionings of all his three localizations of the results spiritualized in his presence, called 'thinking-center,' 'feeling-center,' and 'moving-motor-center.'"[4]

What I'd like to try, is to introduce three different chants, each aimed at one of the centers. Of course, you may, at any time, run with this as you wish. As I mentioned the other day, when we sang the first one of these: feel free to experiment with harmonies, whether consonant or dissonant, feel free to simply listen, bring your attention to sensation, as I know all of you are practiced in doing, because after all, music making is in the body. And there will be various instructions about other exercises to perform while chanting.

I'm intentionally not writing the chants anywhere, or projecting the quotations that I'm reading, because I want us to practice our listening skills: taking things in aurally, through our ears. Whole listening opens us to different energies, and perhaps even to higher energies along its whole spectrum, from the most ordinary to the most subtle.

So, here are some chants, on behalf of the centers. The words of the first one are, "Attend to the living presence while you are alive." This is a quotation from the gospel of Thomas,[5] and in that holy book, the saying goes on: "Attend to the living presence while you are alive, so that when you die and have the desire to do so, you may have the power to attend." All sing:

At - tend to the liv - ing pre - sence. Her and now. At - tend.

I invite you to continue this attention on whole-body sensation as we continue to invoke the other centers.

This next chant is intended to allow some contact with the feeling center. The words are from the Biblical *Song of Songs*, or *Song of Solomon*: "Though I sleep, yet my heart awakes." This melody is a little longer, so just listen as long as you need, until you feel you can enter into it. In addition to this attention to whole-body sensation that we have now opened up, if you wish, bring some attention to your longing to wake up, your longing for reality, whatever form that takes for you.

3 Nicoll, Maurice, *Commentaries on the Teachings of Gurdjieff and Ouspensky*, Volume I, pp. 10–11.
4 Gurdjieff, *Beelzebub's Tales*, p 1172.
5 Gospel of Thomas, logion 59, tr. Lynn Bauman.

All sing:

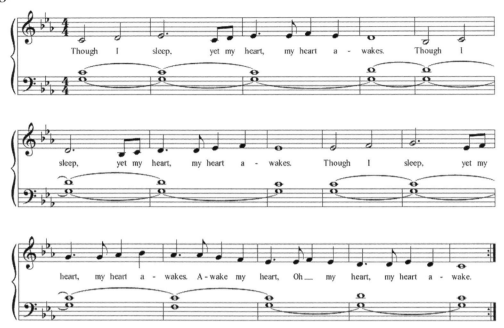

Having invoked the moving center, sensation, some sensate awareness, and the feeling center, let's continue with: how do we use chant to open the mind, or the intelligence? What came to mind to me for this part of the experiment, was a chant with the words, "Every cell of this body sings glory." And for me this relates to the mind, because it's about scale. It's about literal cells of the body, it's about each of us as a cell in some larger body of humanity, it's about humanity–you get the idea. It's about worlds and cosmoses at every scale. What in us comprehends that?

As best I understand mind at this point, (and I hope to have many further and deeper understandings as I go along) mind has to do with this apprehension of the totality of things, as they actually exist. "Every cell in this body sings glory" is a round, it's a two-part round. After we've sung it for a little while, I will begin the second part. So, those of you on the first part, hold your own, and if some wish to switch to the second part, we'll just get the whole thing going that way. All sing:

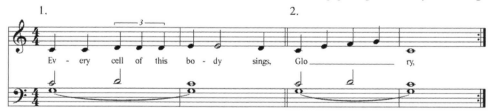

[Interrupts the singing] Ah yes, so here we have the curse of conference room singing. This environment doesn't transmit sound very well, but we also have a tremendous opportunity for listening, for attending in a different kind of way. Those of you on this side of the room are actually quite distant from those on this other side of the room. The harmonium sounds incredibly loud to me, right here next to me. It's a new instrument for me, a smaller one that I bought for traveling. And so I'm trying to play softly, and hear what's going on in the room, and I noticed we got dis-coordinated from each other. So, what kind of attention to this microcosmos – this chant circle, and to your own part in it, and to holding the different parts at the same time – would allow us to remain overlapping in time, in a musical way that makes sense?

So, one part is: 'Every cell of this body sings', and then 'glory' is its own part, and those should fit right on top of each other like that [makes a gesture of one hand directly above the other] for the harmonies to work. So let's try this: open up your attention. We spoke, in an earlier presentation of the auto-stereogram: a visual image that's made of dots, so that if you look directly at it you don't see anything. And so I want you to imagine now, a musical 'auto-audiogram.' We all know about stereo sound, which uses two speakers, four speakers, or even eight speakers. We have in this room far more sources of sound than that. So how do we take these dots of sound, soften our attention to include all of it, while at the same time, being in the flow of each part, and of the whole, to have this fit together, even in non-ideal acoustical conditions. Let's give it a try.

It's still about sense of fun and enjoyment, not, "Oh no, I'm doing it wrong. She's telling me to do it differently." Listen.

[All sing, "Every cell of this body sings glory."]

So you can see it's one thing to receive the instruction, listen, and it's really quite elementary how the two parts fit together, and yet, under the real circumstances, what are the variable factors? We hear some people's voices louder than others. We had difficulty hearing across the room. What began as coordinated becomes dis-coordinated. There's a constant possibility for the renewal of attention – for re-finding our place in this whole – and there will be other opportunities for this as we go along.

So having invoked the three centers by these three chants, I hope you will attend inwardly in such a way as to maintain contact with the three centers. I'd like to reach beyond ordinary consciousness now, to Conscience. I'm going to read again from *The Tales*. We can do this with confidence, knowing that

> ". . . although the factors for engendering in their presences the sacred being-impulses of Faith, Hope, and Love, are already quite degenerated in the beings of this planet . . . nevertheless, Objective-Conscience is not yet atrophied in them, but remains in their presences almost in its primordial state . . . embedded in that consciousness, which is here, called 'subconsciousness'."[6]

And although Beelzebub says that Conscience "takes no part whatever in the functioning of their ordinary consciousness,"[7] he also later says that:

> ". . . the bringing to light of those properties hidden within them, namely, the properties found in their sub-consciousness, turned out to be possible exclusively only with the intentional help on the part of them themselves, that is, with the help of that consciousness of theirs, which with the flow of time had become proper to be possessed by them during their waking state."[8]

So, although objective conscience is buried in our sub-consciousness, Mr. Gurdjieff seems to me to be conveying the idea that the participation of this consciousness is, in fact necessary, and that ordinary consciousness is necessary to access sub-consciousness, where conscience resides.

6 Gurdjieff, *Beelzebub's Tales*, p 359.
7 Ibid.
8 Ibid., pp 536–37.

169

As music to invoke this dimension, I suggest we sing a chant with the words, "Unknowing, abide, in stillness, abide, in patience, in patience possess your soul."

This to me speaks of the subconscious: in our unknowing, we simply abide, and are patient, and this too is an aspect of cultivating or making soul. As an inner exercise, you may already have an exercise that is appropriate to this for you. If you wish, while maintaining this three-centered awareness that we've been cultivating so far, you might also try repeating an inward gesture of releasing attachment to each passing thought. Our ordinary consciousness is connected right into our ordinary patterns of thinking. So as you notice the volume of these thought patterns rising, and see yourself attaching your attention to them, just allow them to be released, with an inward gesture. To abide in unknowing may be aided by such an exercise.

You'll notice this chant is more complex harmonically: if you are interested in singing along with that, there's a chromatic line in the lower part, which I will begin singing after a while. It descends by half-steps. All sing:

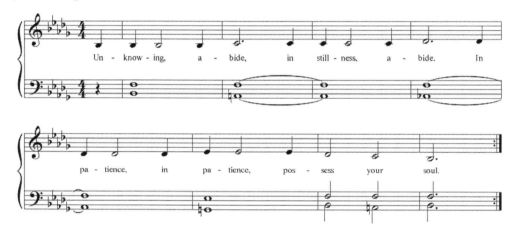

I want to move from here to an exploration of directing our attention to breath and vibration, quite literally, in the body. The bodily experience of breath and vibration has possible pathways to understanding exchange, and the idea of exchange. Remembering, as Beelzebub tells us, that,

> ". . . each of them to the smallest detail is exactly similar, but of course in miniature, to the whole of our Megalocosmos, and in each of them are all those separate functionings, which in our common Megalocosmos actualize the cosmic harmonious Iraniranumange or 'exchange of substances,' maintaining the existence of everything in the Megalocosmos as one whole."[9]

As I continue to speak, bring some attention to the processes of breathing as they exist in you at this moment, with no attempt to change anything. Simply attend to your breathing in any way that your interest is naturally drawn. This could be, for example, the sensation of breath on the upper lip, or perhaps you experience sensation more clearly in the nostrils or in the throat, or perhaps the rise and fall of the chest, or the abdomen. You may even be aware of processes occurring in the lungs or in the bloodstream, related to your body's activity of breath.

It is my belief that the body – my body, your body – already knows how to breath. As with our true selves, this may be covered over with layers of conditioning that affect our breathing processes. But,

9 Gurdjieff, *Beelzebub's Tales*, P 775.

as Anthony Blake was saying this morning, the upper octave is present and sounding simultaneously with the lower octave, and many other harmonics as well.

As you continue to attend to your breathing, I'm going to introduce one other idea that has been perhaps the most profound idea for me about breathing in my entire musical endeavor, whether playing the oboe or singing. And that is simply that the quality of the out-breath is what determines the quality of the in-breath. Or, again I seem to remember someone earlier in the conference quoting Mr. Gurdjieff as saying, "Must make vacuum. Must make vacuum." Our breath is doing this without our assistance, in fact, constantly on our out-breath it's making a vacuum. So our conscious attention to our breathing processes, even in the simplest of ways, in this regard I believe can teach us what it is to make a vacuum.

I'd like to mention another useful exercise for introducing slightly more participative attention into the breathing process. Although we have many breathing exercises from many traditions, including Fourth Way breathing exercises, it is also the wisdom of many traditions that to interfere with the breathing process too much, can be, in fact, dangerous. We don't know what effect it will have on our organism.

So, quite gently, as a way of participating slightly more actively, I invite you on the out-breath, if you wish, to introduce the phrase, "willing release." Experience the out-breath as willing release, or perhaps just hold the question, "What would it be like to experience the out-breath as 'willing release'?"

And on the in-breath, we could introduce the phrase, "Welcome renewal," or the question, "Do I, or how can I, experience the in-breath as 'welcome renewal'?"

Let's simply continue this practice in silence for a brief moment.

I didn't bring a specific chant for the breath; it will, however, be participating in every subsequent chant we do. I invite you to, at any time you wish, to return your attention to the way in which you naturally breath when you sing, and especially to this idea we have directly from Mr. Gurdjieff of making a vacuum.

The other aspect of exchange that I would like to explore is vibration. Singing, and in fact the sound of the voice, whether speaking or singing, is, of course, vibration. And, vibration, in my experience, by its very nature is relational. It transmits through the vibrating air to other bodies, which then vibrate with our speech. A vibrating object is itself fluctuating between two positions, thereby relating them through its energy.

And one way we could begin to explore the vibration of our voices involves the use of primal sounds inherent to us as human beings. So this is the really fun part of the workshop where I'm hoping you'll 'cut loose.' We may even want to stand up and move around a little bit.

So, here begins an exploration of "Ahh." The breath escapes the body on the syllable "Ahh." How is that for you? Engage a few sighs.

[All say, "Ahh."]

Where does that vibration reside in the body, in your organism? How do you experience it?

[All say, "Ahh."]

And we have another primal sound: "Ohh."

[All say, "Ohh."]

What about "Ooh"?

[All say, "Ooh."]

So there's a literal physical vibration of these sounds, and as I'm sure we're all aware. I see so many smiles: this is great. A feeling dimension opens, just by these very simple sounds, and whenever I do this exercise with groups I get the image of young children.

I'd like to introduce one more primal sound. What happens to vibration if we don't actually open our lips and allow the air to escape? We get, "Mmm."

[All say, "Mmm."]

Anyone with children, grandchildren, nieces, or nephews, knows the pure joy of a spontaneous "Mmm" when a yummy food is introduced to that young being of tender age.

So let's invite a bit of that chaos, that 'yawning gap' that allows something new to enter, by engaging in these sounds all together. Make whichever sound seems interesting to you. I invite you to explore your zone of comfort. Where do these sounds resonate in my body? There are so many explorations we could do with this. I invite you, if you're not having a sensate awareness of the vibration of your voice, to simply touch very lightly the surface of the body where you think you may be vibrating. That's one way of exploring these vibrations, to listen to the sound of your own voice, the sound of others' voices. Where is it most natural to find the resonance of these different sounds in my voice and in my body? And, where are perhaps some unexpected, or less comfortable places? For example, do you have a naturally low voice? Well, after a while, maybe you want to try exploring some higher sounds, and where does that resonate in the body? Or vice versa.

So, it's really up to us to find what exploration of vibration resonates, and how we can open ourselves to greater vivifyingness, quite literally in the physical body.

So, here we go. Make sounds however you like.

[All say, "Aah, Mmm, Ooh, Aah, Ohh."]

So there are many fascinating experiments to be done with this form, and variations on this form, with vocal exploration in groups. One of them that began to emerge naturally in the group here today is called 'Toning.' As you can tell, it could become quite chaotic, depending on how much people give themselves to it. In Toning, the structure is usually defined to be that any person can sing any tone they choose. However, once you begin a tone, maintain that same pitch for the duration of the breath. It need not be consonant or dissonant, just any tone you choose.

You can also come up with some quite interesting improvisations in this way by simply introducing to the group a word or a phrase upon which to improvise. And then the parameters of pitch, duration, rhythm, all come into play, and of course, the composition that emerges from this type of improvisation depends on the quality of listening of the group. It's a really fascinating exploration, that if we had more time I would love to go into either of these.

In the interest of exploring other dimensions yet today, and perhaps even having time for questions at the end, I'm going to leave these improvisatory explorations to all of you, in whatever context, and whatever ways may inspire you after you leave here. You may choose to do this for the purpose of exploring these sacred sounds, and perhaps integrating an awareness of breath into that.

I did want to say one more thing about the primal vibrational sounds. These four sounds, when taken together, Aah, Ohh, Ooh, and Mmm–if we do these four in a row, "Aahohhhoohmmm" –we come up with the most sacred of syllables upon which the Sanskrit traditions teach us the whole universe is founded. This is not a tradition to invoke lightly, simply play around with, and I am not a particular expert in it. I have found some fruitful exploration in following the trajectory, the pathway of vibrations through the body of those four sounds in turn, which do follow a specific course of vibration through the body that's quite regenerative.

Working with these sacred sounds, I find myself often drawn to "Aah," as a sound that opens, and at one time I composed a chant to use the sacred sounds, or sacred words in Christianity that have this "Aah" vowel central.

The chant we'll do next has four of these words: "Ave, Salve, Alleluia, Amen." Ave means "Hail," or, "I greet you," Salve, meaning "to save" or "to heal." This is often used in liturgy as "Salve nos," meaning, "Save us, save me." Alleluia doesn't really have a translation, but we usually understand it perhaps . . .

COMMENT: To praise.

FRANZ: To praise or to bless; yes, this is the most common.

And "Amen," which means, "So be it, I accept." It invokes that place of acceptance in ourselves.

As we sing this chant, of course you may explore any dimension of sensation, vibration, or breathing that you wish, but I invite you to specifically begin with the breath. When you attend to the outflow of breath from the body, how does it leave your body? Not trying to do anything, but simply attending to the questions: "How does the breath leave my body, and how does it come back in as I'm chanting?" And when you've found that, experiment with adding to it some awareness of the vibration of your own voice, of the feeling center, and whatever way it draws you to add to the breath in your awareness. All sing:

At this point, I'd like to turn to another exploration of vibration—and this may be pure wiseacreing—but I need your cooperation to find out. I've done this with groups before. Is it possible to explore the Law of Three directly as vibration in sound? There's a chant in the Christian tradition that, perhaps a bit simplistically, but I believe quite clearly introduces this possibility, or at least one aspect of it, to our practice.

One dichotomy that we tend to fall into—one way in which we are 'third force blind' perhaps—is in our division of sound into consonance and dissonance. We tend to view sound in terms of consonance and dissonance, and this often equates also to like and dislike. I like the sounds that are consonant, and I dislike the sounds that are dissonant.

But, vibration is simply itself, in one sense, and then what is consonance and dissonance? We're making that up: what if we made up another experience of sound? In any case, dissonance is just as necessary to what we call Western harmony as consonance, and within every consonant formulation, there is dissonance, and the dissonance is in fact what moves us. And what moves harmonic progressions is the dissonance far more than the consonance.

If I stay on one chord, [harmonium chord sounds], and sing only the consonant pitches, [she sings]—it's lovely, but rather static. And if that's what the angels singing in heaven are doing, then I don't need to be there. But this may relate to our picturings in the same way that we picture God in our strange picturings. We tend to picture heaven in our strange picturings as a place of consonance. Anyone with background in Middle Eastern music, forgive me as I'm about to improvise with little depth of knowledge of this tradition, but the dissonances are where our interest lies. [She sings with a mixture of consonance and dissonance]

So there are those notes that pull or crunch against each other, and that we define as dissonant. We can be aware of dissonances in our experience of singing. We can in fact become comfortable with them, in spite of the fact that those are the notes we've perhaps – because of this intensity of vibration – become conditioned to experience as "wrong notes," or "bad notes," or "notes to avoid."

Let's sing another chant now; this chant has three parts. We're going to work with the first two of them quite a bit, and this will involve dividing us up into groups and listening to each other in some different ways, as we've been doing so far.

The words to the chant are "Veni Sancte Spiritus," or "Come Holy Spirit." It comes from the Taizé tradition. And the first musical line is simple as can be: it's just intoning those words on one pitch, so let's learn that pitch. All sing:

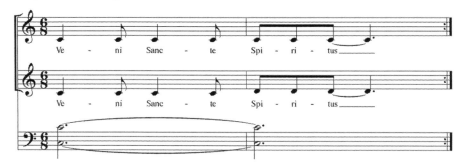

Nothing could be simpler, yes? So that's the first part of the chant. The second part of the chant, rises by a whole step on the word "Spiritus." All sing:

Do you hear how that whole step clashes against the note that's playing on the harmonium? So our first attempt at exploring the Law of Three in music will be to hold this dissonance, to vocally hold this dissonance.

So let's see, how should we do this? If we could, as quickly and simply as possible, divide the room into four quadrants, and have each quadrant form a smaller circle. Within each of these little circles, I'd like you to divide yourselves into two groups, seated in proximity. So one group will sing and hold the first part, and one group will sing the second part. Sit quite close together so you can really hear each other, and feel each other's vibrations.

This will be an experiment, literally in the body, of holding two notes that have dissonance. You could perhaps describe the first note as affirming; the second note, because of its dissonance, we experience as denying. Our first task is to hold these two constant and steady, and with equal valuation.

And so, have you determined who in your groups will maintain the constant note, the first part we sang; and who will go up a step? Just see if you can divide relatively equally and quickly for that purpose.

COMMENT: I'm wondering whether we can have an observer, if that's alright?

FRANZ: It's certainly alright; we spoke earlier of the role of the observer. Actually, this is a good reminder for me. Designate one person in each group to be the observer, please. One person in each group is the observer, who simply listens to the experiment as it is being carried out.

Is it worked out? When the room gets quiet, I'll say the whole thing again.

All right, so we're going to have in each group one person who is the observer. The job of this person is to remain quiet, and simply listen and observe: What do you hear? What do you see going on? If you can keep these observations as physically grounded as possible that would be useful. And so then you have two groups: one group is staying on the lower pitch that stays the same, and the other group is staying on the pitch that goes up. Now those of you singing may have observations of your own of how this task unfolds in yourself. There will be time for discussion afterwards. So for the moment, let's try to carry this out.

I'm going to play just the single note. At some point, I may drop out with the harmonium and leave you on your own to hold these two notes, but to begin we'll have a little help.

Remember, it's "Veni Sancte Spiritus." So those of you singing the lower constant pitch, begin with me, and then I will nod to the various groups and begin the upper one. The second group just remain listening until the constant pitch is established. All sing:

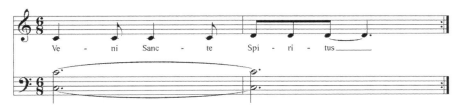

All right, let's switch roles. So if you were singing the note that stays constant, you will now sing the note that moves. If you were singing the note that moves, you will now go to the note that stays constant so you have a chance to inhabit, literally inhabit the other role. If the observer would like to switch, this would be a good point to do that, or you may stay the same.

Okay, let's do this from the other side in exactly the same sequence.

[All sing, "Veni Sancte Spiritus."]

Stop! Ah, that word really works with these groups [laughs]. The Christian contemplative groups I work with don't use the word, stop, so. . . [participants laugh] . . . it just occurred to me I could use that word here.

What are your observations from this little experiment? Why don't we take just a few moments, two or three minutes at most, to share some observations from the observer, and from either role of holding the dissonance, especially as it relates to vibration in the body, but certainly any observations you have to share within your little groups. Go ahead.

[Participants share observations in their small groups.]

If we could bring our discussions to a conclusion, that would be wonderful; and move chairs back to the circle.

So, there is a third voice to this chant, which I actually heard – one group found this voice on its own, which is not surprising – and which takes the dissonance of the first two parts into a larger harmonic world. Perhaps we could chant just a little bit of this. I'm trying to be mindful of the time. There's one whole dimension of the exploration that we haven't come to, which is rhythm, and for comprehending matters of scale, exploration of rhythm is absolutely fascinating.

Anyone who's participated in Movements certainly has a greater awareness of rhythm and of scale than the general population. But even in some Movements classes I've been in, I find that some of the rhythmic explorations that I've done with this chant work, and also in my musical development, are extraordinarily helpful to me, and might be helpful to those of us endeavoring to undertake the Movements as well.

So, if we have time briefly for "Veni Sancte Spiritus," adding a third part. And then, a chant ever so briefly around rhythm that will transition us into the Movements. Here's "Veni Sancte Spiritus." Let's begin with the first two parts, and then I'll sing the third upper part, and I'm sure you'll recognize it.

[All sing, "Veni Sancte Spiritus."]

I find it profoundly meaningful that this chant we're using to explore some basic aspect of the Law of Three is in fact a chant to invoke the Holy Spirit: "Come, Holy Spirit" is what we're singing.

By way of beginning a very brief exploration of rhythm, here is where I want to read the passage from Beelzebub again that has been read several times in presentations this weekend. It's interesting how it keeps recurring: this may in fact be the third time it's been read in a presentation.

For me the exploration of rhythm is a way of opening our awareness of scale, and thus increasing our capacity for finding, for each person finding, their place in the stream of musical unfoldment in time, in this chant circle microcosm that we're participating in right now. When we can do this, that is, having an awareness of scale and finding our corresponding place, it opens the possibility of responding more immediately and appropriately to changing or unexpected circumstances and conditions in other spheres as well.

Or as Mr. Gurdjieff puts it,

> " . . . an all-around awareness of everything concerning these sacred laws also conduces, in general, to this: that three-brained beings irrespective of the form of their exterior coating, by becoming capable in the presence of all cosmic factors not depending on them and arising roundabout them–both the personally favorable as well as the unfavorable–of pondering on the sense of existence, acquire data for the elucidation and reconciliation in themselves of that what is called, 'individual collision', which often arises, in general, in three-brained beings from the contradiction between the concrete results flowing from the processes of the all-cosmic laws and the results presupposed and even quite surely expected by their what is called 'sane-logic'; and thus, correctly evaluating the essential significance of their own presence, they become capable of becoming aware of the genuine corresponding place for themselves in these common cosmic actualizations."[10]

So, not just here, but any participatory music making has this possibility, on a smaller scale than this universe, which is practically incomprehensible in scale. And yet it's the same all the way up and all the way down, isn't it: within ourselves, within the intentional groups in which we participate, and within the Megalocosmos.

So I'd like to do a chant to conclude, a chant that has multiple layers. I suppose you could think of it as a round. I like to think of it as multiple simultaneous layers of words and music, and so we'll learn those first: three parts, and there's a fourth one if we want.

One way of working with rhythm in this regard is to realize that rhythm is a simultaneity: all layers of rhythm, all pulses are present simultaneously at all times. It's a matter of our awareness

10 Gurdjieff, Beelzebub's Tales, pp 755–756.

whether we tap into them, which one we tap into, and whether we can hold multiple of them at the same time. This is one of many things that has become tremendously deepened for me in Movements classes, for which I'm incredibly grateful, involving the whole body in the rhythm and in holding different rhythmic unfoldments simultaneously.

One simple way to practice this here, would be during this chant, to find a pulse. So the basic first line is, "Become a whole world, for a whole world," and this is just very simply sung on one note. So there's the largest rhythm: one repetition of that phrase, "Become a whole world, for a whole world."

[Darlene and participants clap the various pulses during chant from here on. When the word 'clap' is printed, it occurs simultaneously with the word or syllable immediately after it.]

Then we could make it two pulses, "Be-(clap)come a whole world, (clap)for a whole world." We could make it four pulses, "Be-(clap)come a whole (clap)world, (clap)for a whole (clap)world." We could make it eight pulses, "Be-(clap)come a (clap)whole (clap)(clap)world (clap)for a (clap)whole (clap)(clap)world." We could make it sixteen pulses, perhaps at the capacity of the size of our organism. Vibration – rhythm is a vibration, too – depends on the size of what is vibrating.

Another factor to keep in mind as we begin this exercise, is that at the largest and at the smallest scale of rhythm, it becomes easier for dis-coordination to happen. So if you find yourself becoming dis-coordinated with the rhythm of the whole group, return to one of those middle pulses, the four or the eight that we were talking about, and see if that doesn't stabilize you. But realize that even if you're not holding all the pulses at once, the group is holding all the pulses at once. So, at some level of scale, all are held at once, regardless of any dis-coordination we experience.

Why don't we learn two musical parts at once, in the interest of time. The second musical line has the words, "Remember the mercy; remember the mercy." I'm using here the meaning of mercy at its root; mercy and commerce have the same root. In other words, mercy is an exchange. So, "remember the mercy" means "remember the exchange" among and between all these levels of scale that we are contemplating here. Once "become a whole world" gets going, I'll just sing the second part. All sing:

FRANZ: Remember the mercy; Remember the mercy.

I forgot to give the exercise. Find one pulse, and see if you can hold it really strongly, whatever it is. Once that is well established, see if you can find a different pulse and hold it strongly with a different limb. So if your foot is tapping, "1, 2," see if your other hand can tap, "1, 2, 3, 4." As a matter of practicing coordination, all the while you'll be listening and fitting multiple pulses together. If our pulses are coordinated our singing will coordinate, and vice versa. So there's a global listening as well as specific listening, and both specific and a global listening are required to maintain the coordination of the whole.

[All sing, "Become a whole world, for a whole world.
FRANZ: Remember the mercy; Remember the mercy."]

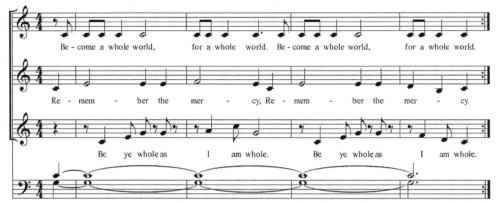

Now there's a third part, which is a little bit complicated rhythmically, so I'll just teach it separately briefly [sings] "Be ye whole as I am whole. Be ye whole as I am whole." It's the old King James English, "Be ye whole as I am whole." This is a command of Christ to be holy – whole – as he is ("I am") whole. I'm going to click my tongue in the rests because they're a little tricky.

[All sing, "Be ye whole as I am whole. Be ye whole as I am whole."]

So let's just conclude with this – chant ourselves out on this – with all three parts layering on top of each other. All sing:

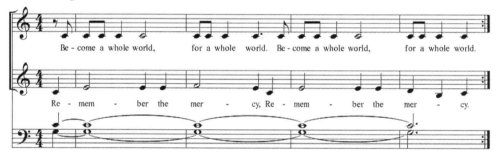

[Darlene: Remember the mercy; remember the mercy.
Be ye whole as I am whole. Be ye whole as I am whole."]

I invite you to remember the mercy. Remember that every large idea is also an embodied idea. The theory and the practice are one and the same: both necessary. I'll end with a quote from Schopenhauer, rather than Gurdjieff: "Music exhibits itself as the metaphysical to everything physical in the world. We might therefore just as well call the world embodied sound as embodied will."

I thank you for your participation and attention.

I'm very sorry there wasn't time for questions. I'd love to hear from all of you about how these exercises resonated with you, how they could be extended, or perhaps used in a Fourth Way context. Please initiate any discussion you'd like to have.

Darlene Franz — dbfranz@uw.edu

··· ∾ ···

My Illustrious Presentation
A Collaborative Picturing

> "... then you will probably acquire the possibility of clearly picturing to yourself and well understand how, ... (*BT* p. 618)

You are invited to participate in a collaborative picturing experiment during the A&E Conference, entitled *My Illustrious Presentation*. This activity aims to explore a section of the text from *Beelzebub's Tales to His Grandson* (*BT* pp. 613-619) in a novel and potentially groundbreaking way.

This collaborative painting/drawing will be created during the conference by any of the conference participants wishing to engage with it. The theme of the artwork is taken from a section of the chapter Russia in *BT*. This section of the text is rich in imagery and may contain significant material accessible through visualization and "mentation by form". The aim of this collaborative "picturing" is to bring out the imagery contained within the text from multiple perspectives of different participants, thus providing new insights that may not be otherwise accessible.

Similar to Tunisian Collaborative Paintings [1], any of the "artists" may add to the work at any time during the conference, but contributors all agree to follow the proposed theme and are discouraged from painting/drawing over anyone else's work. There is no need for an arbiter. No painting or drawing skills are required!

The medium for this work will be a Magic White Board [2] and non-permanent marker pens. The board is installed and pens are provided for participants who may "picture" simultaneously and at any time during the conference.

Audio recordings of the relevant text is available for streaming and download at:
https://soundcloud.com/user675274643/

Apple TTS	Harold Good	Tony Blake

[1] Tunisian collaborative painting. (2012, December 31). In Wikipedia. Retrieved 23:55, December 18, 2014, from
http://en.wikipedia.org/w/index.php?title=Tunisian_collaborative_painting&oldid=530590983

[2] Whiteboard. (2014, December 2). In Wikipedia, The Free Encyclopedia. Retrieved 23:57, December 18, 2014, from
http://en.wikipedia.org/w/index.php?title=Whiteboard&oldid=636302536

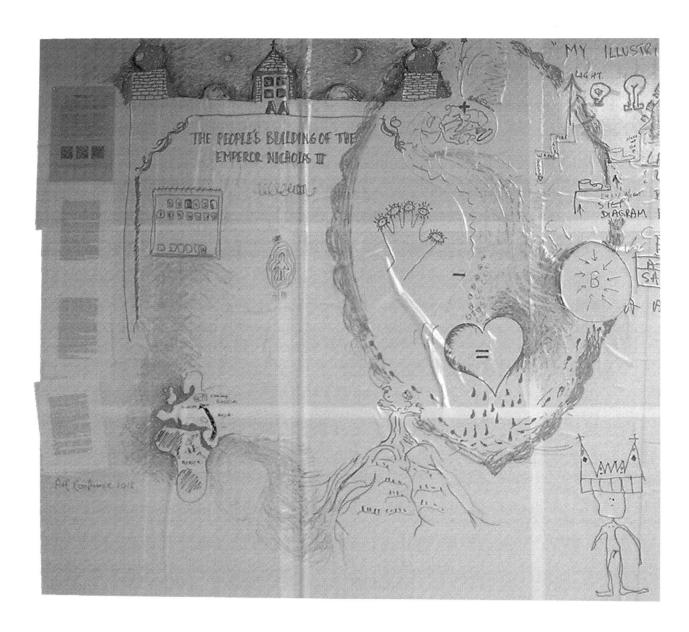

··· ∾ ···

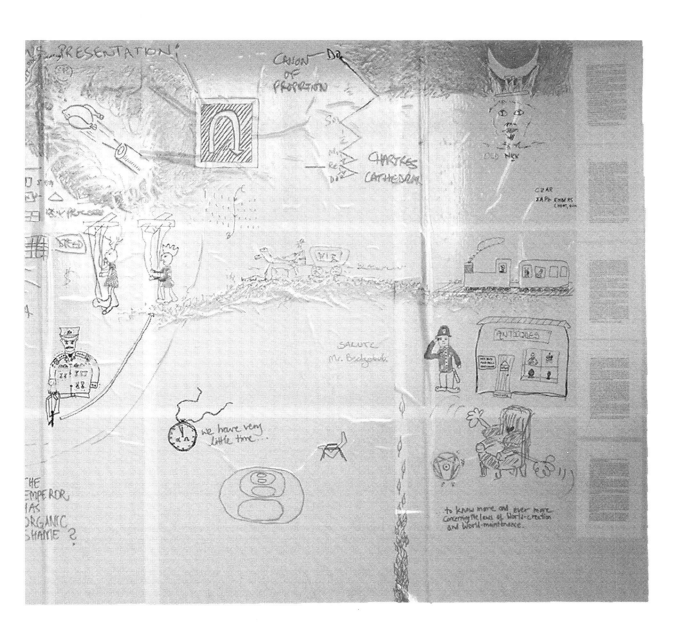

··· ∿ ···

Tetetos Tirzikiano Tokitozine

Toof-Nef-Tef Toogoortski

Tooilan

Took-soo-kef Tookha Tes Nalool Pan Tookloonian Toolkhtotino

Tooloof

Toolookhterzinek Toorinoorino Toosidji

Toosook Toosooly Toospooshokh Toosy

Tralalaooalalalala

Transapalnian Trentroodianos

Triakrkomnian Triamazikamno Tritocosmos Tritoëhary

Trnlva Troemedekhfe Trogoautoegocrat

Trotopine Tsirikooakhtz

Turkestan Turkoman Tzel putz kann Tzimus Uneano

Unter den Linden Urdekhplifata Urmia

Vallikrin Veggendiadi Venoma

Vermassan-Zeroonan-Alaram Veroonk Vetserordiapan Veziniama

Vibroechonitanko vibrometer vibrosho Vietro-yretznel

Viloyer Vitus Vojiano Vuanik Vznooshlitzval Yagliyemmish

Yenikishlak Ypsylodox

Zadik Zalnakatar Zarooary Zehbek

Zernakoor Zernofookalnian Zevrocrats Zilnotrago

Zirlikner Zoostat Zoutine

Zrrt

In gratitude to Dimitri Peretzi and the group in Athens for assembling Gurdjieff's neologisms

Beelzebub's Hoorn

Conference Banquet Address
Delivered on the 2nd of May 2015 in Hoorn, The Netherlands

... Farzin Deravi ...

As far as we know, the Beelzebub of *The Tales* never visited the municipality or the city of Hoorn during any of his sojourns on our planet. This is more than just a little strange, as this lovely town, although admittedly not a centre of culture like Samlios, Koorkalai, Babylon or even Paris, is nevertheless associated, through its name, with a key anatomical feature of supreme importance to all the beings of his planet, Karatas, namely, horns–those hard, pointy projections on the head, consisting of a core of live bone surrounded by a covering of keratin and other proteins. So one would have thought curiosity alone (of which impulse Beelzebub seems to have had plenty) would have drawn him to check out this place, to assess the no-doubt-strange psyche of the three-brained beings who breed there and who would have chosen to name their city after his uppermost extremities.

Hoorn was founded in 716 AD, which, according to Dr. Hugh Hubbard's 2013 All and Everything Conference paper, falls within the period between Beelzebub's fifth and sixth descents to our planet Earth. Legends and myths surround the origin of the city's name. According to Old Frisian legends, Hoorn is derived from the name of the stepson of King Redbad, who was called Hornus. Another account reports the origin of the name as being related to a sign from an early 14th century hanging outside one of the establishments situated on the Roode Steen Square depicting a post horn. The name is also linked to the horn shape of one of its first ports. However, it is probably derived from *Hornicwed*. The medieval meaning of *hornic* is 'corner', and *wed* or *wedor* is water.

All these possibilities for the origin of the city's name bring to mind the related concepts and words in his tales. We have mention of all manner of horns (for example, the powdered horn of the Pirmaral, the Golden Horn, "fine art horns", horned devils and buffalo), and also corns (which are etymologically related to horns), cornucopia (meaning the horn of plenty), hornets, horny fingers, and even corners of restaurants to mention just a few–here and there pointing to possibilities where a "something" may be found.

Would he not have been keen to visit and explore all and every horny connection that may be hinted at by this city's name? Not to mention the chance to sit and relax at the many Chaikhanas of which he was fond, here called "Coffee Shops," where, I am told, not only red and black liquids can be consumed in abundance but also substances of a more potent nature.

I vividly remember my first visit to Hoorn a couple of years ago with Paul, Mariëtte and Clare, and being struck by a number of intriguing signs and symbols dotted around the city, including an impressive unicorn which I have since found out to be part of the emblem for the city itself and used

since the Middle Ages. In addition to its cute unicorn, this emblem also contains a coat of arms, the shield, which shows a horn (of the type that may have brought down the walls of Jericho) held by a blue ribbon. According to a myth, this is the horn of a bull that lost it while pounding the city gate of Hoorn. So the emblem contains two horns, one of a bull and the other of a unicorn.

In the literature the unicorn has been described as "a very fierce animal ... which has the head of the stag, the feet of the elephant, and the tail of the boar, while the rest of the body is like that of the horse; it makes a deep lowing noise, and has a single black horn, which projects from the middle of its forehead, two cubits in length."[1] Does this composite creature not remind you of the emblem of the Akhaldan's so prominent in *Beelzebub's Tales*?

Well, could it be that Beelzebub did visit Hoorn but chose not to mention it to Hassein? I can even imagine him befriending some important power-possessing elderly Dutch being from this area just at the time when the city was being founded, and persuasively suggesting a suitable name for the city —one that perhaps may have reminded him of a city on his own planet. Think of it, Hoorn linking Karatas and Earth ...

Perhaps he knew also that with Hassein's love for us, the unfortunate three-brained beings of planet Earth, he would eventually put two and two together and head here himself in his quest for knowledge.

1 Pliny the Elder, "Book 8. Chapter 31.". Natural History. trans. John Bostock.

Growing horns is normally a slow business. It is a lifetime's work. Yet one of the most powerful images in *Beelzebub's Tales* is that of the gathering to honour him and the process by which all present contribute to the rapid restoration of his horns, a representation of his Reason. Everyone willingly gives of the active elements of their own horns so that Beelzebub's horns may grow, in recognition of his supreme being-efforts.

Whether or not Beelzebub or Hassein visited Hoorn, we are here now. At occasions like this, when we are gathered together in a sincere quest for understanding, we have a genuine opportunity to help and benefit from each other–to grow our "horns." Alas, we have no visible horns to show for it, but we may still grow our virtual horns, in our variety and degrees of Reason–and what better place for that than Hoorn?

Farzin Deravi — f.deravi@btinternet.com

··· ∾ ···

THE THREE SERIES — G. I. Gurdjieff

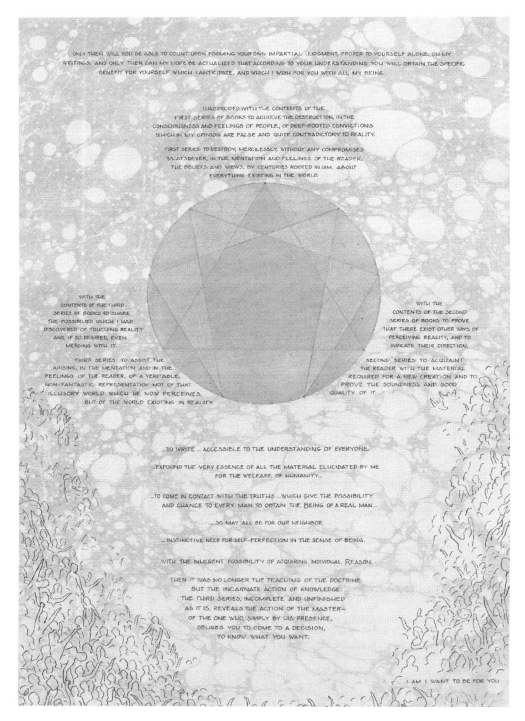

This poster can be purchased on the ALL and Everything website: http://aandeconference.org/
Contributing artists: Bonnie Phillips, Michael Hall, Robert Godon, Amy O'Donnell and friends

Where do we go from here?

ALL and Everything International Humanities Conference 2015

The mission statement was read and further discussion evolved from that.

ALL and Everything Conference Mission

> The ALL and Everything International Humanities Conference is an international forum for the presentation and discussion of studies associated with the exploration of G. I. Gurdjieff's work and legacy and in particular his writings.
>
> The conference aims to provide an impartial, serious, and congenial atmosphere for those who wish to explore these teachings with the hope that, by sharing questions and insights, a wider horizon of understanding and practical incorporation may appear.
>
> The conference is open to all students of Gurdjieff's work and legacy. While providing a framework for structured meetings, discussions and readings, the conference also aims to facilitate interactions to encourage relationships and exchanges among individuals and Work groups.

Topics discussed:

... Time and opportunity was reserved this year for non-verbal impressions and expressions by means of having music at the start of seminars and papers and use of the whiteboard wall on which images could be drawn. Many expressed valuation for this:

~ A wish for an increasing amount of creativity and art.

~ Online submission forms should be more welcome to a diversity of presentations.

~ Experiencing different qualities like movements and chanting instead of just reading was appreciated.

~ The music worked into the beginning of the sessions gave the chance to open another center before the intellectual one was brought in.

~ Music before every presentation to get everybody settled.

~ Opposing views were also expressed, reasoning that the main focus of the conference should be Gurdjieff's writings and that one can only take in so much.

... It was good to see new faces at the conference. We counted twelve different nations represented in this conference. It's an opportunity for people with the same passions to come together and maybe work together in the future.

... Regarding the approach of reading a whole chapter together, the question was asked that when we cannot read the whole chapter, can there be a time for shared views about that part that we could not read together.

... Why were copies of abstracts not available? They should be available online in advance of the conference so participants can be better prepared for the presentations.

... Can we have space to take up a theme or a section of what is studied, so people can come together and find ways to apply the series to one's own practical work?

... The view was expressed that there was too little room for small specific questions/topics. The atmosphere of the same people always speaking made it hard to go and ask such questions. For new people it might be good to have sessions where smaller groups work together.

... There was an introduction of the location for next year's conference, which will be in the Hawthorne hotel in Salem, Massachusetts, USA.

... A plea for volunteers for the 2017 conference is made. The volunteer's responsibility would be the logistic side of the conference, the planning committee provides the content.

··· ∿ ···

Made in the USA
San Bernardino, CA
20 April 2018